Decentralizing Rural Governance and Development

Decentralizing Rural Governance and Development

Perspectives, Ideas and Experiences

Edited by
Anil Kumar Jana

RAWAT PUBLICATIONS
Jaipur • New Delhi • Bangalore • Hyderabad • Guwahati • Kolkata

ISBN 978-81-316-0681-0

Published by
Prem Rawat for **Rawat Publications**
Satyam Apts, Sector 3, Jawahar Nagar, Jaipur 302 004 (India)
Phone: 0141 265 1748 / 7006 Fax: 0141 265 1748
E-mail: info@rawatbooks.com
Website: www.rawatbooks.com

New Delhi Office
4858/24, Ansari Road, Daryaganj, New Delhi 110 002
Phone: 011 2326 3290

Also at *Bangalore, Hyderabad, Guwahati* and *Kolkata*

Typeset by Rawat Computers, Jaipur

Printed at Nice Printing Press, New Delhi

Dedicated

to my students

who motivated me all along to look beyond

Contents

II
Panchayati Raj in India: Experiences and Capacity Building

III
Issues in Decentralization and Panchayati Raj

IV
Decentralizing Development: Including the Excluded

Acknowledgements

The present volume is a product of my long engagement with the issues of rural governance and development carried out in some parts of this state particularly in the undivided district of Midnapore since 1978, in course of interactions with my students in the classrooms as well as with the practitioners and stakeholders outside. They have taught me more than anyone else about the practices and realities in decentralizing development. During the formative years of my teaching career, I had the opportunities to associate myself with the functioning of the panchayats and other grassroots organizations in this district. I relished the experiences in planning and implementation of decentralized development in a remote part of this district while participating at the field-level exercises. As a result, I got the occasion to learn the nitty-gritty of decentralizing development which reinforced my commitment to decentralization.

While recollecting the pleasure of the past, I must remember with a sense of absorbed gratitude and profound regards the inspiration and guidance that I received from Late Binoy Krishna Choudhury (Minister of Land, Land-reforms and Panchayats, WB) Late Satyabrata Sen (Chairman of the First State Finance Commission, WB) and Late Professor Ajit Narayan Bose (IIT, Kharagpur) while familiarizing myself with the process and practices in village-based decentralized planning. The three colourful personalities and activists of alternative development model helped me a lot in inventing an objective framework of understanding decentralization and demystifying development without which, I doubt, if I could sustain my interests for long years.

My interest in the present academic choice and focus owes much to the wisdom of a good number of well wishers and friends but I am mostly indebted to Professor Mohit Bhattacharya and Professor Asok Kumar Mukhopadhyay who almost religiously inspired and motivated me to take up the assignment in the greater interests of the students and practitioners. In fact, the title of this volume is the product of their collective intellectual acumen. They have also eagerly contributed their papers to make this venture a success notwithstanding their tight schedules. All the contributors are a blend of academics, practitioners and field-level activists across the state whose insights and academic sagacity have helped the enrichment of the volume. I find no words to acknowledge their enthusiastic response when I requested them for their contributions.

Thanks are due to my colleagues at the department for providing a supportive space in which this work could be pursued. I would like to convey good wishes to my students with whom I could converse day by day on different issues and problems of politics and development. I intend to dedicate this book to them as a mark of life long bonds between a teacher and his students, which I have been enjoying all along. I also like to appreciate the help of Shri Jagadish Mahata who provided necessary assistance in preparing the manuscript. I owe special thanks to Mr. P. Rawat and others of Rawat Publications for taking a keen interest in bringing out the volume.

Last but not least, my greatest debt has always been to my wife Krishna. This publication and much else beyond this would have not been materialized without her companionship, encouragement and support over the years. I am also thankful to our Anindya for his inspiring youthful confidence and uncompromising attitude towards injustice, which I try to follow quite unsuccessfully at this age of mine and that too in this era of individual materialism.

Midnapore
29 June 2014

Anil Kumar Jana

Contributors

Alok Kumar Mukhopadhyay is a retired IAS officer and formerly District Magistrate and Director of the State Institute of Panchayats and Rural Development, West Bengal.

Anil Kumar Jana is Professor of Political Science with Rural Administration, Vidyasagar University, West Bengal.

Apurba Kumar Mukhopadhyay is a faculty member in Political Science and Political Studies, Netaji Institute for Asian Studies, Kolkata.

Asok Kumar Mukhopadhyay is former Netaji Subhas Chair Professor of Political Science, University of Calcutta, and former Emeritus Fellow in Political Science, University Grants Commission, New Delhi and former Professor at Indian Institute of Public Administration.

Buddhadeb Ghosh is a Senior Fellow, Institute of Social Sciences, formerly belonging to the West Bengal Civil Service.

Budh Bahadur Lama teaches in the Department of Political Science with Rural Administration, Vidyasagar University, West Bengal.

Chanchal Chakrabarti is a former Reader in Political Science, Rashtraguru Surendranath College, Barackpore, Kolkata.

Debnarayan Modak is a Professor of Political Science and Director, School of Humanities and Social Sciences, Netaji Subhas Open University, Kolkata.

Dibyendu Sarkar is Joint Secretary to the Government of West Bengal and Coordinator of Mahatma Gandhi National Rural Employment Guarantee Scheme, West Bengal.

Jhumpa Mukherjee teaches Political Science at St. Xavier's College, Kolkata.

Kumkum Chattopadhyay is an Associate Professor in Political Science at Bethune College, Kolkata.

Mohit Bhattacharya is former Vice-Chancellor of the University of Burdwan and former Centenary Professor in Public Administration, University of Calcutta and Emeritus Fellow of the UGC in Political Science.

Prabhat Kumar Datta is Centenary Professor of Public Administration, Department of Political Science, Calcutta University and Former Adviser, Institute of Local Government and Urban Studies, Government of West Bengal.

Saktipada Pal is a former Reader in Political Science at Kharagpur College, Midnapore, West Bengal.

Soma Ghosh, Associate Professor, Department of Political Science, Sarojini Naidu College for Women, Kolkata.

Tapan Kumar Das is an Associate Professor in Political Science, Dum Dum Motijheel College, Kolkata.

Utpal Chakraborty is a member of the West Bengal Civil Service (Executive) and former faculty member at the State Institute of Panchayats and Rural Development, West Bengal.

Introduction

Anil Kumar Jana

Decentralization has become both the dominating ideology and a practice of governance throughout the world and especially in the developing countries of the Third World. It has also been accepted as an alternative to the centralized governance that had earned much disapproval and discredit in the post-cold war situations, when the socialist world headed by the USSR collapsed and the welfare state system began to trudge after a long and strenuous journey through development administration and populist politics. In some countries, especially in the West, decentralization became a catchword in deciding strategy to overcome the problems of fiscal mismanagement and bureaucratic inefficiency. While considering decentralization as a 'rage' in matters of governance, Pranab Bardhan[1] identified certain important factors interacting in the process of revisiting the idea. According to him, a great loss of legitimacy of the centralized state and the resultant belief in decentralized governance as an alternative channel in extending a host of benefits directly to the people, comparatively at lower costs with the help of technological development and through inter-governmental competitions having checks and balances, coupled with effective monitoring may be viewed as responsible factors[2] in popular approval of decentralization. As a result of all these, decentralization had been 'at the centre-stage of policy experiments' since early 1990s in a large number of developing countries in Asia, Africa and Latin America[3] and about eighty-one countries belonging to different parts of the world took steps towards democratization.[4]

Interestingly, people from both the left and the right soon began to appreciate, though for diverse purposes and in different degrees, the resurgence of the ideal as a process of reallocating power and resources from a higher and central authority to lower levels of government and bringing it closer to the people. Professor Bardhan also notes this swing to the idea of decentralized governance when a vast range of social thinkers – from post-modernists, multicultural proponents and free market economists – to environmental activists, to the supporters of indigenous technology and development dubbed as 'anarcho-communitarians'[5] had been clamouring for decentralizing development. However, different scholars and adherents consider the case for decentralization from diverse dimensions – the first category seeks both political and economic decentralization, while the second concentrates on devolution of political power with little or no economic power. The third approach puts emphasis on economic reforms with little or no transfer of political powers. But, in spite of different visions, there is nonetheless a meeting point that decentralization is vital for democratization and good governance. The urge for decentralization in India is, however, more political. The actual assessment of the nature and scope of decentralization in India can be made only through examining the extent of devolution of powers, functions and resources to the institutional bodies organized at local levels and also the extent of autonomy enjoyed by such bodies. It is yet to be convincingly established whether the policy of economic reforms and structural adjustments had the determining impact on the constitutionalization of local governance in India or whether granting of constitutional status to the PRIs was a part of the politics of globalization, notwithstanding that there is no doubt in the fact that the Seventy Third Amendment Act is also a product of a long chain of decentralizing experiments carried out in India long before attaining independence and a host of recommendations of various committees and commissions in post-Independence period.

Perspectives of Decentralizing Development

The question of nation building occupied the central place after Independence. The need for creation of a new type of political and institutional structure became necessary for discharge of a new set of functions for the people of India, who fought so resolutely for *swaraj* or self-rule as visualized by Gandhi. But the spill-over of the pre-Independence structural configurations was so massive and widespread that it was difficult to overcome the administrative legacies of the Raj.

The Constitution of India is closely modeled on the Government of India Act 1919 and 1935, which were products of British interests in India. The Act of 1935 had its roots in the Regulating Act of 1773 (the first attempt of the British Parliament towards institution building in India) and developed through the Act of 1858. It is an irony of history that the ruling elites, who fought the British Raj and criticized its machinery vehemently before 1947, became the enthusiastic takers of the institutions created by the Raj. Thus, the same set of institutions – the federal structure, the office of the Governor, the steel-frame bureaucracy and the All India Services – was borrowed and affixed to the Constitution of India. In tune with the centralizing trends of the pre-Independence era, the Central government was bestowed not only with a larger share in financial and administrative areas but also with effective powers of control over the states. Similarly, prohibitory restrictions were also imposed on the fundamental rights of the citizens. The emergency provisions were incorporated in the Constitution in order to empower the Union to teach the units should they fail to fall in line with the Centre. Though administrative structure was thus modeled on the pre-Independence configurations, it exhibited serious departures from the western model on the pretext of facilitating national integration and social cohesion. The legacies of the British administration created the major incongruity – between the old structural framework and the emerging bunch of functions in a changed philosophical environment of a sovereign, democratic republic committed to social justice, liberty and equality. Hence, the question on the justification of the structural continuities in a new ideological milieu becomes pertinent. India also inherited the economic legacies of the British Raj, which was reflected in acute poverty, stagnant industry and declining agriculture. In such a situation, to reinforce its legitimacy, the new leadership introduced centralized planning for national development.

The first four decades of development administration in India (up to 1994) can be viewed through a succession of three overlapping phases of its growth and development, each of which may be identified according to the focus:

(i) The first two decades, specifically the period up to 1970, was marked as the phase of development administration. Development functions were added with greater emphasis to the regulatory functions that already existed with a view to accelerating the welfare objectives. All-out attempts were made for achieving multi-sectoral coordination among the functionaries engaged at the field levels for speedy socio-economic changes. All these led to the development of a robust administrative machinery organized into multiple line departments, which ultimately created problems of coordination and brought challenges to the efficiency and effectiveness in administration.

(ii) The second phase started around 1970 with the failure of the Panchayati Raj and the Five-Year Plans to get rid of poverty and social chaos. Different sectoral schemes were introduced to launch a direct attack on poverty, which represented a shift towards centralized concept of sectoral development at the grassroots. The approach initiated was essentially bureaucratic, and with the decline of panchayati raj bodies, the role of people in planning and implementation of rural development programmes and projects was missing.

(iii) The last phase starts with the constitutionalization of the local government in both rural and urban India. The Amendment Acts were passed in 1992 and subsequently the states passed the conformity Acts by 1994. This phase has greater implications for decentralization and has raised new issues and challenges that need to be addressed for the smooth and effective functioning of local self bodies.

The Community Development Programme was the first attempt in rural development in a comprehensive manner under government initiative. Prior to Independence, since the beginning of the first quarter of the last century, certain attempts were however made to find out appropriate models for physical, economic and cultural improvements in the villages of India through effective use of own resources. Mahatma Gandhi, Rabindranath Tagore and V.T. Krishnamachari were the leading personalities and social thinkers who came forward with their own ideas and experiences. Gandhi raised a huge contingent of village-level volunteers and started his Sevagram (Wardha) programme designed on the basic objectives of decentralizing comprehensive rural reconstruction. Krishnamachari organized his village reconstruction movement at Baroda. After initial attempts in East Bengal (now Bangladesh), Rabindranath began his experiments at Sriniketan (Birbhum) in West Bengal with the goal of making people self-respectful and self-reliant. These programmes, no matter how far sustainable and productive, were the products of imagination to protect Indian tradition and culture from the onslaught of western mechanical materialism and provided clues for future government initiatives for decentralization in rural development after Independence.

The Community Development Phase

The Community Development Programme was launched with a view to bringing about 'an all-round improvement of the villages and those who inhabit'.[6] Though the programme was intended to be a people's programme with government participation, popular participation was structured at various levels through the formation of advisory committees consisting of officials and non-officials under overall leadership of the bureaucracy. Hence, the CDP and subsequently the National Extension Programme (1953) had nothing to strengthen local government institutions. This was the beginning of contradictions in designing the structure of local governance in India after Independence: the two systems, the residue of the local bodies created by the British and the bureaucracy-dominated community development-extension programme, working parallel to each other and both directly and indirectly, were engaged in the accomplishment of the same objectives. The Community Development Programme and the NES together introduced an integrated development administration at the district and block levels and created a base for management approaches in rural development which still act as brakes in the process of decentralizing rural India. It took considerable time to realize the need to reinvigorate the panchayati raj bodies when the Balwantray Committee attributed the failure of the Community Development Programme to the absence of popular initiative and participation at the grassroots level and recommended the creation of a three-tiered structure of administration in the districts above the villages. The Committee observed eloquently: 'So long as we do not discover or create a representative and democratic institution which will supply the local interest, supervision and care, ... invest it with adequate power and assign to it appropriate finances, we will never be able to evoke local interest and excite local initiative in the field of development'.[7] The observations made five decades earlier equally apply to the present-day situation in structuring and functioning of the local bodies in our country.

The debate between the forces of decentralizing governance and parliamentary representative democracy in India has a long history since the days of Constituent Assembly when the idea of village panchayat was discarded as 'a sink of localism, a den of ignorance, narrow-mindedness and communalism' (Ambedkar).[8] While moving the objective Resolution in the Constituent Assembly in 1947, Jawaharlal Nehru tried to tune up the mindset of the House by putting greater emphasis on industrialization and evading the issue of establishing village *swaraj*.

The heat generated was put to rest through the inclusion of a directive to the state 'to organize village panchayats as units of self-government' in Article 40. But the debate was not closed and it had been on the agenda of a good number of commissions and committees that dealt with the issues of development, decentralization and people's participation. The recommendations and suggestions made from time to time ultimately culminated in the Seventy Third and Seventy Fourth Amendments. Thus, the constitutional amendments have a direct linkage with the dilemma among India's ruling elites led by Congress and the dilemma is ideological in nature. It may not be a mere coincidence that the philosophy of liberalization was also accepted as a part of India's policy-making during the period. The global phenomenon of decentralization took place concurrently with the liberalization of world economy and the development of the 'third wave'. The Amendments though not a part of the framework of globalization, the pervasive forces of globalization exerted profound impact on the process of democratization in India.

Pre-Independence Legacy

The Indian political leaders or the Congress had no comprehensive plans for local self-governments in rural India in the pre-Independence era. Lord Ripon contemplated his views to give the people of India the first lessons in popular and political education in his Resolution of 18 May 1882. The Indian National Congress came into existence in 1885 and was indifferent to the views expressed by Ripon based on an ideology of paternalistic benevolence pursued in India by the British. The Congress raised the issue and demanded village panchayats only in December 1909 at the 24th Lahore Session. But, subsequently, the demand disappeared from the Congress agenda, excepting occasional references in individual speeches.[9] After the pronouncement of the Government of India Act 1919, the 'Diarchy' and limited 'Provincial Government' were introduced and local government became a provincial subject. The Congress failed to prepare a blueprint of local level reforms even when Gandhi was devising his constructive programmes for regeneration of Indian villages. Following the Government of India Act 1935, the Congress put more focus on national issues and left the local issues to the wishes of the local leaders and provincial governments.

Thus, confusion in ideology is very much a part of Congress policies and hence it could not take coherent views about rural local self-government in the pre-Independence period and that continued in the post-Independence period as well. This neglect of the local-self governments in the ideology of the Congress remained almost unchanged till 24 November 1957 when PRIs emerged in India. After 75 years, we find the same logical consistency that Ripon's Resolution finds its place in the recommendations of the Balwantray Mehta Committee for 'Democratic Decentralization'.

Towards Institutionalizing Panchayati Raj

This dilemma of the Indian National Congress became more pronounced when the need for creating new structures was felt after Independence for discharge of new functions. Reform of the discredited bureaucratic machinery to absorb the demands and pressures of the people accumulated over the years was a necessity. There was also the need to devise a new strategy and make necessary administrative changes so as to enable the people to participate in the emerging political process. The leadership met the challenges of development and nation-building through creation of a state system based on Western liberal ideology by incorporating the British parliamentary model of government. The leadership responded to the changed situation without formulating any well-conceived strategy of change, but by implanting almost the entire political and administrative structure developed by the British in India. The spillover of the pre-Independence structural arrangements created by the British Raj in India was so massive and widespread that it becomes extremely difficult to consider the achievement of Independence as a turning point in India's politico-administrative history.

The cumulative effects of all these inconsistencies and incongruities are profound in the structural design and activity mapping of the

PRIs in India. The growth and development of these institutions of self-governance may be viewed as a movement all along a Functional – Non-functional Scale: Productive (1957–60), Counter-productive (1961–65), Unproductive (1966–77), Under-productive (1978–93), and Functionally confused (since 1994).

Within a very short span of time after their establishment, the Panchayati Raj Institutions became counter-productive instead of being supportive of economic justice and social change. The rural kulaks and the expanding bureaucracy soon captured these institutions. The Asoka Mehta Committee rightly described the situation – The Panchayati Raj Institutions are:

> usually dominated by economically or socially privileged sections of society and have as such facilitated the emergence of oligarchic forces, yielding no benefits to the weaker sections. The purpose of the Panchayati Raj Institutions has also been vitiated by political factionalism, rendering developmental thrust either warped or diluted. Corruption, inefficiency, scant regard for procedure, political interference in day-to-day administration, parochial loyalties, motivated action, power concentration instead of service consciousness – all these have limited the utility of Panchayati Raj for the average villagers.[10]

During the first three decades of panchayati raj in India, many changes and experiments were carried out in organizations, structures and functioning of these institutions. Various committees were formed starting with the Balwantray Mehta Committee in 1950s. Subsequently, Asoka Mehta Committee, Dantwala Committee, Hanumanth Rao Committee and the CAARD (G.V.K. Rao Committee) were appointed to identify the level and method of decentralization and development in which people's participation could occupy the position of centrality. But, all the initiatives and experiments dealt with the peripheral aspects and failed to involve people in the process of decentralization. The experiments undertaken in four decades also failed to resolve the duality and contradictions between the bureaucracy-led development administration and decentralized governance. The policy formulated and actions devised by the policy-makers and bureaucrats had helped to sustain this situation all along. With the introduction of PRIs in India, attempts were made to make these institutions ineffective and subsequently, the Intensive Agricultural District Programme (IADP) was launched to bypass the Panchayati Raj Institutions. The introduction of poverty alleviation programmes under bureaucratic control was not merely a superficial change; it intended to paralyse the panchayats as organizations of rural people for their development. The shift 'from the community or area development concept in favour of a sectoral professional (no involvement with community) approach'[11] was the result of the confusions from which the leadership had been suffering since the days of Lord Ripon.

Gradually the panchayats started to decline due to bureaucratic monopolization of development administration and political indifference and ultimately, it became unproductive. The institutions had been suffering from financial crisis since their formation in absence of any viable source of resource mobilization and scheme of financial devolution. The resources of the panchayats were insufficient in making them operative in discharging the functions which were assigned to them. It was felt that these bodies needed to 'be revitalized and endowed' with necessary powers and resources to make them effective.[12] These also began to suffer from a legitimacy crisis soon when elections to these bodies were overdue. 'Elections have been put off on one pretext or another like drought, floods, census, general elections, delimitation reservation, etc. and the term of the existing bodics has been extended or the bodies have been superseded.'[13] In such a situation, centrally-sponsored schemes (CSS) and various sectoral schemes of different departments were introduced and subsequently, the concept of 'community' development was replaced by 'rural' development in 1971. Naturally, the panchayats became inoperative for all practical purposes in the changed situation created by structural constraints: insufficient funds, declining role and inadequate staff strength.

During the Janata Government, fresh attempts were made for the revival of the Panchayati Raj Institutions. Following the recommendations of the Asoka Mehta Committee (1978), some of the states renewed their initiatives to organize these institutions through amendments in their existing laws. Some states like West Bengal, Karnataka and Kerala made some progress in revamping the institutions and evidence suggests that the state governments took steps for holding elections to the panchayats and involving them in planning and implementation of rural development programmes. While considering the involvement of political parties in panchayats positively, the Asoka Mehta Committee could not resolve the structural issues involved in decentralizing rural India. The Committee expressed its preference for two-tiers – 'a district-level Zilla Parishad and a Mandal Panchayat', but allowed the continuance of the other two tiers for some time. Though it recommended adequate devolution of powers and functions with proportionate financial resources to the local levels and pleaded for transfer of the district-level development officials to the zilla parishad and lower tiers, most of the state governments preferred to remain silent on these issues and in absence of constitutional provisions, they started to move as they liked. As a result, the efforts towards developing a genuine decentralized structure of local government did not materialize.[14] However, the experiences in West Bengal, Karnataka and Kerala were encouraging and strengthened the urge for consitutionalization of the system. The idea of district government[15] also kindled the imagination of the activists.

Constitutionalization of Decentralization

The Seventy Third and Seventy Fourth Amendments are attempts to clear the inconsistencies and incongruities experienced over the years in the process of democratic decentralization in rural India. Through these Amendments, a scheme of economic development and social justice based on self-governance has been worked out. The 'institutions of self-government' have been constitutionalized (Article 243G) with the creation of a three-tier panchayati raj structure developed on the gram sabha, the foundation of local democracy. The Amendments also include certain exciting aspects and institutions, having far-reaching implications on the structural mapping and functional expectations of these local governing bodies. Emphasis on regular elections of panchayats at an interval of five years, reservation of seats for women and the marginalized sections of the society, financial resource generation and provisions indicating the devolution of a good number of functions to the panchayats through their inclusion in the Eleventh Schedule, and provisions for new institutions like the District Planning Committee, the State Finance Commission and the State Election Commissioner reflect the new dispensation of the democratizing development in India. It is quite natural that this structural reorganization would strengthen the process, which has been on the agenda of institution building for local democracy for a period of more than four decades. The state governments passed their conformity Acts by the middle of the Nineties (23 April 1994), but most of these fall short of making panchayats the 'institutions of self-government'. A close review of the direction and the outcomes as evident raises doubt. The moot point is whether the attempts led the system towards deepening of local democracy, which goes beyond the confines of efficient delivery of services, or if the scheme is incomplete and incapable of accomplishing the functions as visualized in the Amendments.

A review of the Amendment by the scholars exhibits the limited focus of the Act, which raises the scope of both structural and functional variations in the conformity Acts in absence of any clear ideological persuasions. The structure-functional inconsistencies dominate the Amendment and as a result, the new institutional structure created within the established structural framework is incapable to discharge the development functions outlined in the Act. Under the new framework, the gram sabha occupies the key role because it is the only institution which provides the scope for direct participation of the people. But the gram sabha, as the studies suggest, has become almost dysfunctional in absence of necessary constitutional provisions. The limited focus has created spaces, which are being utilized by a variety of institutions engaged in minimizing the role of the Panchayati Raj Institutions.

Incomplete Decentralization

The attempt towards decentralizing development is no doubt historic and the direction of the amendment is very clear, which seeks to make the panchayats 'institutions of self-government' in an autonomous situation. This autonomy arises when there is the total devolution of three Fs – Functions, Functionaries and Funds. The Amendment sets out the direction but leaves the responsibilities to the states to decentralize powers and functions relating to the subjects identified in the Eleventh Schedule. All the states passed conformity Acts without detailing out the functions of the PRIs. In most of the state Acts, there is simply the reproduction of the items listed in the Schedule. The status accorded to the panchayats as 'institutions of self-government' implies that these bodies as a whole should be considered as the 'third stratum' of governance along with the governments at the Centre and the states. Responsibilities and functions of the governments are classified through incorporation of three lists in the Constitution: *Union List, State List* and *Concurrent List.* But there is no such list as *Local List,* which is necessary to ensure autonomy for the local bodies. In fact, the Amendment is a reflection of the ambiguities and incongruities among the different forces and trends. In a sense, it is an act of compromise between the Centre and states in which the states retain the power to restrict the functioning of the local bodies, if they desire.[16] Even after the Seventy Third Amendment, local government finds its place in the State List (vide entry no. 5) and hence it is a state subject to be guided under Article 162 of the Constitution. Thus, the PRIs are institutions of self-government under the control of the state government. In other words, autonomy of panchayats largely depends on the political will of the state governments.

Critical reviews done by the experts reveal the lack of clarity in the functional assignments made in the Eleventh Schedule. Since the subjects mentioned in the Eleventh Schedule are state concurrent, the institutional arrangements depend on respective state legislations. It is found that all the states have not yet transferred all the subjects to the panchayats and excepting only a few of them have transferred all the subjects to all the tiers without clearly dividing the activities which makes the PRIs functionally confused. Of the three states (Karnataka, Kerala and West Bengal), Karnataka had completed the task of activity mapping in respect of all the 29 items covered under the state Act in August 2003, followed by Kerala covering 26 subjects, earlier transferred to the panchayats through state Act. It is interesting that the Third State Finance Commission in Karnataka has proposed a new set of activity mapping for PRIs, though already done previously, for better coordination and effective implementation of programmes.[17] The progress in West Bengal is comparatively slow. Thus, the activity mapping on the basis of the principle of subsidiarity and the entitlement from below has not yet been completed, though decided on several occasions. The basis of autonomy at different tiers of PRIs should be the entitlement from below, i.e. the gram panchayats should perform such functions as they can do at their level, and the block level and district-level panchayats should be given the leftover functions. Thus, the gram panchayats should have the priorities and shall be the primary repositories of the devolved functions. The inadequacy of the scheme of devolution of functions becomes all the more exposed when the status of the central government vis-à-vis the panchayats in respect of the subjects included in the Eleventh Schedule is examined. Out of the 29 subjects included in the Schedule, 26 are dealt with by the various departments of the Centre and the plan expenditure made on these subjects exceeds 70 per cent of the annual central plan budget. By creating a separate Ministry of Panchayati Raj, the central government has taken right steps but it is only a half-hearted measure. It should have been the Ministry of Local Government, bringing both the rural and urban bodies under a single roof. But what is left for the panchayat when there are two ministries at the Centre – a powerful Ministry of Rural Development and a separate ministry for looking after urban affairs.

Various state governments have created new organizations and agencies for delivery of services covering the subjects included in the Eleventh Schedule of the Constitution. Out of the 29 items provided in the Schedule, 16 subjects are related to social sectors, including education, health, social welfare, minor irrigation, etc. which should come under the exclusive domain of the panchayats but different states have constituted multiple agencies outside the structural framework of the panchayats. Multiple functional agencies with diverse channels of fund flow render the PRIs ineffective and inert, apart from creating duplication and non-sustainability of the programmes. Again, the spaces, left vacated due to gradual reduction in government's involvement in the spheres of social welfare, are being captured by NGOs and 'parallel bodies' backed by foreign donors, the World Bank, the US Government.[18] The Janmabhoomi Programme launched in Andhra Pradesh is a classic example of the formation of such parallel bodies that threaten the very existence of the panchayats at the village level. The rural bureaucracy has been given wide powers under the programme and they are allowed even to appropriate funds from the centrally-sponsored schemes, ignoring the local level panchayats. The functions discharged under the Janmabhoomi Programme are similar to those of the panchayats and include education, health, community development. Resources are made available from JRY fund and Rural Water Supply Scheme.[19] The formation of the village education committees in Andhra Pradesh is another case of violation of the spirit of the Amendment. Powers and functions related to the management of 'Social forestry and farm forestry' are assigned to the panchayats in Eleventh Schedule but these functions are taken away from the panchayats in some states and assigned to some non-elected bodies, and a huge amount of funds is dovetailed from the state budgets. The joint forest management committees (van panchayats) in Uttarakhand are guided by the *patwaris* and not the panchayats. These are even formed by the *patwaris* and not by the people. Under World Bank projects, Pani Panchayats have been created in Odisha for management and distribution of water with the help of user associations. The big landlords control these associations and the poor farmers are excluded. It may be pointed out that the process of devolution of functions, funds and functionaries to the PRIs in Odisha is very slow and 'the overall devolution is limited to 11 departments covering 21 subjects in a very truncated form'.[20] The case of village development committees constituted in Haryana, though representative in character and headed by the sarpanchs, is a glaring example of sidetracking the gram panchayats. These bodies are empowered to execute development functions with flow of funds through the Haryana Rural Development Fund Administration Board. All these are new types of agencies, not representative in character and mostly being captured by the traditional rural kulaks, trying to regain the control they lost, through backdoor manipulation in absence of strong mobilization of masses, especially the poor and the deprived. These are parallel bodies with wide powers and bureaucratic support, having far-reaching implications on decentralizing development in India.

The hijacking of the roles and functions of the panchayats by these parallel organizations has created the problems of overlapping jurisdictions, lack of representative character and absence of social accountability and people's participation. These parallel organizations are statutory bodies, which can be reshaped or dissolved by the respective governments. But there are other centres of powers and influences in rural India, which necessitate a fundamental structural change, almost revolutionary. The formation of the non-elected service delivery agencies is a global phenomenon and necessarily a part of liberalization-privatization framework. The emergence of the *quasi-autonomous non-governmental organizations* (Quangos) is now a much publicized subject in the contemporary debates on decentralization. Functions and funds available to the local bodies are increasingly being channelized to these bodies and the elected local bodies are being marginalized. Hence, there is the need for structural changes in the organization and functioning of the local bodies in India for strengthening the process of decentralizing development as visualized in the Amendments. 'Clearly, successful devolution is unlikely unless it is supported by the line departments of both the central and the state governments' in India.[21] The caste panchayats, the traditional village panchayats like *Khaps* in Haryana etc. still exist as centres of power in rural areas. Even in remote parts of a progressive state like West Bengal, the dominance of caste panchayat, similar to *Khaps*, has attracted attention for different reasons.[22] In some cases, unopposed panchayats are rewarded (Madhya Pradesh) and the two-child norm receives social backing.[23] Literacy qualification criteria for elected members of the panchayats (Chhattisgarh) bring

Mill's views on universal suffrage into the agenda for reforms. Provision for empowerment is not enough in itself, there is the urgency in creating enabling conditions.

Again, there are attempts on the part of some state governments to curtail the areas of jurisdiction of the panchayats through introducing amendments to the state Acts. Karnataka, once considered a pioneer one in the sphere of introducing a scheme of effective decentralization, now seeks to reverse the whole process. Recently, the government has passed an Amendment in the state Act empowering the MLAs to approve the list of beneficiaries for certain rural housing schemes bypassing the panchayats.[24] There has been a trend in Karnataka over the years to withdraw the powers given to the panchayats one by one. The purpose and status of decentralization will be tarnished seriously if the government moves further in bringing about such changes to the existing Act.

Decentralized district planning is one of the major strategies in the decentralization development project and for this purpose the Amendment includes the provision for creation of the district planning committees (DPC) to consolidate the plans prepared by the panchayats and the municipalities in the district and to prepare draft development plan for the district as a whole (Article 243ZD). The constitutional provision is no more than a pious wish. There is no time-frame in respect of formation of the DPCs, though the constitution of the state finance commissions is time-bound. Moreover, the composition, functions and activities of the DPC are left to the states, making room for variations and delays. Still, the DPC has not been constituted in all the states in India. Even in some states where it is constituted, it is chaired by a minister or a government official (government official in HP). Again, Gujarat has nominated district planning boards instead of DPC, and Maharashtra has a district-level body with an equal number of elected and nominated members. In some states, the DPC seldom meets and when it meets, it is chaired by a minister (Madhya Pradesh, Chhattisgarh) to finalize the draft plan.

West Bengal and Kerala (leaving behind the success stories from Karnataka in view of the current recentralizing trends in the state) are the two states where some serious experiments in decentralized planning were carried out in the backdrop of successful land reforms and organized political mobilization of the masses. In spite of the seeds of 'contradictions and the yearning for decentralization' in the Kerala Panchayat Raj Act, 1994,[25] People's Campaign for Ninth Plan was launched in July 1996 in Kerala to enable the local bodies to prepare their plan proposals and the same was completed to some extent successfully. The uniqueness of the developments in Kerala is that the Kerala Panchayat Act has been amended fifteen times till August 2010, as a result of which the system of decentralized development and planning has been completely institutionalized and an elaborate arrangement of laws and structure has been developed afresh to translate political will into administrative actions.[26] But the Coastal Management Zone Notification and Kerala Tourism Act 2010 negate the rights of the PRIs in matters relating to the affairs of local tourism, which falls under the jurisdiction of local bodies.

In West Bengal, decentralized district planning was initially introduced in 1985–86 but the success was extremely limited and the primary goal of development through effective decentralization remained mostly unfulfilled. After the growth and sustenance of the panchayats and municipalities and the formation of the constitutionalized district planning committees in West Bengal in 1994, decentralized planning was launched afresh and now the government has assumed the role of facilitator in the functioning of the local bodies and the implementation of development plans. The process of decentralized planning and development could be consolidated in view of the penetration of the ruling parties in the remote parts of the state and the mobilization of the poor and marginalized sections of the community as a social force for reforms and development. But the success is partial. It is doubtful if the objectives and spirits of decentralized planning have been internalized in the structure and functioning of the state government and the local bodies. It is also an issue of debate whether the government has been pursuing a policy of controlled decentralization. The recent development that took place in *Singur* in establishing a Tata Motor company on agricultural land has added new dimensions to the debate. The urge for industrialization, (a necessity, no doubt) and consequential process of conversion of agricultural land for setting up of industries at least were not taken up for consideration of the DPCs concerned. The post-facto consideration of issues after finalization of the plan and acquisition of land thereof does not promote the process of decentralizing development in any way. It may be mentioned that several central and state Acts such as the Coal Bearing Areas Act (1957), Coal Mine Act (1974), and Environmental Protection Act

(1986) have a conflicting nature with many provisions of the PESA and limit the process of decentralizing development in scheduled areas.

Dispersion of fiscal responsibilities and funds across the different tiers of the government is an essential element in decentralizing process. The Amendment, while dispersing the functional responsibilities to the PRIs and recognizing the need for fiscal devolutions (Articles 243-H and 243-I), has remained almost silent on the issue of devolution of funds, excepting the incorporation of a provision for appointment of state finance commissions in the states. The scheme of revenue raising and expenditure responsibilities of the Centre and the states is demarcated in VII Schedule. But there is no such provision relating to local governments, nor does the Amendment mention the issue of resource raising assignments for the local bodies. 'The Amendment proposes various taxing powers, sharing of taxes and duties, grants-in-aid for the consideration of the states for bestowing upon the PRIs'[27] There is no clear policy in the Amendment in respect of grants to the panchayats. As a result, there is a wide variation across the state Acts and practices in respect of tax and non-tax resources. While some states have made provisions in this regard, some others have left the issue to the state finance commissions for rationalizing the scheme of grants at the substate level. A review of the enabling provisions regarding tax assignments, fees, tax sharing and grants-in-aid provisions adopted in the states reflects only duplication, discrepancy and confusions.[28]

The role of the SFCs is not also encouraging. The delays in constitution, frequent reconstitution, delays in submission of reports and delayed tabling of ATR more often make the SFCs dysfunctional. Again, there is a different kind of problem with the SFCs. Most of the reports of the state finance commissions do not address the problems in concrete terms and also fail to give a clear view on the authority and responsibilities assigned to the local level bodies.[29] Since the composition of the SFC is not outlined in the Amendment, sometimes it becomes a product of a nexus between the bureaucrats and the state politicians for keeping the PRIs under their control. The extent of central grants is increasing through the CSS, which now constitutes a major part of gram panchayat budgets. The Finance Commission recommends grant to the PRIs for a period of five years but most of the grants are matching in nature. Moreover, release of grants without clear outlines of divisible pool and evaluation of vertical gaps between revenue assignments and expenditure commitments at different levels of the PRIs leads to the development of dependency syndrome.

Though the gram panchayats throughout the country have been given some taxing power, the block and district-level panchayats are deprived of the same in some of the states. The generation of own resources at different levels is also minimum for political reasons and hence there is the need for incorporation of some mandatory measures for resource mobilization and a provision for conditional non-matching grants from the Centre and the states. The rationality and appropriateness of the continuity of the MPLAD scheme and (CSS) need a closer and objective study to promote fiscal stability of the panchayats.[30] In addition to these schemes, there are some 26 sectoral programmes implemented by the Centre which clash with the subjects included in XI Schedule. The extent of devolution of funds and the financial autonomy ratio can be understood by the fact that in 2011, the allocation in the central budget for the Ministry of Rural Development was ₹ 89,578 crore (revised) as against ₹ 5,710.70 crore for the Ministry of Panchayati Raj (including BRGF grant). Apart from the scheme and project covered under the Ministry of Rural Development, there is separate allocation (around ₹ 80,000 crore in the budget for the year 2011–12) for some major flagship programmes under different ministries of the central government.[31] As a part of liberalization-privatization programme, the State is gradually withdrawing itself from providing social services and in such a situation the question of greater financial devolution in favour of the states does not arise.

Besides devolution of functions and funds, devolution of functionaries is an essential conditionality for decentralizing development, which is neglected in the Amendment. Under the provisions of the Constitution, there is no provision for creation of cadres for management of local governments, but 'integrated development requires integrated staff structure ... and the staff should be under the control of an elected body'.[32] The issue of transfer of functionaries has not yet attracted the serious attention of the state governments, excepting those of Karnataka and Sikkim. These two states have transferred functionaries relating to all the 29 subjects. Maharashtra has created district service for Class III and IV categories of staff who are placed under the control of the zilla parishad. But majority of the states (Assam, Bihar, Haryana, Punjab, Rajasthan, Tamil Nadu, etc.) are yet to initiate steps and some others (West Bengal, Kerala, Maharashtra, Himachal Pradesh) have transferred functionaries ranging from two to 18 of the line departments.[33] The decisions of the first round table of the panchayati raj ministers (July 2004) for building up a cadre of officials and technocrats for PRIs are yet to be implemented. Though the central government declared its policy to have a separate cadre for panchayati raj and advised the states to follow up, it did not spell out the time-limit for implementation.[34]

The existence of the District Rural Development Agency (DRDA) in some of the states and absence of clear guidelines for merging the DRDA with the zilla parishad or the district planning committee interferes with the functioning of the elected local bodies. It was created in early 1980s to activate people's participation and ensure flexibility in implementation of rural development programmes, but now unnecessarily occupies a certain space after the constitutionalization of the PRIs and the DPCs. The existence of such a parallel structure simply strengthens bureaucratic powers and needs to be merged with the panchayats. The executive officers for panchayats in some states, including West Bengal, are recruited and controlled by the state government but attached to the panchayats. The Block Development Officer is appointed by the state government and is a civil officer of the government but works as the executive officer at the middle-tier panchayats in most of the states. Similarly, the officers attached to the zilla parishads as secretary or in ex-officio capacities are deputed by the state governments. The government appoints some other panchayat functionaries also. The intuition of hierarchical principle in public services – central, state and local – dominates the behaviour and activities of the bureaucracy and the panchayats are at the receiving end.

The objective of the Amendment is clear and the whole scheme is to empower people through panchayats, which shall function as 'institutions of self-government' (Article 243G). Whatever the confusions and contradictions that may exist, the role of the gram panchayats in general and the gram sabha in particular is crucial in the entire decentralization project. Under the Amendment, the gram sabha is supposed to act as an engine of people's direct participation. But the dismal picture in the functioning of the gram sabha became an all-India phenomenon within a couple of years and the Government of India has been continuing special campaigns through the observance of the 'Year of Gram Sabha', in recognition of the potentialities and to energize gram sabhas with the necessary package and incorporating action programmes. These institutions build trust in panchayats and legitimize community actions. There are more issues involved in the functioning of these institutions, but information gathered so far does not allow looking at those issues. However, the low level of people's participation in the functioning of these institutions is the major problem at this stage since the danger to democracy does not emanate from the Opposition, but from the increasing absence of people and the opposition. In spite of these facts, the picture is not totally bleak. Some states are carrying out the new experiments. There are even PILs demanding panchayati raj elections and the judiciary is responding in a positive manner.

But the progress is tardy. Confidence of the people is yet to be built in the effectiveness of the gram sabha. Sometimes, the gram sabhas appear to be government departments rather than institutions of the people. Studies conducted in different parts across the country reveal almost the same picture. These are in fact democratic deficits and quite natural to be traced everywhere in India. But the effectiveness of the gram sabha is structurally constrained.

In some states like Kerala, Karnataka and Andhra Pradesh, gram sabhas are comparatively active. In West Bengal, the gram sabha has no significance in view of the creation of gram sansads and gram unnayan samitis. But women hardly attend the meetings of the gram sabha and the officials struggle for managing quorum. From field studies, it is revealed that indifference, ignorance, illiteracy, lack of awareness, patriarchal values, poverty and engagement in outside daily works are responsible for non-functioning of the gram sabha in different states. In one or two states, conditions are lacking in the tribal areas to give effect to the provisions of the Panchayat (Extension to the Scheduled Areas) Act, 1996 (PESA). The Act provides a framework for establishing *gram swaraj* as visualized by Gandhi.[35] In Kerala, the participation of people is slightly better because of the density of population and people's campaign launched previously. In Madhya Pradesh, the rate of women's participation is better and in Kerala it is around 30 per cent, due to the formation of a large number of SHG groups in both the states. It is found that in most of the meetings of gram sabha, the problems are identified but the elected members cannot suggest solutions. Hence, there is the need for capacity building for the members of the gram panchayats so that they are empowered to play a leadership role in development planning. The participants, the average people of the gram panchayats, should be made aware through a process of awareness building with continuous dissemination of information and general campaign preferably on the lines followed in Kerala, so that they may be really empowered. This empowerment may enable them to understand not only why they are poor or disenfranchised, but also what they can do about it, through their 'institutions of self-government'. The usual assumption is that power is to be transferred to the people – but the holders of power are seldom ready to relinquish it, hence the situation may lead to the degeneration of democratic decentralization into controlled decentralization. In West Bengal, the rates of participation at the meetings of the gram sansads are slightly better than those observed in case of the gram sabhas. It is found that the meetings are held almost regularly in all the gram sansads, each having coverage of 700 voters on an average.

Subsequently, the gram unnayan samitis (GUS) are also established at the level of the gram sansads within the gram sabhas to provide a regular forum for the rural people for their continuous involvement. The creation of the gram sansads and gram unnayan samitis aims at increasing participation of people without creating additional tiers of the PRIs at the field level. The gram unnayan samitis are essentially bodies outside the structural framework of the panchayati raj and different in composition and functioning. Though time is not ripe yet to make an assessment of these bodies, micro studies conducted in three blocks in Midnapore (unpublished) reveal that so far these are acting as complementary organizations, not parallel agencies. The criticisms sometimes leveled against the GUS in West Bengal are unfounded as it in no way hinders the functioning of the gram panchayats. The whole perspective in West Bengal is quite different and the ideological persuasions of the parties are also different. It is the only state in India which has been holding panchayat elections in time at regular intervals of five years till 2008. The government has been trying since 2005–06 to make the institutions work in an effective manner. In addition to all the statutory changes, the government has introduced the World Bank-supported programmes of Institutional Strengthening of Gram Panchayats (ISGP) in 1,000 gram panchayats covering nine districts of the state since 31 August 2010 to activate and strengthen the GPs as institutions of self-government. The programme consists of four components: block grants to the gram panchayats; empowerment and capacity building; strengthening the monitoring and supervisory role of the PRIs; and management and implementation of programme-related activities.[36]

The above review does not negate the view that the scheme for decentralizing development of rural India is an incomplete state of affairs; the hierarchical structure of policy-making is in no sense weakened. Major decisions still flow from the top to the bottom with the exception that the political and administrative elites share some powers of decision-making with people. Without land reforms and mobilization of masses through grassroots level organizations, this balance in the co-relation between the elites and the people cannot take a reverse direction. Decentralization and decentralizing development require structural changes, new set of institutions and systems, which can be built up effectively on the axis of these two forces.

The rural community in India is basically organized on feudal and semi-feudal structures, occasionally intervened by class considerations and as such effective decentralization is always a conflict-prone area. The state governments led by the ruling groups and elites seek to exert and retain their control over the rural population through the institutions of local governance. Cohesion and unity in the thinking and approaches are gradually declining in the organizations of political parties under the all-encompassing impacts of the liberalization-privatization framework. Group hegemony and individual materialism and self-interests within the organizations have become the determining considerations to which the public organizations succumb. Powers and authority are necessarily concentrated in the hands of a few in the parties. The interests of the ruling groups are linked to those of the dominant sections active in the rural organizations. The leadership of the local-level organizations is equally allied with the dominant groups in the government. These groups and for that matter the governments in such situations prefer to decentralize power and authority to that extent in which their dominance and control remain unaltered. In extreme cases, the local leader also identifies himself with the party and the panchayats, compounding his personal interests with those of the local organizations and the party, which in turn control such organizations. Hence, devolution or delegation of powers to the people becomes tailor-made or meaningless description of functional reality. 'Merely giving a vote or instituting a "gram sabha" have not assumed any participation by the "people", though pumping in a great deal of money into these areas has, after leaking into various intermediary hands, shown some improvement of the rural areas. Still it is not proved that decentralization *per se* is instrumental in whatever has happened. The local bodies do not seem to have made any great impact on democratic participation by the people'.[37] The observations were made three decades back and still have equal relevance.

Organization of the Volume

Most of the discourses on decentralization are normative in approach in the sense that almost all of them seek to examine the nature and evaluate the impact of decentralizing practices on the socio-political and economic landscapes of the society under study in order to have an in-depth understanding of what actually is being done at the grassroots levels, and how and in which manner the implementation of the portfolio of development functions takes place. The basic objective of this book is to bring together the findings and studies contributed by academia, experts, bureaucrats and development practitioners from a broader dimension in which theories, ideas and experiences are blended together in an interacting manner. The book is divided into four interrelated but identifiable sections. *The first* section deals with the theory of decentralization and the ideas of two great thinkers and activists. *Section II* is devoted to the constitutionalization and the functioning of panchayat raj bodies in India, highlighting the experiences and the need for capacity building. In implementation of any model or system of governance, there are always certain developments and issues interacting upon one, another that determine the course and future of the experiments. These issues are included in *Section III.* The last *Section (IV)* intends to highlight certain innovative decentralizing experiments tried in the state having both explicit and implicit implication for inclusion of the excluded. The contributions made by individual writers are introduced in these sections in a comprehensive manner with the obvious purpose of giving almost a synoptic view of their discussions for which I present my apologies to both the contributors and the readers for causing inconveniences, if any, by way of repetition.

The first article contributed by Mohit Bhattacharya indicates the scope and limit of the first section of this publication. Bhattacharya in his paper has made a brief focus on various aspects of decentralization realizing through establishment of local government. The author considers decentralization from a normatic perspective as being instrumental in creating an enabling environment in which people, especially the marginalized category, finds a scope for playing the role of decision-makers. In the context of achieving the Millennium Development Goals and re-inventing government, the role of local governments is interestingly acclaimed. While explaining the concept of decentralization in a broader context of human development and presenting a brief outline of major 'waves' of decentralization, the author examines the perspectives in which decentralization has become a dominating phenomenon to promote democratic governance, thereby reinforcing mutually capabilities and broadening the scope of human development. A genuine decentralized system ensures a participatory democratic process, and combining pro-people growth, brings 'economic and political democracy closer in the shortest possible time'. The author has reiterated the point what Anil Bhaduri emphasized elsewhere. Bhattacharya traces the benefits of decentralization like 'accountability, responsiveness, equitable and cost-effective local services available through people's participation at the grassroots, and cites the instances of success stories from Brazil and Kerala. But at the same time, the parameters of effective local governance demand that the holders of public faith and trust must act effectively and fairly. That is why the issue of capacity building emerges and the author indicates the need of institutional capacity building at all levels to institutionalize the system of decentralization. The issue of capacity building has also been discussed elsewhere in this volume.

The issue of decentralization is always linked with the issue of political power since it aims at empowerment – based on political and administrative pluralism. Herein lies the constraints and challenges to the decentralized framework. The priorities and perspectives of decentralization have changed (*rather diluted*) considerably with the emergence of the concept of local governance encompassing diverse actors, citizens' groups and stakeholders beside local government, which has complicated the functioning of decentralized local bodies. In his concluding note, the author looks to appropriate local leadership to overcome the additional challenges of good governance providing an opportunity for giving the poor a sense of fuller participation in governance to bridge the gap between ideas and their applications in democracy.

Since the beginning of the last century, some nationalist thinkers and social reformers started their experiments for organizing the people in rural areas for community development based on cooperative efforts without turning to the government for financial support. Mahatma Gandhi and Rabindranath Tagore are the most prominent among them who have made lasting contributions in the sphere of developing concrete ideas for rural development in India.

The fact that deserves attention of the scholars and academia is that no individual thinker has ever made so much contribution in recent times as M.K. Gandhi had done in a comprehensive and organized simplicity in offering a clear programme of rural development based on a decentralized political system. In fact, since Independence, the policy-makers and planners have been trying to realize Gandhi's ideas of *gram swaraj* through various programmes and experiments starting with community development in early 1950s to most recently the legislation to provide employment guarantee for the rural poor. In the intervening period, constitutional amendments (1992) have been passed to institute panchayats throughout the country to strengthen the process of decentralization of decision-making and financial powers to the grassroots levels. Anil Kumar Jana in his paper has made an attempt to explain Gandhi's views on decentralization and development and to find out their relevance in the present context.

The contributor has explained the process of culmination of Gandhi's ideas of development into his views on decentralization and panchayati raj with a view to eradicating poverty and reducing the gap between the rich and the poor. In doing so, the author has discussed in brief the background in which Gandhi began to articulate his views and the influences exerted by Tolstoy, Ruskin, Thoreau and others on him. The contributor elaborates Gandhi's concept of development based on utilization of indigenous resources and human labour for 'a higher standard of life' in a non-violent decentralized system, which could be established through creation of panchayats at different levels starting from the villages. Citing primary sources, the contributor has explained Gandhi's views on the nature and functions, besides rationale, of the 'little republics' and has tried to examine relevance of his views in the present context in spite of much repeated limitations. He has also picked up the concept of 'aparigraha' and other propositions on which Gandhi's concept of decentralization is built up and has tried to understand the relevance of these elements in the context of changing perspectives of modernization and nation-building that has taken place in post-Gandhian era. There is also the urgency in close introspection of Gandhi's ideas to see if these could provide some solutions to the multifarious problems that beset our society today. Finally, the author concludes with a rider that Gandhi's ideas like those of other thinkers are time and situation-specific which demand their reinterpretation and adaptation with necessary modifications to fit well into the domain of the current development discourse.

Rabindranath Tagore is another personality who was much inspired by the new wave of 'back to the villages' movement that swept over a large part of rural and semi-urban India in early years of the 20th century. While staying in East Bengal (1890–1915) to supervise the family *zamindari,* he gathered his first-hand experience in planning and undertaking rural development programmes at *Shelaidah* and *Sahajadpur.* Later, he shifted his focus to Sriniketan (1922) in West Bengal and tried with his experiments until 1941, before his death. During all these years, Rabindranath tried to popularize cooperative principles, scientific methods and modern techniques of agricultural development, idea of rural reconstruction based on indigenous resources, scheme of education and development, and the concept of environmental protection. Rabindranath, like Gandhi, had his own views on education in which he laid emphasis on establishing linkages between soul and mind of the learners for a greater cause of the country.

Tagore's achievement in diverse fields of creative art and literature are highly applauded but his contribution to development discourse is not much cited. Kumkum Chattopadhyay in her painstaking researches has explored all the major issues of Tagore's model of rural development and highlights the basic features of his experiments. In fact, the development experiment started by him continued to flourish for more than two decades under his own active supervision and even today, Sriniketan moves forward with its growth, though slightly in a different way. The author rightly points out that Tagore's concept and programme is also 'eco-friendly' and possibly sustainability of the model is the main reason. The contributor has picked up the core areas of experiments outlined and implemented in two phases: pre-Sriniketan and Sriniketan, and has traced the linkages between the two. The principles of *Samavayaneeti,* which constitute the essence of Tagore's ideas, schemes of development of agriculture and rural reconstruction and his views on education, are analysed in this paper. Tagore's views on *swadeshi samaj* and emphasis on indigenous resources and knowledge, as the author points out, have been applied by the poet himself in building Sriniketan and Shantiniketan. Viswa-Bharati University incorporates rural reconstruction and development in its academic curricular. All these contributions reflect the novelty in Tagore's ideas which stimulates the author to consider Rabindranath Tagore as an alternative development thinker.

Two decades have passed since the passing of the two Constitutional Amendments in 1992 according constitutional status to the panchayats and municipalities to function as the third tier of governance in India. It is also worth mentioning that the Seventy Third

Amendment made certain institutional innovations, including the creation of *gram sabhas (*village assemblies), which contain the potentialities of strengthening local democracy by making these bodies more direct and inclusive. As a result, the political landscape of the country has considerably changed: now it comprises a large number of institutions involving almost three million elected representatives, of which more than a million members are women. The experiences gained during these years naturally raise the basic issue of the effectiveness of these institutions in playing the role designed for them as 'institutions of self-government'. Moreover, there is always the problem of viewing development as preceding the political dimensions of local government.

The papers contributed by Asok Mukhopadhyay, Prabhat Datta, Budh Bahadur Lama, Apurba Mukhopadhyay, Debnarayan Modak and Soma Ghosh are directed towards finding answers to some of the questions covered under these broad issues in this section of the volume. Apparently, the picture that comes out as a whole contains both the achievements and the failures in transforming the socio-economically inegalitarian society of India into a politically egalitarian and viable set-up. Hence, the issue of capacity building comes to dominate the priority areas, which have also been considered by one of the above contributors, while Asok Mukhopadhayay introduces the constitutional perspective of the decentralizing exercises confirmed by the Seventy Third and Seventy Fourth Amendment Acts to the Constitution.

Though there are different perceptions about development, there is an agreement that radical changes in politico-economic policies and structure of a country is required for bringing about necessary changes in improving the living conditions of the people. This realization by the policy-makers in the face of failure of bureaucracy-led development administration in early decades of Independence in India has finally resulted in the constitutionalization of local governments. Asok Mukhopadhyay in his paper has dealt with the situation in explicit terms that prevailed in the Indian administrative system prior to the Seventy Third and Seventy Fourth Amendments and also the experiments carried out previously for development at the ground level. The increasing gap between the government and the people was becoming clear and visible which posed major problems in good governance and this was reflected in various reports submitted by different committees and commissions appointed by the central government.

Though the author does not have any illusion in considering the Amendments as moving towards establishing a 'third tier of representative government' or district governments in a multi-level federal system, as perceived by a section of enthusiastic intelligentsia, he believes that the nature and ambit of these Amendments provide 'a fine format for good governance' in the present-day context. In his anxiety for success of the scheme of decentralization, the author identifies the major constraints, both structural and ideational, standing in the way of implementing the constitutional mandate in letter and spirit. The author is also very much critical of the role of bureaucracy especially at the state levels. He strongly urges the leadership to undertake a serious exercise for working out a complete scheme of decentralization and allocation of powers and functions among the Centre, states and local government bodies on the principles of subsidiarity. Decentralization is based on a clear demarcation of functions, authorities and entitlements. Though the frontiers of different tiers of government have been made more visible through the Amendments, many grey areas still persist. Hence, the contributor suggests the formulation of a comprehensive policy and building an institutional framework for making decentralized governance in India more viable and effective since decentralizing for development is not a mere political catchword, nor is it an administrative expertise only but also a living philosophy for the people.

Prabhat Datta has a definite point in examining the nature of decentralization in India which has made the process altogether inadequate. While tracing the origin of the decentralized system of governance in an otherwise centralized set-up commissioned by the British, he refers to the perception of the Congress party for a strong Centre which has produced a centralized federation in India. Thanks to the hegemony of the Congress at both the Centre and the states, coupled with the absence of a sufficient challenge until 1967, there was no major tension or conflicts between the Union and units to demand a review of the Centre-state relations. The post-fourth general elections held in 1967 gave a new twist to India's federalism when the demand for redrawing the federal map gained momentum and serious thinking began to dominate the election agenda and political conclaves. For other reasons as well, the situation was moving towards culminating in a new direction and in the process the Seventy Third and Seventy Fourth Amendment Acts were passed in 1992, thereby strengthening the blueprint for a multi-level federalism.

In this paper, the author also seeks to examine the constitutional position of the local government system and its inherent implications on decentralization in India. He scrutinizes the various provisions of the Amendment as well as the states' conformity Acts to point out the vulnerabilities of the panchayati raj bodies in absence of necessary and steady devolution of 3Fs – functions, funds and functionaries – by the states to the different tiers of the panchayats. Most of the states, excepting only a few, have adopted a reluctant attitude towards transforming these bodies into effective institutions of self-government. Beside these gaps and limitations, there have been certain unusual developments emerging from both the Centre and the states which seek to deliberately cripple the functioning of these fragile institutions. The provision of allocation of central funds for the members of Parliament, which destroys the very spirit of decentralization, has been dealt with by the author at length. The constitution of grassroots level parallel bodies in some states, launching of various CSS, both in urban and rural areas, jeopardize the effectiveness of the local elected bodies, at times simply making them implementing agencies. The attempt for implementation of certain policies in respect of urban areas uniformly throughout the country without considering the localness of the localities goes against the spirit of decentralized local governance. The state of affairs in planning and implementation of decentralized planning is highly deplorable, which pinpoints the callous attitude of interests on the part of the government. The author concludes that the issue of the third stratum in India's federal system is a far cry even after the constitutional Amendments, and he puts all his hopes in new social movements in strengthening the process of decentralization.

The article contributed by B.B. Lama is devoted to an overview of the system of participatory democracy in the context of functioning of the panchayats in India. At the beginning, the author explains the concept of participatory democracy as a method of intensifying and authenticating people's role in determining the course of their development and identifies it as a component of the New Democratic theory. Though there is always a challenge in creating opportunities for larger participation in increasingly complex and differentiated societies, the contributor citing arguments from Kothari's *Rethinking Democracy* makes a strong case for participatory democracy for people's role in decision-making and policy implementation. While justifying the need for participatory democracy, Lama makes a brief survey of the historical evolution and expansion of the panchayat system in India, referring to the Constituent Assembly debate on the proposal of inclusion of provisions for panchayats in the Constitution after Independence and the subsequent dilemma confronting the political leadership of the country in magnifying the role and effectiveness of these grassroots organizations. The enactment of the Seventy Third Amendment, 1992 has apparently put an end to the ongoing debate but has brought certain issues hitherto unknown to the policy-makers. The spirit of the Amendment, in the author's view, seeks to heighten the role of the 'gram sabha' and other tiers of the panchayats to ensure the functioning of participatory democracy, though in a very limited scope. The conformity Acts passed by different states and certain procedural and administrative actions have created entropy in transforming representative democracy into a participatory one. However, there is a silver lining in the functioning of the system in some states, including West Bengal, the author points out, which makes us confident of a better tomorrow.

Thus, the contributions made by Prabhat Datta and B.B. Lama focus mainly from an all-India perspective. Apurba Mukhopadhyay concentrates his discussions on the functioning of panchayats in West Bengal through contextualizing decentralizing experiments to the political developments and ideological perspective in India. While refering extensively to previous findings drawn by a good number of scholars, Apurba Mukhopadhyay has convincingly established the case for decentralization under a pro-people active state to counter-balance the forces of inegalitarian growth. He thinks that the case for local governance in India is not an act of the State based on democratic ethos, but by the dictates of the IMF-World Bank. On the contrary, the author asserts, the practice of decentralization in a few states, especially in West Bengal, is no doubt an exception which had its origin in the Left front regime. Even prior to the Seventy Third Amendment Act, Mukhopadhyay lucidly traces the perspective of decentralization in West Bengal. The decision of the state government to revitalize the panchayats through direct elections and to involve the newly-elected bodies in rural development and other related activities, including implementation of land ceiling provisions, identification and distribution of surplus land to the landless and recording the names of sharecroppers in order to protect their rights against forceful eviction, led to a change in the pattern of rural leadership. All these ultimately helped the process of decentralization which struck roots deep into the soil.

The author has neatly summarized the changes that have taken place in West Bengal landscape and has elaborated the political impact of all these changes on democratic governance in general and on the functioning of panchayats in the state in particular. He comes to the conclusion that 'the panchayats in West Bengal do not represent a mere change ... These are to function as an alternative structure of people's power, bridging the gap between state and civil society up to a certain level ...' though viewing in an ideal type formulation, 'gram panchayats in West Bengal are yet to evolve as institutions facilitating "cooperative decision-making", taking gram sansads and gram unnayan samitis into full confidence'.

Now Apurba Mukhopadhyay turns his focus to the debate on depoliticized development based on civil society-NGO collaboration as proposed in neo-liberal circles and its counter discourses and practices developed in the era of globalization. Citing the examples from South Korea, he tries to address the issue of relationship between development and democracy and to explore the Leftist strategy pursued in the state for participatory rural development. But there were certain failures and serious mistakes in the experiments under the Leftist dispensation, he points out, which led to popular discontent and alienation. And as a result, the Left has been given the third major defeat in a row in the last concluded panchayat elections (2011), preceded by its defeats in the 2009 Lok Sabha and 2011 Assembly elections. The post-panchayat elections have brought the issues of adopting an effective strategy of decentralization to absorb the shocks of neo-liberal policies and making 'participation-in-development' an actuality through involving people not as passive beneficiaries of development, but as active and dynamic partners in decentralizing development.

While making an attempt to present an overview of the functioning of panchayats especially in West Bengal during the last twenty years, Debnarayan Modak raises the issue of capacity building for streamlining the activities and strengthening the institutional framework of these grassroots level organizations. Capacity building seems to be the way in the opinion of the author to make panchayats the engines of development and to help overcome the hurdles standing in their way of becoming institutions of self-governance. According to the author, capacity building is a broader concept which includes the state's and panchayat's ability to overcome opposition in order to fulfill the objectives through optional use of resources by rational choices and strategic planning. Moreover, to enable the panchayats to function effectively, there is the urgency in developing behavioural and functional skills of the members and functionaries of panchayats to realize the dynamics of social, political and economic perspectives of rural transformation and development and to work in close cooperation with local people in formulation and implementation of specified programmes and activities. Hence, capacity building is also intended to develop and empower every member to take part in the process of decision-making without any apprehension and dilemma through a process of building of opportunities as well as abilities to accomplish the desired objectives.

After explaining the issue of capacity building, the author examines the implications of the two Amendments on the functioning of the PRIs in general and the *gram sabha* in particular and points out that enactment of law and taking certain administrative measures are not sufficient enough to ensure effective decentralization and that certain conditions are necessary for success of local government. And here again, he raises the issue of capacity building and highlights the role of both the central and state governments in making the panchayats empowered, enabled and accountable in discharging their constitutional obligations. Though the panchayats have stuck to the roots in West Bengal in view of the changes through successive amendments in the state panchayat Act, followed by political commitments, still there are certain lapses and gaps. The roadmap published by the state government of West Bengal for strengthening decentralization is also reproduced by the contributor, which indicates the present state of affairs. In conclusion, the author observes that in spite of certain deficits in the functioning of panchayats in the state during the Left regime, there are enough evidences to confirm the proposition that the experiments in decentralization over the years have progressed steadily in the desired direction, which could be given a further push by the new regime by moving towards consolidation of decentralized democracy.

The vital need for capacity building of the elected representatives and panchayat functionaries is thus widely acknowledged and certain steps in this direction have been outlined in the paper contributed by Modak. Soma Ghosh, on the other hand, seeks to focus our attention to a specific area of common concern which necessitates capacity building for women's empowerment at the state's initiative at the first instance. Ghosh begins her analysis with a panoramic view of the growth and changes in the role of the state from the 18th to the 19th and the 20th centuries. At the beginning, the author explains the situation in which the state was advised to retreat or withdraw itself from all activities excepting those pertaining to certain core areas of governance. After exploring the IMF–World Bank touted minimalist state and market-friendly approach, which ultimately culminated in the theorization and emergence of the idea of good governance necessitating and promoting people's participation in development, the author seeks to concentrate on the issue of people's participation at local levels.

The panchayati raj bodies in India provide the extended scope for women's participation after the 73rd and 74th Amendments. Quoting from a reply to a question in Parliament, the author has traced the increasing trend in women's participation at all levels of panchayats moving above 35 per cent in 2010, much above the stipulated one-third requirement in the Amendment. Though the system has been working quite well in this direction in West Bengal since 1978, the author observes that the system has failed to ensure empowerment of the poor and the marginalized, especially women, and raises a very pertinent question that whether the panchayats are capable in changing the social perception about women in which a secondary status is reserved for them.

She also examines the reasons behind the situation. The reservation of seats for women in Parliament and state legislatures is a long-pending issue. As a remedial measure, the author justifies the need for capacity building for women members at local levels in particular and women in general at all levels and identifies the critical areas, methodology and the measures to enhance women's access to production process, suitable working conditions, productive endowments and finally to decision-making both within and outside the family. In her article, the author proposes pro-active roles of the district administration in the empowerment process through creating mechanisms for 'information exchange, conflict resolution, joint actions, strategic planning and enhancement of public awareness.' The contributor concludes her write-up with the suggestion that the governments should take the entire responsibility of capacity building of women and making the panchayats gender-sensitive.

Decentralization in governance of a country is not a strait-jacket arrangement but rather a 'mosaic' comprising a variety of issues, actors and diverse elements, including constitutional structure, relationship between the government and the people, role of bureaucracy and voluntary organizations, structure and role of political parties, methods of people's participation, concepts and practices in respect of relationship between economic and social structure and the like. It has a changing character. As a result, a certain type of decentralized system that works excellently in a particular country may become dysfunctional in another country. Again, activities of different tiers of government may also overlap and interpenetrate one another. Hence, successful implementation of decentralizing policies depends a lot on a host of factors and a number of actors, which necessitates the understanding of the contours of the role and relationships involved in the system. This section of the present volume is devoted to explore this contours while examining the experiments in decentralization that has taken shape in West Bengal in the last three decades following the revival of panchayats in the aftermath of Asoka Mehta Committee. In this section, the issues involving bureaucracy, parties, decentralized planning and political will of the ruling regime are included to make a comprehensive understanding of the functional domain of the panchayats as contributed by the authors: Alok Mukhopadhyay, Buddhadeb Ghosh, Sakti Pada Pal and Chanchal Chakrabarti.

The paper contributed by Shri Alok Kumar Mukhopadhyay, formerly district magistrate and head of State Institute of Panchayats, is in fact a critical account of his interactions and encounter with people's representatives during the Left Front regime in West Bengal. The author recollects the experiences he had during the period of transformation of the decorative panchayats into effective ones, changing the nature of line of communication and decision-making culminating in the establishment of legitimacy of the elected representatives. The change reinforced the demand for a legitimate share in administration in favour of the panchayat representatives, which led to the development of an atmosphere based on cooperation and occasional conflicts between people's representatives and state bureaucracy especially at the lower levels. Adopting an ecological approach, he tries to explain the changes in the functioning of the PRIs since the beginning of 1990s, marked by introduction of economic reforms, demolition of Babri Masjid and the enactment of twin Amendments in 1992 in which the bureaucracy reoccupied the driving seat in the decentralizing process, which was successfully steered towards consolidation of the system over a decade. The relationship between the representatives and bureaucracy got new twists and turns at this juncture. The situation confronting the system has been better explained by the author himself:

> There was plenty of money for implementation of schemes under different names, all carefully designed with detailed guidelines. Even funds released as untied grants under dispensations of Finance Commissions were subject to bureaucratic value judgement ... A time was soon reached when the prime concern of panchayats was to receive funds, spend them, submit utilization certificates and face audit, and all this strengthened the hands of bureaucracy.

The above observation may appear to be curt but not costive. Within a short span of time, panchayats in fact became merely delivery and implementing agencies of the government at the field levels. Democratic decentralization took the shape of *controlled decentralization* (term used and emphasized by the editor) worked out by a crafty bureaucracy and endorsed by a weary political leadership. Corruption and misappropriation of public funds were nothing new under such a situation. At the same time, a new urge emerged in government circles in ensuring transparency and accountability for good governance in the functioning of the rural local bodies and there were mixed experiences. Different methods and techniques, both institutional and procedural, were worked out but again, as the author points out, all these resulted in 'a hopeless dependence on appointed officials' and thus further bureaucratization of panchayats took place by the middle of the first decade of this century. Most of the steps initiated to strengthen the process of participatory decision-making were reduced to mere formalities heavily dependent on official intervention. Even the creation of a body like gram unnayan samiti (GUS) for effective people's participation failed to gear up mobilization of people. Thus, the author concludes with a sense of circumvention that the constitutional spirit of making the panchayats institutions of self-government has been betrayed with due respect by providing a room in the Acts and statutes and also treating these bodies as extension counters of the governments. In the concluding part of the paper, the author, however, cites some inspiring examples, though only a few, which raises hope that effective decentralization could be materialized in an atmosphere of complementary roles involving the bureaucracy, political elites and panchayat functionaries, if a proper scheme of decentralization is designed.

Decentralized district planning now constitutes an important element in India's framework of multi-level planning. Prior to the Amendments in 1992, there was some sort of district planning which was primarily a process of data-collection but not final decision-making at the lower levels. The practice followed was that plans prepared at the local levels used to be modified at higher levels without taking the views of lower units into consideration or even without reference to them. Moreover, the planning exercise hardly involved participation of people in either designing or implementation of planning. In fact, since its introduction in India after Independence, planning has always been sectoral rather than spatial. Planning at the national, state and district levels was nothing but a break-up of sectoral or departmental programmes. Local government was never involved meaningfully and closely in planning efforts.

Buddhadeb Ghosh, having a standing experience in both bureaucratic kingdom and academic domain, in his contribution has succinctly identified the constraints on institutionalizing decentralized planning in India and before raising the issues has made a quick survey of the planning process that preceded the present methodology. Prior to constitutional amendments, the author points out, the practice followed in respect of district plan was purely 'an aggregation of departmental schemes' and the same was far from actual planning. Afterwards, some experiments in decentralized planning were started in West Bengal and Karnataka in mid-1980s under the leadership of panchayats with initial success, but the practice could not be sustained after a few years. After the twin Amendments, an all-out attempt was made in different parts of the country to try for decentralized planning and Kerala came forward to show how a holistic approach could be adopted in formulation of decentralized plans. West Bengal also made some new experiments in a scattered manner.

However, the author does not share the common perception of 'a multi-level planning regime' being created through the Amendments and explains very meticulously the inherent inconsistencies and deficiencies that make the Amendments edentulous instruments to fulfill the long-cherished aspiration for an effective decentralized direction. The devolution of functions to the panchayats, if any, under Article 243G, especially in sub-clause (b), the author rightly points out, makes the panchayats simply implementing agencies, not autonomous institutions. Moreover, the functional jurisdiction of panchayats and the devolutions of powers and functions are left to the state governments to decide. One of the most interesting innovations in the Amendments is the provision of the District Planning Committee and decentralized planning. But while the constitutional provisions are laudable on these counts, the restrictions imposed on the scope of their functioning to the preparation of 'a draft development plan for the district as a whole' betray both the scope and spirit of decentralized planning.

There are also certain conceptual and institutional problems that hinder the process of developing multi-sectoral decentralized planning at different tiers of panchayats. The author specifically raises the issue of integration of departmental multi-sectoral schemes into the gram panchayat level planning, apart from the problems relating to the issue of implementation. Similar types of problems also confront the policies outlined at the panchayat samiti and zilla parishad levels. Thus, there are more grey areas 'covering conceptual, institutional and operational' aspects that deserve minute attention of the policy-makers, experts and field-level practitioners so as to make decentralized planning an effective method of development. The findings and observations made by the contributor of this paper lead us to take a serious note of the conclusions and recommendations arrived at three decades back by the Hanumantha Rao Committee on district planning: 'For decentralized planning to make headway, institutional mechanisms have be made more broad-based with the active involvement of local representatives and endowed with a greater degree of autonomy in local decision-making. Simultaneously, several administrative and financial delegations as well as other measures have to be systematically worked out.'[38]

In modern democratic systems, political parties attract more public attention than government because they ensure peaceful change of regimes, people's participation in the functioning of the system, articulation of public interests and socialization of democratic values in an organized manner and hence, their importance is widely acknowledged. The primary function of political parties is to organize and aggregate public opinion and transmit the same to government, thereby reducing the gaps between the people and their government. Representative democracy is based on this relationship. Naturally, the issue of involvement of political parties becomes pertinent in case of local government and it is not an exception to the functioning of panchayats in this state.

Amidst a broad collection of mixed and varied debates on the role of political parties in localized decentralized government operating through panchayats, Sakti Pal endeavours to reach to an ultimate resolution with a different style in presentation. His attempt at round-whole and compact discussions consisting of a number of key questions conveys a message bearing contextualized answers, involving effectiveness and relevance of political parties in the third stratum of governance in India. He starts his discourse with a reference to the recommendations of Balwantray Mehta Committee, which emphasized non-political and non-party based panchayats, directly elected at the village level and indirectly at the intermediate and district levels. Essentially the panchayats formed party-less in form, but in spirit became the carrier of vested interests recoiled by rural *kulaks* and upper-caste elites of the society. The Congress, having been in the centre of power, dominated these new-born institutions. Naturally, the non-party based panchayats, the contributor points out, became party based in reality.

Then the author seeks to examine the changed political situations that warranted a decline in hegemony of the Congress after the fourth general elections (1967) landing in coalitional political arrangements devised by some regional and non-Congress political parties in subsequent years. The new situation led to the revival of fresh interests in revitalizing panchayats through effective decentralization of power and functions to the lower levels from the Centre on Gandhian principles, which culminated in the constitution of the Asoka Mehta Committee by the Janata government at the Centre in 1977. It recommended establishment of party-based panchayats as institutions of local level governance, bidding goodbye to the non-party or party-less Gandhian formulations. The whole country, including West Bengal, set the ball rolling in trying afresh the appropriateness of politically-oriented local bodies in decentralizing development.

In West Bengal, the Left Front government reorganized the local bodies holding elections in 1978, taking a cue from the Asoka Mehta Committee on party-based composition with a view to strengthening its political base in rural segments. Subsequently, after the Seventy Third Amendment in 1992, the panchayats were accorded constitutional status. The concluding part of the article focuses on the issue whether party-based panchayats are capable of meeting the main plank of ensuring autonomy of the grassroots organizations in furthering the cause of decentralizing development with special emphasis on experiences gained in Kerala and West Bengal. The author highlights a point that the leadership in Kerala has been able to create a space for people's effective participation in local governance, adopting the formalities of party-based formulations in their own way. He concludes with his observation that the issue of non-party and/or party-based local government has almost been settled in India in favour of the latter by the people themselves through their massive participation in the process.

Decentralization may differ in extent to which it can meet the democratic requirements as it vacillates in respect of having autonomy from higher levels of government. Whatever may be the situation, reflection of democratic ideas and functioning is at the heart of decentralizing practices. It is a fact that there is something more to democracy then to elections, but notwithstanding, elections are vital and essential elements in building a decentralized system of governance.

One of the innovative features of the Seventy Third Amendment is the provision for holding regular elections to the panchayats at an interval of five years under the superintendence, direction and control of the state election commissions constituted at the states by the Governor concerned. After the Amendment of 1992, all states passed state conformity Acts incorporating the changes introduced in the Constitution but some states did not organize elections to the panchayats in due time, even after long expiry of their terms. Some states conducted elections for one or two tiers of the PRIs and withheld election for the other levels for sometime, which led the Supreme Court to advise those states in August 1997 following a writ petition (no. 719 of 1995) to follow the constitutional mandate. But due to absence of political will on the part of some state governments, holding of elections was delayed. Such an attitude indicated their reluctance in sharing power with decentralized local bodies, which ultimately impeded the process of institutionalizing the third stratum of government at the local level. Hence, it is not surprising that in Jharkhand, the elections were held after 32 years in December 2010 and in Jammu and Kashmir, these were conducted for the first time in April 2011.[39] West Bengal was the only major state which organized regular and timely elections to these local bodies at an interval of every five years since 1978 to 2008 during the Left Front rule. Actually, while in power, the Left had never postponed or delayed panchayat elections even when elections were delayed in other states, including Karnataka and Kerala. These states once stood at the forefront along with West Bengal and Tripura in carrying out new experiments in revitalizing panchayats. The Congress-led UDF government delayed the elections for a considerable period till the second half of 1995.[40]

However, despite its leading role in decentralizing development, West Bengal earned a bad name when the last panchayat elections (2013) were delayed and rescheduled in a very undesirable situation, having an adverse implication for strengthening decentralization in the state. The entire story behind such an unprecedented situation and events orchestrated prior to the elections in 2013 in West Bengal has been meticulously examined and restructured by Chanchal Chakrabarti in this section. He has focused on the main issue of contention between the state government and state election commission, both mandated by the Constitution to comply with and oversee the implementation of constitutional provisions religiously and not to hold back the spirit of the Constitution. It is a fact that the events sought to deface and defile the Constitution, no matter where the responsibility lies, and the readers are at liberty to draw their conclusions, if they so decide. Chakrabarti rightly indicates a very fundamental issue which constituted the debate and other issues cropped up merely as by-products in course of the debate. The main issue involved in this case relates to the status and authority of State Election Commission (SEC) vis-à-vis the state government, precisely based on the primacy pertaining to conduct of panchayat elections.

The author identifies the issues one after the other and tries to explain the constitutional position and refers to the debates in the Constituent Assembly to have a general understanding about the position of Election Commission (at that time there was no question of SEC). The Left Front government also failed to appreciate the need for having a definite focus on the role of the commission while amending the state panchayat Act in keeping conformity with the spirit of the constitutional Amendments. The formulation of the provisions in the Constitution may not be very specific though the spirit and objectives are much clear to rule out the scope for such debates. Nonetheless, the author traces the acrimonious exchanges at times between the parties. The whole situation reflects the 'lack of political will' of the presiding regime. The Governor, the head of the state, and the High Court, both the institutions created to serve and protect the Constitution, tried to bypass the real issue and adopted a policy which ultimately delayed the solution. Very interestingly, the High Court in fact on one occasion became interested in taking over extra-judicial functions, calculating the requirement of forces for holding peaceful elections. However, the role of the Supreme Court, the author points out, was highly praiseworthy and befitting of the constitutional position of the apex court which helped to overcome the impasse centered on the holding of elections. Reviewing the situation and the facts that happened, Chakrabarti raises the basic question about the prospects of local democracy if this continues to happen in future.

Decentralization is an ideal instrument for promoting and strengthening grassroots democracy and this aspect has been widely recognized in literature concentrating on participatory democracy and development. Additionally, decentralization also helps to counter the secessionist trends of the deprived and alienated minority and exclusive policies of the majority through creating new avenues for local community as a whole, with a strong sense of cultural identity in socially or ethnically heterogeneous states. This dimension of decentralized governance has vital implications for India's development practices because of her complex multicultural composition. The main focus of this section of the present publication aims at exploring the perspective and progress in the direction of accommodating the issues of identity of diverse ethnic groups as well as negotiating with empowerment of the poor and other marginalized categories of the society. It is a fact that following the Seventy Third Amendment, decentralizing initiatives have started moving towards empowering both politically-alienated ethnic groups and the excluded poor to come out of the vicious circle of circumscription, both economic and social. The achievements in the post-Seventy Third Amendment period are relocating the traditional centres of power and power is also fast permeating down with devolution of functions and finances from the centres to the peripheries.

In Section IV, four papers are included of which the first two seek to highlight the experiments being carried out to give vent to the hopes and expectations based on indignation and distraction of the two ethnic communities – the *Lepcha* and the *Gorkha* in the district of Darjeeling in West Bengal. Two other papers contributed by two development practitioners and field-level experts have tried to address the issue of empowerment of the marginalized rural people through implementation of the rural employment guarantee scheme (MGNRES) in the state in general and in a backward district in particular. In these two contributions, the authors using intensive data and participant observation have made attempts to focus on the nature and extent of inclusion objectively as clearly as possible. Moreover, all these papers are interesting in a sense that attempts are made by the contributors to look into the issue of inclusion and empowerment not from the pure traditional efficiency perspective of public administration hitherto followed in understanding decentralization, but from the viewpoint of accomplishing identity and empowerment in a democratic set-up.

Tapan Kumar Das begins his analysis of political mobilization of the Lepcha, raising a very pertinent question on the appropriateness of a politically constituted panchayat to address the issues and problems of the marginalized ethnic communities living in different parts of West Bengal, having a decentralized system of rural governance. In other words, how far do the panchayats act as an instrument of inclusion of a marginalized community in the face of strong opposition from another comparatively larger ethnic community? In spite of Subhas Ghishing, formerly head of the Darjeeling Gorkha Hill Council, having a very negative perception about panchayats, the author observes that gram panchayats were the only institutions in which participation of local people was ensured though the Lepcha were suffering from political indecisions in absence of an articulating leadership. From analysing the available data on the voting behaviour of the Lepcha, Das finds that participation of the Lepcha at the panchayat level is more clearly perceived but diffused at the parliamentary and assembly elections. It is also ascertained from the field study conducted by him that objectives of panchayats are not approachable to the tribal community and hence panchayats remain to be alien institutions to the hill politics - though used by certain sections of them for concentrating power, acquiring positions in leadership. After examining the trends in hill politics, the author concludes that the Lepcha have always remained under-represented in political decision-making and they have no political party of their own. As a result, the contributor comes to the conclusion that empowerment through self-governance remains a fantasy for the Lepcha minority.

Jhumpa Mukherjee in her article has tried to trace the developments in the Darjeeling Hills since the middle of 19th century when the British took over the administration of this area to find out an appropriate framework of governance to meet the hopes and aspirations of the Gorkha, who have developed a perception of crisis in their identity. She has also made an in-depth study to explore if the crisis is moving towards resolution with the formation of present GTA in 2011. While doing so, the author has examined the interplay of socio-psychological issues in implementing development agenda in a decentralized political arrangement. She has unearthed the contemporary roots of the problem in the failure of the States Reorganization Commission to properly comprehend the issue of autonomy of the Gorkha and in the malfunctioning of the Hill Council headed by Subhas Ghishing. In her view, the present Gorkhaland Territorial Administration aims at development in a decentralized framework bypassing the crucial issue of identity of the community, while decentralization also calls for democratic integration of cultural diversities. However, she concludes with a bit of confidence that the creation of GTA 'reflects an appreciation of the political and cultural identities of the Gorkha' in the Darjeeling Hills.

The Seventy Third Amendment has accorded constitutional status to the panchayats, the third stratum of governance at the local levels, thereby opening the scope of direct democracy at the grassroots and intensifying new dimensions in rural development through greater representation and people's participation. Since the commencement of this 'largest experiment in local democracy' ever known to the other part of this world, two decades have elapsed with mixed experiences in successes and failures, leaving apart the issue of balancing each other. But the paradox still haunts: the panchayats are mandated by the Constitution 'to function as institutions of self-government' for 'implementation of schemes for economic development and social justice', while a host of schemes including some flagship programmes of local development including MPLAD have been launched by the central government, apart from the proliferation of a large number of parallel bodies and non-governmental organizations at the behest of the governments, both central and state, penetrating into the functional domain of the panchayats.

But it is perhaps an exception that the panchayats are given their legitimate role in planning and implementation of the National Rural Employment Guarantee Scheme intended for empowerment and capacity building of the disadvantaged and marginalized category in rural India. The parent Act allocates the principal role to the panchayats – gram sabha, gram panchayat and intermediate panchayat – right from recommending projects to monitor execution of works, to conduct regular social audits of all the projects taken up under the scheme. As a result, the capabilities of the panchayats and local people have increased while meeting the challenges of planning and implementation. Quite naturally, the scheme is viewed as providing new perspective and scope for institutionalizing and strengthening decentralization at the local levels based on participatory process. In a way, the whole exercise involves far-reaching implications for politics of inclusion.

The last two papers, arranged thematically in this publication, are contributed by Dibyendu Sarkar and Utpal Chakraborty. These seek to explore the development and empowerment effects of the National Rural Employment Guarantee Scheme on poor and disadvantaged rural households in general and women in particular in this state. Both the papers are self-explanatory and additional introduction may be considered inessential.

Dibyendu Sarkar in his contribution starts with a survey of the employment generating schemes launched since the beginning of 1960s and makes a distinction between the previous programmes and the present rural employment guarantee scheme after highlighting the salient features contained in it. While evaluating performance appraisal and reviewing the progress in implementation, he identifies the problems and constraints standing in the way of its complete success and suggests necessary modifications in procedure and planning of action programmes for decentralizing development through diversification in selection of projects, convergence with other schemes and inter-departmental programmes, so as ensure inclusive growth and development. However, he points out the dichotomy between the dynamics of labour potential in the scheme and the creation of sustainable assets which need to be addressed along with the issue of balancing between the supply-driven and demand-driven essences. The author also suggests rethinking on the schemes usually undertaken and according emphasis on development of agricultural potential through land-based and water-based activities. Though the progress in implementation of the scheme is quite satisfactory in West Bengal, the author concludes there is no alternative but to put faith in strong policy intervention coupled with a commitment to changes with a view to realizing the objectives in an effective and sustainable manner.

In the second article on the impact of the scheme, Utpal Chakraborty has advanced his argument in considering the scheme (MGNREGS) as a paradigm shift in policy-making on rural development. After analysing the report submitted by Mihir Shah Committee on the nature of the scheme unprecedented till the middle of the last decade, the contributor moves his analytical tool to present the performance appraisal of the scheme from 2006 to 2012 with the help of some tables. Citing the findings from a study conducted in the district of Birbhum in West Bengal, the author points out that income generated from participating in work under the scheme is being used by the poor in the villages for strengthening future economic prospects of the households through starting own ventures. The author also indicates how participation of women workers brings empowerment effects on decision-making within and outside the family. The decision-making process in the family has become decentralized as a result of this change, the contributor points out. Identifying the constraints in implementation of the programme, the author summarizes the key issues and suggests intervention measures involving social mobilization for smooth sailing of the programme to realize the goals of the scheme.

The attraction of decentralization is not merely confined to local development. It is also commonly associated with a wide range of political objectives. It is widely acknowledged since the days of liberal thinkers of the West that decentralization strengthens accountability and responsibility and also provides a training ground for people's participation in governance and political leadership. When direct participation of people is not rationally possible, decision-makers are elected and accountable to the citizens who participate in the political life of the local communities or regions in different ways.

These are some of the issues and functional experiences which guided the interplay of Panchayati Raj Institutions, bureaucracy, political parties and government in the process of decentralization and development in this state over a period of more than three decades, excepting the last two-three years, presided over by the Left Front government. In the last panchayat elections (held in July 2013), the Left Front phase of panchayati raj in West Bengal has come to an end, and a new regime has taken over the control of the rural citadel of power. The present government has adopted almost the same policies of the previous government with more reform sensitivity towards liberalized mode. The initiatives taken previously by the Left in strengthening institutionalization of panchayats are not moving well –

may be in absence of a clear policy vision of the new government. Now it is a matter of conjecture to presume whether the progress achieved in decentralization all these years in West Bengal would move further towards consolidation or initiate a reverse trend as has been the case in Karnataka.

We may conclude with a note that since the middle of 1990s, local democracy has been taken seriously by the government and policy-makers in India. Prior to the Seventy Third and Seventy Fourth Amendments, decentralization was being viewed simply in terms of creating certain structures and assigning some functions, mostly of voluntary nature. Decentralizing development was fully considered to be the concern of the states based on the recommendations of different committees and commissions endorsed by the central governmental and devoid of constitutional mandate. Now the focus has shifted from a structure-functional perspective to a larger one with multi-dimensional directions involving social, political, economic, cultural and human aspects. The developments in the aftermath of the Amendments present a picture moving towards reforming, invigorating and strengthening local democracy in India. It would not be an overstatement that the progress is on the wing steadily, though a little slowly. The present status of the process of rural decentralization in India may be gauged from the table reproduced below. Indeed, now, decentralizing rural development has become a dynamic concept couched in human dignity.

The present volume is an attempt to examine the process and extent of decentralizing rural development in India over the last two decades following the historic Amendments of 1992. The overall assessment offered by the contributors based on their own analysis and researches in this field reflects the present directions noticeable under this process. The common thread uniting the papers included in this publication highlights the thesis that the Amendments, backed by an interplay of diverse socio-political forces, have made the changes in the 'oceanic circle' of Indian society that is capable of ushering in a great beginning to provide a legitimate share for the timid millions in the democratic power structure of the country. A churning process has begun, which is being observed by the contributors with an outlook of social scientists more concerned with society and its transformation.

Table 1 *Decentralization in Rural India: Overall Devolution Index (2012-13)*

Ranks	*States*	*Frame work*	*Functions*	*Finances*	*Function aries*	*Capacity Building*	*Account ability*	*D*
		D_1	*D2*	*D3*	*D4*	*D5*	*D6*	
1.	Maharashtra	48.95	56.31	55.50	75.37	75.00	76.64	64.04
2.	Karnataka	67.55	57.96	49.97	63.12	79.04	69.73	62.22
3.	Kerala	41.34	52.86	48.52	68.55	58.77	64.64	55.41
4.	Rajasthan	68.33	52.97	35.61	40.90	79.43	57.25	52.10
5.	Tamil Nadu	69.84	52.33	46.26	39.23	63.40	52.97	52.05
6.	West Bengal	56.84	50.57	35.41	37.67	81.18	53.96	49.81
7.	Madhya Pradesh	60.37	52.61	34.44	39.45	51.41	62.50	47.26
8.	Chhattisgarh	53.75	37.53	31.77	33.68	78.52	48.27	44.61
9.	Haryana	70.39	31.14	36.91	50.19	42.68	46.09	43.63
10.	Gujarat	54.58	38.92	26.55	53.18	46.61	43.76	40.75
11.	Odisha	66.50	51.46	35.11	28.55	19.14	53.04	40.01
12.	Uttarakhand	54.00	53.90	27.23	32.02	43.24	52.85	39.37
13.	Uttar Pradesh	60.02	41.04	26.17	28.57	45.88	41.06	37.34
14.	Assam	44.69	42.76	23.13	21.66	67.84	37.65	36.89
15.	Himachal Pradesh	56.19	22.43	34.92	35.35	36.15	44.32	36.83
16.	Goa	50.70	17.78	18.69	48.23	32.87	41.72	31 77
17.	Punjab	60.24	24.25	17.37	23.64	38.67	46.74	31.23
18.	Bihar	49.78	39.44	19.40	24.29	42.01	21.60	29.90
19.	J&K	15.38	15.28	28.01	23.98	51.61	35.15	28.85
20.	Jharkhand	55.01	18.97	13.95	23.52	46.11	28.48	27.25
North-Eastern States								
1.	Tripura	48.10	46.03	28.37	53.34	29.71	46.91	39.72
2.	Sikkim	68.56	45.07	31.37	29.25	41.72	36.30	39.12
3.	Manipur	29.52	12.22	24.00	20.41	45.13	27.27	25.91
4.	Arunachal Pradesh	30.88	17.22	25.17	10.14	34.67	24.85	23.67
Union Territories								
1.	Lakshadweep	48.89	20.79	7.33	39.82	30.95	28.29	25.07
2.	Daman and Diu	56.04	3.43	8.03	33.56	0.00	30.11	18.08
3.	Dadra and Nagar Haveli	28.60	1.11	0.78	39.17	20.85	33.22	17.25
4.	Chandigarh	24.16	7.22	25.86	18.80	0.00	8.14	15.30
National Average		51.40	34.06	29.45	36.99	49.33	43.33	38.52

Note: Detailed explanation and analysis is available from the source mentioned below.

Source: Strengthening of Panchayats in India: Comparing Devolution Across the States, (New Delhi: IIPA, 2013), 5.

Notes

1. Pranab Bardhan, 'Decentralization of Governance and Development', *Journal of Economic Perspectives*, Vol. 16, No. 4, 2002, p. 185.
2. Ibid., p. 186.
3. Ibid., p. 185.
4. *Human Development Report 2002*, New Delhi: Oxford University Press, 2002, p. 63.
5. Bardhan, op. cit., p. 186.
6. *Hindustan Times*, 3 October 1952, quoted in L.C. Jain, *Grass without Roots*, New Delhi: Sage, 1985, p. 41.
7. *Report of the Team for the Study of Community Projects and National Extension Service*, Vol. I, New Delhi: Balwantrai Mehta Committee, Government of India, 1957, p. 5.
8. H.D. Malaviya, 'Constituent Assembly Debates', reproduced in *Village Panchayats in India*, New Delhi: All India Congress Committee, 1956, p. 258.
9. M.K. Gandhi, *Young India*, 17 September 1925; 28 August 1924; 26 March 1931; *Harijan*, 26 and 28 July 1946; *Collected Works of Mahatma Gandhi*, Vol. V, Ahmedabad: Navajivan Publishing House, 1956.
10. *Report of the Committee on Panchayati Raj Institutions*, New Delhi: Asoka Mehta Committee, Government of India, 1978, p. 67.
11. L.C. Jain, *Grass without Roots*, New Delhi: Sage, 1985, pp. 37–38.
12. *Report of the CAARD*, New Delhi: G.V.K. Rao Committee, Government of India, 1985, paras 6.9 and 6.10.
13. *Report of the Committee on Panchayati Raj Institutions*, op. cit., para 6.9.
14. Abdul Sab Nazir, 'Towards a Four-pillar State', in George Mathew (ed.), *Panchayati Raj from Legislation to Movement*, New Delhi: Concept Publishing Company, 1994, p. 53.
15. Nirmal Mukherjee, 'The Future for District Governance', *Administrative Arrangements for Rural Development*, NIRD: Proceedings of the National Workshop, 1985, pp. 197–204.
16. Kamala Prasad, *Indian Administration*, New Delhi: Pearson Longman, 2006, p. 281.
17. *Panchayati Raj Update*, July 2009.
18. N. Jayal, A. Prakash and P.K. Sharma (eds), *Local Governance in India*, New Delhi: Oxford University Press, 2006, p. 14.
19. Ibid., p. 15.
20. *Panchayati Raj Update*, August 2007, p. 7.
21. Jayal, Prakash and Sharma, op. cit., p. 16.

22. *Telegraph*, Kolkata, 24 and 25 January 2014.
23. *Panchayati Raj Update*, July 2006, p. 3.
24. *Panchayati Raj Update*, May 2007, p. 8.
25. V. Ramchandran, 'Kerala', in George Mathew (ed.), *Status of Panchayati Raj in the States of India*, New Delhi: Concept Publishing Company, 1995, pp. 105–115.
26. Anil Kumar Jana, *Administering District Plans in India*, New Delhi: Concept Publishing Company, 2004, pp. 98–109.
27. M. Devendra Babu and N. Jayaramaiah, 'Financial Relations between the States and Local Governments', *Indian Journal of Public Administration*, Vol. L, No. 3, July–September 2004, p. 763.
28. M.A. Oommen, *Devolution of Resources from the State to the Panchayati Raj Institutions*, New Delhi: Institute of Social Sciences, 1995, pp. 34–73.
29. *Report of the Eleventh Finance Commission*, New Delhi: Government of India, Ministry of Finance 2000–2005, para 8.116.
30. Editorial, *Hindu*, reproduced in *Panchayati Raj Update*, December 2005, p. 3.
31. *Kurukshetra*, New Delhi: Government of India, Publication Division, April 2011, pp. 4–6.
32. *Report of the Committee on Panchayati Raj Institutions*, op. cit., Chapter VIII: Dualism in Staff Structure.
33. Mahipal, 'Panchayati Raj and Rural Governance: Experience of a Decade', *Economic and Political Weekly*, Vol. 39, No. 2, 10–16 July 2004.
34. *Panchayati Raj Update*, May 2006, p. 5.
35. Mahipal, 'Gram Sabha in Fifth Scheduled Areas: Precept and Practice', *Kurukshetra*, Vol. 10, No. 10, May 2013, pp. 10–15.
36. G.O. No. 4316/1 (1397) /RD/O/DPF/1E-12/10pt-II dated 19 July 2011.
37. K. Seshadri, 'The Unresolvable Debate of Centralization versus Decentralization', *Indian Journal of Public Administration*, Vol. 31, July–September 1978, p. 676.
38. Anil Kumar Jana, *Administering District Plans in India*, New Delhi: Concept Publishing Company, 2004, Appendix I, p. 315, (para 3.8).
39. *Panchayati Raj Update*, April 2010 and December 2010.
40. *Panchayati Raj Update*, April 2008.

I

Decentralization: Theory and Ideas

CHAPTER 1

Decentralization and Local Governance

Mohit Bhattacharya

At the outset, it needs to be clarified that 'decentralization' involves measures to decongest a congested centre. It can take many forms – administrative and political. Local government, by contrast, is an institutional form to create locally elected democratic bodies basically accountable to the local populace. The term 'local governance' connotes a network of local organizations subsuming the civil society organizations, local functional groups, and even influential individuals involved in some way or the other in the delivery and management of local public services such as health, primary education and so on. Local government like a municipality or a panchayat is just a part of the network constituting 'local governance'.

Decentralization: Contemporary Trend

There is today almost universal agreement among academics, practitioners and development stakeholders that decentralization as an important aspect of 'good governance' is necessary to assure democratic governance for human development. Decentralization and local governance are increasingly recognized as basic components of

---

The author gratefully acknowledges very helpful suggestions and references from Professor Anil Kumar Jana, Department of Political Science, Vidyasagar University, West Bengal.

democratic governance. It is now widely acknowledged that they provide an enabling environment in which decision-making and service delivery can be brought closer to the people, especially to the poor. Decentralization is instrumental in the overall issue of re-inventing government and is essential to achieving the internationally set Millennium Development Goals (MDGs). Under the combined pressure of accelerating globalization and persistent demands for deeper and expanded democratization, central governments everywhere are seeing their traditional roles continuously challenged. Re-inventing government would then require revisiting the nature and role of the state itself and the sharing of political power and administrative responsibilities.

Explaining Decentralization

The term 'decentralization' is, however, not free from ambiguities. Norman Uphoff, an acknowledged authority on the subject, explains the concept thus:

> The term decentralization implies that one is moving away from centralization, a preexisting condition. Centralization has in fact been the dominant form of governance for many centuries in most parts of the world. Starting roughly 250 years ago, there have been a variety of movements and proposed methods for moving away from central government rule, in one way or another diminishing it, so that a whole range of economic, social and political values can be better served. These values include efficiency, equity, accountability, and participation, to name several of the most prominent. In the literature on public administration, a distinction has been commonly and usefully made between *deconcentration* and *devolution*, considered as two contrasting forms of decentralization.[1] In the first, either decision-making is transferred from the centre, i.e. from the capital city to regional or district capitals, or authority is transferred to officials in the latter; in either case, regional or district decision-makers remain accountable to the government at the centre. With devolution, real authority is conferred on decision-makers at lower levels of government and they are responsible to members of the public in their area.

It is in the sense of what Uphoff terms 'devolution' that 'decentralization' is currently being discussed in the context of 'development'. Academics, administrators, policy-makers, and donor agencies are virtually unanimous on the virtues of decentralization, which, in their view, takes the heavy load of governance off the shoulders of central governments, brings 'government' close to the people and makes them active participants in the system of governing. The overall process thus leads to a salutary 'deepening' of democracy. Decentralization, in this sense, serves the twin purposes of 'institutional' strengthening in the interest of better democratic governance, and effective and accountable 'delivery of services' to the localities. Another benefit is what Mill termed 'political education' of the citizens.

Three 'Waves' of Decentralization

Three waves or generations of federalist/decentralization theories may be identified in this context.

1. The first wave relies on the works of Montesquieu and the authors of the classic Federalist Papers, namely Hamilton and Madison, who were primarily 'normative' theory builders. Their main concern was to 'constrain the malevolence of public officials, for which purpose governments should be small and separated, and only functions affecting wide areas such as defence and monetary policy should be assigned to central government.
2. The second wave is associated with the theory of 'fiscal federalism'. Almost in opposition to the first version, the assumption here has been that governments are inspired by 'public interest', which justifies their existence. The benefits of decentralization are similar to those generated by market competition. Decentralized government allows a better matching of the 'performances' with the 'policies' by bringing governments closer to people and thus increasing efficiency.
3. The third wave (representing second generation of fiscal federalism) replaces the benevolent government assumption with a more realistic one of self-serving officials and politicians. In this version, 'institutions' are critical in determining the effects of centralized or decentralized governments. Hence, what is important is to examine the political, legal-constitutional and economic contexts within which institutions exist and operate.

Multiple Sources

Robert Ebel, an eminent fiscal expert, gives the reasons for the universal spread of decentralization in recent times. As he observes:[2]

The western world sees decentralization as an alternative to provide public services in a more cost-effective way. Developing countries are pursing decentralization reforms to counter economic inefficiencies, macroeconomic instability, and ineffective governance. Post-communist transition countries are embracing decentralization as a natural step in the shift to market economies and democracy. Latin America is decentralizing as a result of political pressure to democratize. African states view decentralization as a path to national unity.

Contemporary decentralization discourse is the result of a convergence of multiple ideas, more important among which are:

- In a sense, it is a revival of the old libertarian view of local institutional development a la Mill, Tocqueville, Bryce and others.
- The other impulse can be traced to the contemporary 'democracy wave' sweeping the globe as described by Huntington.
- Another motivating factor is our increasing concern today about 'environment' and natural resources conservation which, as revealed by many research evidences, need to be locality and people-based.
- Also, there is now a world-wide shift of emphasis in the governance process from 'bureaucracy' to 'people', implying thereby a call for a new mode of 'participative', 'accountable' and ' transparent' governance.
- Last, but not the least, even in terms of efficiency, the donor agencies and development consultants are increasingly advocating more and more people-driven, 'inclusive' and 'participative' management of local development projects.

Professor Pranab Bardhan, an economist of international fame, wrote in his seminal paper[3] on 'Decentralization of Governance and Development' that decentralization is a rage in today's world. The important reasons suggested by him in this context are loss of legitimacy of the central state and a corresponding belief that decentralization (as against the 'predatory state') can bring a range of benefits directly to the local people. It is good to have more intergovernmental competition and attendant checks and balances. In this view, decentralization is supposed to make government more responsive and efficient. Professor Bardhan also points out that technological changes have made it easier to arrange supply of services in smaller market areas, and transaction costs are much less in decentralized operations. Explaining the popularity of decentralization, Professor Bardhan writes:[4]

These potential benefits of decentralization have attracted a very diverse range of supporters. For example, free-market economists tend to emphasize the benefits of reducing the power of the overextended or predatory state. In some international organizations pushing structural adjustment and transitional reform, decentralization has sometimes been used almost as a synonym for privatization; similarly, in the literature on mechanism design, an informationally decentralized system of individual decisions coordinated by a price mechanism is pitted against a system of central commands and plans. Even those who are convinced of the pervasiveness of market failures are increasingly turning for their resolution to the government at the local level, where the transaction costs are relatively low and the information problems that can contribute to central government failures are less acute. They are joined by a diverse array of social thinkers: postmodernists, multicultural advocates, grassroots environmental activists and supporters of the cause of indigenous peoples and technologies. In the absence of a better unifying name, I would describe this latter group as 'anarcho-communitarians'. They are usually both anti-market and anti-centralized state, and they energetically support assignment of control to local self-governing communities.

Bardhan and Mookherjee[5] have further elucidated decentralization in terms of 'participatory democracy'. As they have argued:

From the standpoint of politics, decentralization is typically viewed as an important element of participatory democracy that allows citizens to have an opportunity to communicate their preferences and views to elected officials, who are subsequently rendered accountable to for their performance to citizens. Apart from actual outcomes in terms of policies, their detailed implementation, and their impact on economic well-being, popular participation is valued for its own sake for a variety of reasons. It can promote a sense of autonomy in citizens, enhance social order by promoting the legitimacy of the state, and limit pressures for separatism by diverse regions or ethnic groups.

Benefits of Decentralization

To reiterate, democratic decentralization is now regarded as beneficial both for economic growth and as a means of achieving the MDGs. It is often claimed that decentralization increases popular participation in decision-making because it brings government closer to people, making it more accessible and knowledgeable about local conditions and more responsive to people's demands.

Central governments located far away and preoccupied mostly with national and regional issues, fall short of adequately and efficiently providing services essentially local in nature. The cause of decentralization has been advanced on a number of grounds as under:

(i) Local authorities tend to act more in line with local preferences and conditions, and their response to local needs is more expeditious. Decentralization provides opportunities to marginalized sectors of the community, like women in some countries, minorities, etc. to participate at the local level, enabling a more sensitive approach to policy formulation and implementation.

(ii) Because decentralization tends to enhance transparency and accountability, the amount of money wrongfully diverted away from development often declines. The Human Development Report (2003) underlines that in 55 countries, decentralization of government spending was closely associated with lower corruption among bureaucrats and reduced rent seeking by private parties – leaving more money to spend on basic services for poor people.

(iii) Decentralization increases effectiveness in service delivery, like reducing absenteeism among government employees, for example, in local schools and health clinics because elected officials receive complaints from their constituents and can improve discipline.

(iv) Decentralization provides bureaucrats with early warnings of potential disasters, enabling quick remedial action.

(v) Decentralization makes development projects more sustainable and cost-effective because local people are more likely to be involved in their design, execution, and monitoring.

(vi) Decentralization encourages communities to find solutions to their everyday problems, yielding innovative ideas, which are more attuned to local conditions.

(vii) Decentralization provides opportunities for more people, including the under-represented groups (like women in some countries, the poor, minorities, etc.) to participate in decisions that affect their lives.

Because of a greater degree of accountability, responsiveness and participation, effective decentralization has been accepted axiomatically as an institutional device that makes the provision of local (social and economic) services more efficient, equitable, sustainable and cost-effective. It is now widely acknowledged that through community participation in decision-making, planning, implementation and monitoring and backed by appropriate institutions and resources, decentralization can go a long way in improving the quality of life, particularly of the poorer and the marginalized sections of the population.

Constraints on Decentralization

It is naïve to think that decentralization at one go will bring about all the desired results. Certain preconditions of successful decentralization, as the UNDP's Human Development Report (2003) has listed out, are the following:

1. Effective state capacity;
2. Empowered, committed and competent local authorities; and
3. Engaged, informed and organized citizens and civil society.

The other important factors to make decentralization a success are:

(a) Decentralization requires co-ordination between levels of government and more regulation – not less – to ensure basic transparency, accountability and representation.

(b) The state also has to raise adequate fiscal resources to support decentralization.

(c) For the above to be achieved, effective state capacity is necessary. Alongside this, local 'governance capacity' is of paramount importance.

(d) Furthermore, to ensure that the decentralization effort is not hijacked by the local elites, and there is broad-based popular participation, both a strong state and a mobilized civil society are required.

Appropriateness of 'functions' to be decentralized, adequacy of fiscal resources to be transferred to the sub-national government, efficacy of administrative and legal setups and sufficiency of technical/skilled personnel at all levels of government are important ingredients for successful decentralization.

Additionally, the perceived constraints regarding decentralization, which should be taken seriously while designing decentralization, have been identified as under:

- The political and institutional inheritance of the country from the colonial period is an important factor to be reckoned with.

Decolonization proceeded roughly parallel between Anglophone and Francophone Africa, namely during the 1960s and early 1970s, yet the structures, functions and administrative processes, in the French-speaking colonies, were regarded as more centralistic than the ones left behind by the British. Thus, history of administrative development in a country needs to be taken into account.

- Capacity deficits both in institutions and skilled personnel are considered to be real constraints in the actual implementation of decentralization policies.
- Another important constraint is the mismatch between the vertical plane of decentralization, which involves transfer of power from the centre to sub-national structures, and the horizontal plane, which involves empowerment of grassroots communities to decide and to plan, manage and implement specific programmes.
- The other constraint is the inability to make the transition to people-centred governance, with its commensurate implications for participation and empowerment, even where formally, through laws and rules, an enhanced space for decentralized decision-making has been created.
- Arising from the above is to question how far decentralization, be it political, fiscal or administrative, can be planted and nurtured if the institutions and political process responsible (including the individuals and political parties in power) is itself compromised and flawed.
- The absence or ill-working of accountability and transparency from the centre to the periphery and vice versa again constraints the cause of decentralization. Traditionally, such accountability was conceived hierarchically – that is, from below: from sub-national authorities to central government. Increasingly, the demand by the civil society organizations is that accountability must also operate in the reverse direction, that is downwardly, from the sub-national authorities to the communities and to civil society.

In a recent World Bank publication,[6] questions have been raised about why one should worry about decentralization, despite its universal popularity. As the document points out, based on industrial countries, the literature on decentralization is usually normative and empirical. There is an assumption here about the existence of certain institutions (e.g. stable central government, strong civil society, etc.) that are usually very weak in developing countries. To achieve allocative efficiency gains from decentralization, traditional public finance literature related to fiscal decentralization relies on 'voice' and 'exit'. Dissatisfied citizens, according to this view, can vote the local leaders out of power, and they can even leave a locality ('voting with their feet'),[7] if they do not like the package of local taxes and public services offered by local bodies.

The situation in most developing countries is very different. Local governments in many developing countries are often not responsive to their citizens, and decision-making is rarely transparent and predictable. It is not so easy for poor citizens to leave a locality to show their displeasure.

The other aspect of local level decentralization that needs proper design and care is its 'instrumentalist' dimension. In other words, efficient and equitable delivery of local public services is as necessary as the successful operation of the democratic processes. The track record of local democratic decentralization in this respect is, however, a mixed one. Local government has in many instances not been able to 'manage' local services cost-effectively and to the satisfaction of the general public. Cases are not rare where the poor and the socially marginalized have not had their proper share of the local services.[8]

Weak and fragile democratic systems render the electoral system a highly problematic method of achieving accountability. Effective local participation can overcome weak formal election systems, but powerful elites make this difficult in most situations. Also, because of political reasons and weak central monitoring and supervision, oversight of local government's functioning usually goes by default. The net result of such institutional weaknesses is that 'accountable' local government is a rare institution in most developing countries.

Rhetoric of Decentralization

It has been usually noticed that politicians have often used the slogan of democratic decentralization as rhetoric to strengthen their own power base rather than to genuinely improve governance. In practice, the lack of willingness of the Centre to relinquish or share power has been a major impediment to effective decentralization. In fact, because of the state of power politics in a country, the inability to make the transition to a people-centred governance, with its commensurate implications for participation and empowerment, is perhaps a bigger bottleneck in the process of decentralization than legislative changes. Also, lack of public awareness and an absence of a culture of participation and a weak 'voice' of particularly the poor and marginalized sections of the population have inhibited the development of decentralized local governance. The tendency in most cases has been that as a matter of fact, the decision-making process is dominated by local elites and government functionaries with little, if any, participation by the masses.

It needs cautioning that decentralization is necessary but may not be sufficient for deliberative participation at the local level. Hence, participatory governance deliberately promoted by local government is considered a corrective remedial measure necessary to remove 'democratic deficit'. Participatory governance focuses on empowerment of citizens, and is related to competence, empowerment and capacity building especially of the marginalized groups. In this connection, the experiences of 'public budgeting' in the city of Porto Alegre, Brazil[9] and People's Planning in Kerala[10] deserve special mention as successful examples of participative local planning and governance. These instances are closely associated with the issue of power – creating avenues for voice to the voiceless. Benefits are expected to follow as a matter of right (bringing in 'human dignity')[11] from the active participation of the otherwise marginalized and excluded categories.

Capacity Building

Managing a decentralized and people-centric government is, however, not a bed of roses. One has to echo in this context the sentiment of Woodrow Wilson, the founder of public administration. Wilson made a profound statement that 'it is getting harder to run a constitution than to write one'.[12] This applies equally well to actually 'running' a decentralized local government. Designing a proper decentralized system is no doubt the first priority; but once the system is put on the ground and activated, there are mundane but most difficult issues that need to be faced regarding how best to 'run' the system on the ground – to raise revenues, manage services delivery in accordance with the people's needs, motivate employees, and more importantly, to take the people along in a true participative manner. It is in this context that the crucial issue of institutional 'capacity building' confronts the policy-makers and administrators at all levels involved in the process of 'running' the decentralized system.

The following observation from the World Bank document[13] on 'Rethinking Decentralization', as earlier quoted, deserves special mention in this context:

Increasing fiscal, political, and administrative responsibilities and setting clear rules holding each tier of government accountable for those responsibilities lead to an important set of questions: Does the public sector – that is, central and local governments – have the capacity to support and manage decentralized responsibilities? Does it have the political capacity to identify and respond to individual preferences? Does the central government have the administrative capacity to provide technical and financial support where appropriate? Do local governments have the capacity to deliver promised services at low cost? Political capacity has to do with the channels for local participation and administrative capacity with the processes required of central and local administrators and with their training. The evidence on these issues is sparse.

Planned and imaginative efforts are, therefore, of paramount importance to build 'capacity' at all involved levels, particularly at the local government level, to enable the newly-introduced system to function efficiently and effectively in accordance with the design as conceived and planned.

Turning to the nitty-gritty of the actual governing process, it has been rightly put:[14] 'To debate whether decentralization is good or bad is unproductive and misleading since the impact of decentralization depends on design.' Beyond design phase, details of a functioning system that can really live up to the expectations of the design framers need to be meticulously worked out.

Thus, it is essential to consider the wide range of issues that influence decentralization. Traditional 'fiscal federalism' approach has been the starting point in terms of devolution of powers among levels of government. Beyond this, what is needed is a stronger focus on institutions – both the rules that influence the behaviour of actors at different levels of government, in the private sector as well as the civil society. Decentralized local 'government' today is conceived in a much broader term as 'local governance' – taking in its sweep the familiar institution of local government, the private sector, the civil society actors, the citizens qua citizens as well as in discrete functional groups (e.g. parents, women's group, the local youth, etc.). Additionally, there is today a broader and enhanced focus on openness and transparency, accountability and social audit. It is not enough to have internal hierarchical accountability; local government must at intervals face the people as real stakeholders interested to find out what is actually happening on the ground and inside the organization.

Summing Up

Practically speaking, decentralization is an issue about which it may truly be said that 'the devil is in the details'. To quote the World Bank document again (1998):

Much research needs to be done – primarily in case studies – on a variety of important issues, particularly with respect to the outcome of alternative institutional changes. These include but are by no means limited to the effect of intergovernmental transfers on local tax efforts and service expenditures, the effect of fiscal decentralization on macroeconomic indicators and capital market development, alternative forms and methods of strengthening local institutional and service delivery capacity, assessments of the extent to which different decentralization initiatives improve (or worsen) governance, and potential uses and limitations of user charges as a means of financing decentralized services.

Gone are the days of euphoric attachment to local government conceived purely in terms of deepening of 'democracy'. In today's context of increasing popular vigilance and impatience about the quality and quantity of services being delivered, local governance has turned out to be much more complicated a task for which appropriate local level leadership seems absolutely necessary.

Notes

1. James Fesler, 'The Political Role of Field Administration', in Ferrel Heady and Sybil Stokes (eds), *Papers in Comparative Public Administration*, Ann Arbor, MI: University of Michigan, 1962.
2. Robert Ebel and Y. Serdar, 'On the Measurement and Impact of Decentralization', *Policy Research Working Paper 2*, Washington, DC: World Bank, 2002.
3. Pranab Bardhan, 'Decentralization of Governance and Development', *Journal of Economic Perspectives*, Vol. 16, No. 4, 2002.
4. Ibid.

5. Pranab Bardhan and Dilip Mookherjee, 'The Rise of Local Government: An Overview', in Bardhan and Mookherjee (eds), *Decentralization and Local Governance in Developing Countries: A Comparative Perspective*, New Delhi: Oxford University Press, 2007.
6. Jennie Litvack, Junaid Ahmad and Richard Bird, *Rethinking Decentralization in Developing Countries*, Washington, DC: World Bank, 1998.
7. Charles Tiebout, 'A Pure Theory of Local Expenditure', *Journal of Political Economy*, Vol. 64, No. 5, 1956.
8. See, in this context, Omar Azfar, Satu Kahkonen, Anthony Lanyi and Patrick Meagher, 'Decentralized Governance and Public Services: The Impact of Institutional Arrangements', *Working Paper No. 255*, College Park: University of Maryland, Centre for Institutional Reform and the Informal Sector, September 1999.
9. See Social Development Notes, 'Case Study 2, Porto Alegre, Brazil: Participatory Approaches in Budgeting and Public Expenditure Management', Washington, DC: World Bank, March 2003, Note No. 71.
10. Patrick Heller, 'Building Local Democracy: Lessons from Kerala', paper prepared for the Workshop on Poverty and Democracy, February 2006, pp. 17–18. Also, Anil Kumar Jana, *Administering District Plans in India: Issues, Constraints and Choices*, New Delhi: Concept Publishing Company, 2004, pp. 98–109 and 426–434.
11. See, in this context, Amit Bhaduri, *Development with Dignity*, New Delhi: National Book Trust, 2005.
12. Woodrow Wilson, 'The Study of Administration', *Political Science Quarterly*, Vol. 2, June 1887, pp. 197–222.
13. Litvack, Ahmad and Bird, op. cit.
14. Ibid.

CHAPTER 2

Gandhian Approach to Development and Decentralization

Perspectives and Relevance

Anil Kumar Jana

Mahatma Gandhi's views on development and decentralization are necessarily the product of his contempt for centralization of political power and authority, even based on majority rule, since he had all along nourished a vision in the dignity and freedom of the individuals and nurtured their capacity in bringing about an economic and social revolution from the below 'along non-violent lines'. Gandhi's obsession with non-violence and passion for individual freedom led him to develop his scheme of decentralization, which, he believed, could provide the scope for participation of individuals in the management of their community affairs. Gandhi strongly believed in decentralization of political power through cooperatives and local self-government for change and improvement in such a way as could promote cooperation, progress and happiness at all levels. He always stood for a *higher standard of life* and not merely a *higher standard of living*. Thus, development was basically a human problem for Gandhi which could be achieved under decentralization.[1] Gandhi's concept of development and decentralization is an integral part of his attitude towards individuals, state and society in their mutual existence.

Gandhi was a great personality in Indian politics and political thinking, a humanist and a great social reformer having the ultimate goal of transforming the social system to be based on human values and morality. He was a man of religious and spiritual temperament who believed in the totality of human life and discarded the idea of strictly bifurcating social, economic, political and religious activities into different compartments.[2] In fact, there is no space in human life left untouched in his thinking: his philosophy is all-pervasive and complementary. Gandhi was a strong idealist and, at the same time, also a keen pragmatist. As a result, his ideas reflect a fine moral treatment of political issues through a happy blending between philosophy and reality as well as between religion and politics.[3]

Introduction

There are always some problems in understanding Gandhi's philosophy dispassionately. Scientific analysis and study become possible when the attempt is based on objectivity and detachment. But there is a group of thinkers who seek to attach some sort of sacrosanctity to what Gandhi opined, while there is a category of analysts who make an oversimplification of his ideas in an attempt to fit his views into a particular model. They try to put his ideas into a strait-jacket classification: utopian, idealist, reactionary, pragmatist, and spiritualist, secular, radical liberal and even revolutionary. There are critics who like to discard Gandhi's ideas as outdated on the logic that his model of self-sufficient and glorified village is no longer sustainable in the present context since 'global village' has replaced the desired 'glorified village'. In view of all these one-sided and diverse attempts to explain Gandhi's philosophy, renewed interest and debates among the scholars and social scientists have arisen in recent times. Even some post-development thinkers of the West like Wolfgang Sachs appreciate Gandhian philosophy of village reconstruction for transformation of society while discarding the Western model of so-called development. Another problem lies in the fact that there is a lack of continuity in Gandhi's thinking and philosophy. Gandhi himself was conscious of this limitation, and at the same time he was modest in his approach. He was also not interested in ensuring continuity and internal consistency in his writings. Such a conclusion may be arrived at from examining his interactions with Louis Fischer.[4] There is also confusion among the Left intellectuals. The communists had developed since early 1920s a very negative perception of Gandhi's views and efforts.[5]

Naturally, there has always been a scope for distortions and debate. Gandhi was never a political thinker in the conventional sense or a model builder. He was a practical man with a religious bent of mind and his philosophy was grounded in practice. He had developed his own philosophy that shaped his political views. His ethical and humanist approach to diverse social problems made him both rational and uncompromising towards injustice and oppression. Truth, non-violence and purity of means have always been his guides to actions. His political ideas are thus completely based on ethical grounds. His mission is always directed towards finding out 'truth'.[6]

Philosophical Foundation of Gandhi's Ideas

M.K. Gandhi was not a theoretician *par excellence*; he was a man of action – a *karma yogi*, who wanted to build a new society based on truth, non-violence and morality. His political views and thinking emerged in course of his 'passive resistance' and developed against the Apartheid policy in South Africa and fight against British imperialism in India in the first half of the 20th century. During the initial years of his stay in South Africa, he was influenced by Tolstoy's *Kingdom of God within You* and developed his ideas about a non-formal, non-violent and decentralized politico-economic system. Besides it, John Ruskin's *Unto This Last* had made such an imprint on him as he was inspired to translate it and give the name *Sarvodaya* (development of all) for the Gujarati translation. In fact, Gandhi had learnt three things from Ruskin's book: Individual's good through collective welfare; equal dignity of labour and the right to earn livelihood through work; and the realization of one's life through manual work.[7] In fact, Gandhi was largely influenced by Tolstoy, Romain Rolland, Thoreau, Ruskin and others. There were very lively correspondences between Gandhi and Rolland. The influence of Thoreau was so intense on Gandhi that he preached the statement of Thoreau – 'that government is best which governs the least.'[8] Again, the impact of Tolstoy on Gandhi was so profound that he wanted to put the ideals of *Sarvodaya* into practice in his later life and started his experiments with his philosophy in line with the Phoenix settlement and Tolstoy farm. Though Gandhi expressed his views on different occasions on various complex and controversial issues involving society, politics, economics, civilization, religion and morality, he was never interested in building a political philosophy. He had always tried to apply his own experience based on truth to find out solutions to earthly problems. Morality had always been a source of his political thinking.

To Gandhi, politics and economics could not be separated from religion, which provided a moral basis to all activities. He compared politics with 'a corpse only fit to be buried'[9] and asserted that the whole of man's activities comprised an 'indivisible whole' that could not be separated into a watertight compartment and which interacted with one another.[10] Similarly, Gandhi believed in the unity and indivisibility in a nation's life since the world was an aggregate of such individuals.[11] Thus, for Gandhi, politics without religion was polluted; and politics minus morality needed to be abandoned.[12] The essential purpose of practising religion by an individual, in his view, is to make oneself an integral part of mankind which is possible through political activities.[13] Gandhi's excellence lies in the fact that he has presented politics to common man skillfully in the cover of religion. The political philosophy was settled in this way on religion, truth, morality, justice and non-violence and Gandhi was not ready to sacrifice one for the other. In spite of disorganization in Gandhi's socio-political ideas, there was no lack or inconsistencies in his reverence to anarchist philosophy, which was an essential element in his attitude towards, State and government. Again, his views on the state and government led to the growth of his ideas of development and decentralization.

Concept of Development

Gandhi believed that the state represented an organized power and violence through coercion and compulsion[14] to regulate the national life through representatives. But if the national life became perfect and self-regulated, no representation would be necessary, Gandhi asserted at the same breath, and a state of enlightened anarchy would come to exist.[15] Thus, in Gandhi's views, the state had no place in society. But his anarchism was of a different type, qualified by the principle of non-violence, while a state could never be totally non-violent.[16] The vision of this 'enlightened anarchy' dominated Gandhi's views on development and decentralization which emerged from his concept of *swaraj* – self-rule and self-restraint in all fields of life: social, economic, political and moral.

Gandhi conceptualized the goal of enlightened anarchy in three stages: *Swaraj* would be the first stage to be based on immediate nationalization; in the second stage, the objective was to establish *Gram Swaraj* or village republics by non-violent means; and the final stage or the highest stage would be achieved through *Ramraj,* a kind of pure democracy which would reflect people's sovereignty based on pure moral rights.[17] Gandhi's concept of *Swaraj* was based on 'truth and non-violence', which could be realized only 'in the simplicity of village life'.[18] Gandhi strongly urged the need for revitalization of village community in all its aspects – economic, moral and political, since he was convinced more than anybody else: 'if the village perishes, India will perish too. It will be no more India.' The concept of *Gram Swaraj* was necessarily a comprehensive view involving moral, ethical and economic aspects. The economic aspect was directed towards a new economic and social order labeled as 'constructive programme'. The constructive programme was a set of activities originally outlined in 1908 for rural development based not only on material values, but also on cooperation, compassion and equality. For Gandhi, it was also a programme for building new institutions and values through individual and collective efforts of community people in a voluntary manner.

Though Gandhi had deep regards for individual freedom, he considered unrestricted individualism as the law of the beasts and always wanted 'to strike the balance between freedom and social restraint ...'[19] Gandhi was convinced that the country would achieve *poorna swaraj* (complete independence) through total acceptance and implementation of the constructive programme. Though he was not completely opposed to the idea of centralized planning, nor heavy industries, he rather endorsed such programmes strictly under certain conditions. His faith in the development of small and cottage industries, however, was both unconditional and unbound. Gandhi's scheme of rural reconstruction was man-centred and non-exploiting in nature, specifically designed to create job opportunities for hundreds of rural youths under peculiar economic conditions dominated by huge population and scarce capital.[20] Gandhi visualized his ideal village as 'a complete republic, independent of its neighbours for its vital wants and yet interdependent for many others in which dependence was necessary.'[21] Thus, he accorded top priority on production for consumption within the village. The following major areas of reconstruction programme may be identified out of Gandhi's 'Eighteen Point' programme:

(i) Labour-intensive, diversified, individual and cooperative farming supported by cattle-based economy to ensure food supply, conservation of soil and maintenance of animal and plant life. Use of animal waste for production of compost and prevention of pollution to ensure cleanliness.

(ii) Development of cottage and other village industries as ancillary to agriculture.

(iii) Maintenance of ecological balance so as to ensure interdependence and symbolic relationship among man, animal and plant.

(iv) Full utilization of village resources like land, cattle, capital, machinery through organizing cooperatives to minimize costs and accomplish possible goals.

(v) Protection of natural resources to ensure sustainable development.[22] He further included clothing, housing, education, water supply and recreation in the list of activities for the villagers. Along with these, programmes like khadi, communal harmony and removal of untouchability were also included in the development scheme of *village swaraj*.

Gandhi's ideas of development had their origin in the recognition of the importance of indigenous resources, both natural and human, and the objective of their proper utilization for progress and development of human beings and humanity. Gandhi was confident that such development, if properly undertaken in a community effort at the village level, would usher in the highest intellectual, moral, economic and political advancement of all. He was convinced at the same time that development of the country was not at all possible without a growing household sector at the bottom of the society, though the possibility of development of an ideal society through such constructive efforts seemed to be quite surprising to the later political thinkers.

The above programmes for development in villages constituted the Gandhian alternative of non-violent change for a just society as against the modern state based on power and violence. Because of his firm belief in the anarchist propositions, Gandhi proposed his programmes based on voluntary and autonomous space for community action as a substitute for state and government. No doubt, the main objective in outlining the programmes of rural development in line with his Phoenix experiment (South Africa) was the establishment of a social order completely devoid of poverty and exploitation through a system of decentralized production and distribution. The programme of rural development was designed to create job opportunities for hundreds of village people so as to involve them in productive activities. This aspect of immediate benefits to the people through creation of employment on a mass scale and availability of goods to ordinary consumers through decentralized economy has also been advocated in subsequent years.[23] In spite of his unpleasant experiences with the realities of villages surrounded by heaps of dirty refuse and offending smell, Gandhi was confident of their transformation by the villagers themselves.[24]

Decentralization for Development

Gandhi's urge for decentralized development and passion for non-violence led him to his concept of decentralization of economic and political power through formation of village panchayats, though he did not consider the involvement of panchayats in implementation of his constructive programmes. To Gandhi, political organization was not an end in itself but one of the means of realizing a higher standard of life. Gandhi's view on decentralization had its foundation in his appreciation of the existence of panchayats in 'innumerable village republics', which were destroyed by the policies of revenue collection by the British Government.[25] Gandhi's interest in the working of panchayats can be traced to the non-cooperation era when these bodies undertook the responsibilities of settlement of disputes in rural areas in an attempt to abnegate the formal courts of law. Gandhian approach to decentralization was based on the principles of local initiative, consensus in decision-making, informal and personal relationships among the community people in managing their own affairs. In his scheme of decentralization, Gandhi envisaged a broad classification of functions and responsibilities at different tiers of the *Gram Swaraj*,[26] which exhibited his concern and maturity in his thinking. At the same time, the main rationale of decentralization was also clearly spelt out in his ideas:

(i) Decentralization of power is necessary for enhancement of quality of life, protection of individual freedom and development of moral values.

(ii) It is the best antidote to centralized authority, which can only be sustained and defended with physical force.

(iii) Both economic and political decentralization are interlinked. Economic decentralization cannot be ensured without decentralization in political structure and authority.

(iv) Decentralization insists on use of local resources and promotes self-sufficiency at local levels.

(v) Non-violence is possible in a decentralized system and centralization is inconsistent with a non-violent society.[27]

Gandhi's views on decentralization originated from his concept of *Swadeshi,* which involved three basic elements: (i) concept of self-sufficient village republic as the primary unit of production, consumption and exchange of goods and services, thereby leaving the supply of such things as could not be produced to the immediate neighbouring villages;[28] (ii) use and reliance on native polity and indigenous institutions and to help rectification of defects, if any, in them; and (iii) to strengthen self-reliance of the primary and basic units in the villages and society and nourishment of village industries to make them grow more efficient and self-sufficient.[29] Gandhi had earlier expressed his views on *swadeshi* in a Missionary Conference in 1915.[30] To Gandhi, *swaraj* was a multi-dimensional concept; it meant 'self-rule', 'self-reliance' and 'self-restraint' in all aspects of life – political, economic, social and moral fields.[31] Self-reliance and self-rule were considered two most vital elements in Gandhi's concept of *swadeshi,* which could not be realized if people turn to the government for all the necessities involving their daily life and in such cases *swaraj* would become a painful event, Gandhi emphasized.[32]

In Gandhi's scheme of decentralization, independence and autonomy of all the tiers were protected and the higher units did not have the power to coerce and control the lower units; rather, they derived their strength from the lower units. The higher units were required to provide advice, information, guidance and coordination for enhancement of skill and capacity at all levels.

Gandhi opposed concentration of power and authority and hence he advocated complete decentralization of the villages – 'little republics' in his realm of imagination – since he sincerely believed that real democracy could not be realized by some twenty persons sitting at the top but has to be made effective at the bottom of villages by the people themselves.[33] In his broad conception of the organization of the ideal society: 'Panchayat will be the legislature, judiciary and executive combined to operate for its year of office.'[34] To strengthen his idea, Gandhi added: 'Any village can become such a republic today without interference.'[35] But it should be noted that a panchayat in his view could not work in isolation, but would very much remain a part of the national life.[36] Thus, it will involve a free and voluntary relationship within the republic. In order to comprehend his idea of decentralization in its totality, the following erudite statement made by Gandhi is worth repeating:

> Indian independence must begin at the bottom. Thus, every village will be a republic or panchayat, having full powers. It follows, therefore, that every village has to be self-sustained and capable of managing its affairs, even to the extent of defending itself against the whole world ... In this structure, composed of innumerable villages, there will be ever widening, never ascending circles. Life will not be a pyramid with the apex sustained by the bottom. But it will be an oceanic circle whose centre will be the individual always ready to perish for the village, the latter ready to perish for the circle of villages, till at last the whole becomes one life composed of individuals, humble, sharing the majesty of the oceanic circle of which they are integral units ... Therefore, the outermost circumference will not wield power to crush the inner circle, but will give strength to all within and will derive its own strength from it ... We must have a proper picture of what we want, before we can have something approaching it. If there ever to be a republic of every village in India, then I claim variety for my picture in which the last is equal to the first or, in other words, no one is to be the first and none last.[37]

From the above statement, it is clear that Gandhi was more practical in his approach to decentralization. In fact, he was eager to let his 'ever widening, never ascending circle' move all over the world so that the idea of a world-wide state could emerge as a larger form of *gram swaraj*. Moreover, the scheme reflects Gandhi's originality and depth about the organizational structures and their interrelationship within the gram panchayats. According to Gandhi, the power structure in the panchayats would not be pyramidal-like in which the base carries the peak but, on the contrary, it would be like oceanic waves encircling the individuals at the centre. Thus, the functions of the panchayats would be distributed between different levels of the panchayats on the 'principles of subsidiarity', and not of subordination in his scheme of government. It is highly interesting that the contemporary policy-makers are now thinking in terms of adopting this principle so as to enable the panchayats to function 'as units of self-government' effectively in an autonomous situation.

Gandhi had unbound faith in people's democracy and hence direct election of members of the *gram swaraj* (at the village level) each year was vital in the whole system. Gandhi suggested that the village panchayat would be composed of five elected representatives (men or women) to organize village-level functions in an atmosphere of face-to-face communications among the villagers. He also outlined a broad category of functions to be discharged at the villages and it included production of food, khadi, cotton, hand-made cloth and other daily necessaries, besides organizing village and cottage industries, cooperatives, practice of *charka*, rural sanitation, supply of drinking water, *nai-talim* (education), village hospitals, prevention of public nuisances, maintenance of cleanliness, etc. within the villages.[38] In Gandhi's view, the primary units of the panchayats were responsible for planning and execution of all functions and responsibilities at the village levels with cooperation from the community people and only such items as could not be undertaken at this level had to be vested in the district panchayats comprising the heads of the *gram panchayats*. Again, the left-out functions of the districts were to be transferred to the state level (provincial) panchayats consisting of the representatives from the district panchayats. Accordingly, the All-India Panchayat (national) would be formed for a period of three years with the presidents of the provincial panchayats as members. The functions of the panchayat at the national level were proposed to be confined only to certain specific matters, including communications, currency, foreign trade, external affairs, defence and heavy industries.[39] But the national panchayat would remain accountable to the village panchayats for proper discharge of these functions and thus the villages were considered as complete republics with wide and comprehensive functions embracing almost all aspects of community life. Thus, in all the cases, the role of higher level bodies of panchayats in relation to the lower level organizations were confined to rendering advice and guidance – 'advisory and not mandatory'.[40]

Gandhi was deeply committed to the abolition of exploitation of all sorts and wanted reconstruction of Indian villages into complete republics as units of self-governance. He believed that such republics could be built up on the foundations of local resources and institutions to ensure human dignity to all men and women so as to transform 'mechanical man' into a 'living personality' and thereby, giving them a taste of ideal life.[41] Hence, he proposed to revitalize the ancient practice of village arbitration and settlement of disputes by assigning judicial functions to the panchayats in order to provide speedy and cheap justice to the villagers. However, at the same time, he was cautious enough about the possible mistakes and, therefore, suggested keeping serious matters reserved for the district and higher courts.[42]

Relevance

Gandhian approach to decentralization and development has come under serious scrutiny from a number of scholars, both Marxist and Liberals. Besides, the relevance of his concept of decentralization at the village levels has been questioned. In general, the Liberals as well as the Marxists consider Indian villages as backward, conservative and anti-technical. While emphasizing the need for 'harmonious interactions' between the towns and the villages, Rabindranath Tagore equated, without a bit of hatred, 'rustic' with 'mind's narrowness' as existed in rural India.[43] Karl Marx himself described these village communities 'as the solid foundation of Oriental despotism ... superstition', deprived 'of all grandeur and historical energies' and 'contaminated by distinctions of caste and by slavery.'[44] In a similar way, Ambedkar asked: 'What is the village but a sink of localism, a den of ignorance, narrow-mindedness and communalism? I am glad that the draft constitution has discarded the village and adopted the individual as its unit.'[45] In fact, in most cases, there was always an apathy among the Westernized educated intellectuals towards village organizations.

There are some inherent confusion in Gandhi's views on development and decentralization. There are also some contradictions, which undermine the relevance of his ideas. His attitude towards use of machinery in economic development and his over-emphasis on *charka* (hand-spinning) as the centre of village industry are severely criticized though Gandhi claimed it to be the easiest, the cheapest and the best.[46] Gandhi advocated the use of *charka* as part-time employment by rural people in lean seasons as a supplement to agriculture, which reflects pragmatism in his approach. But the problem emerges when there is a conflict between people's initiatives for rural development programmes and state-directed national planning based on heavy industry. There is no wayout in Gandhi's scheme of development in such situations though he modified his views later to some extent.[47]

Gandhi is not against the use of machinery as such; he is opposed to capitalism Which is a product of indiscriminate use of machinery. The common perception of his antipathy towards machinery is in fact the product of some of his comments in *Hind Swaraj*.[48] There is another issue that emerges from his apathy towards urban settlements and this is a much-repeated criticism. Gandhi had developed a negative perception of the cities as being associated with the imperialist forces in plundering of rural resources. But the abolition of towns and cities was never a part of his agenda. Rather, he had a goal of establishing rural-urban cooperation through reforms in city life. Gandhi always believed in ensuring identical access to food, shelter, clothing and living conditions for both rural and urban people in his scheme of development.[49] On this point, there is a close proximity between Gandhi's views and the Marxian outline of a socialist society drawn in the Communist Manifesto. Another problem is that Gandhi's entire scheme is based on local considerations and not on a general plan of universal application. Even he was not interested in entrusting the implementation of his constructive programme directly to the panchayats. The ultimate goal of his constructive programme was the replacement of the state which, in his views, was an instrument of organized power and hence it was quite illogical to expect that the state would invite, in the final analysis, its own extinction. This is a major inconsistency in his construction of ideal society, which is perhaps the product of his commitment to the anarchist view of development, combined with his passion for morality and individual liberty.

However, it is not out of place to point out that the policy-makers and the development experts in India have been seriously contemplating to realize the basic objectives of Gandhi's *Gram Swaraj* through a number of programmes and experiments, starting with the community development in 1952 to the most recent NREGS with the prefix – 'Mahatma Gandhi'. The ratification of the Seventy Third and Seventy Fourth Amendments to the Constitution passed in 1992 incorporating the mandatory provision of *gram sabha* at the grassroots testifies to the importance of Gandhian ideas in the Indian context. Hence, in order to assess the relevance of Gandhian scheme of decentralization and development, there is a need to trace the major propositions inherent in his scheme and examine their relevance in post-Independence India. The Gandhian approach to decentralization is based on at least five such propositions which may enable us to assess the applicability of the scheme. These are:

(a) The implementation of communitarian principles in the villages is feasible.

(b) Production, distribution and exchange of goods and produce can be organized without interference from the state or government.

(c) Settlement of disputes and arbitration of conflict are possible in the villages by the panchayats.

(d) The want and expectations of people at the community level are low and, therefore, they will not engage themselves in aggressive competition for personal gains.

(e) Since people are guided by the principles of 'plain living and high thinking', they will practice the doctrine of *aparigraha* (non-possession).[50]

These propositions are too simplistic to be viewed as the guiding determinants of economic development in subsequent decades after 1950s. There have been sea-changes in development concepts and indices during this period. The policy of planned economic development adopted in India in early 1950s is directed towards modernization of agriculture and establishment of heavy industries under the command economy of the state. As a result, the scope of further growth and development of self-reliant agriculture and fragmented cottage industries became obviously limited. The pressing need for rapid socio-economic development at par with essential requirements of welfare state in the context of scarcity of capital, efficiency and effectiveness have created a different perspective. Naturally, the goal of planning and development formulated at the national level and followed by the states has turned to be antithetical to Gandhian principles. The cardinal elements of the national strategy for development and industrialization include: (i) Economic development through establishment of heavy industries, if required, with foreign assistance; (ii) use of modern technology and, if necessary, import thereof for speedy modernization of the country and its economy; (iii) use of modern implements, chemical fertilizers, high-yielding variety of crops and machineries for augmentation of agricultural production with a view to eradicating poverty through Green Revolution; and (iv) organizing a strong and hierarchical bureaucratic machinery to accelerate the process of growth. All these elements have strengthened the process of centralization in their combined interactions that negate the sustenance of self-reliant village economy and traditional institutions. In spite of occasional modifications and structural adjustments, Nehruvian model of development is still recognized as the accepted national model of development, which is contrary to the Gandhian model of indigenous, self-reliant decentralized development.

In post-Independence India, there have been certain fundamental changes in our attitude towards life and thinking which have made the

Gandhian approach to economic development and decentralization outdated. Gandhi's concept of decentralization is much relevant to an agrarian society characterized by traditional loyalty, technological backwardness, undifferentiated social structure and communitarian values, which no longer determine social movements today. Moreover, rapid improvements in daily and household necessaries as a result of advances in science and technology have also changed lifestyles and standard of living. As a result, the concept of plain living, an avowed principle popularized by Gandhi, has given place to competitive and comfortable living. Today, people have no liking for what their neighbour produces; rather, they wait for the fresh consignment from the West. Secondly, Gandhi's doctrine of *aparigrah* and minimum want no longer attract people today. The allurement of acquisitive society and sophisticated standard of living, not higher standard of life as depicted in Gandhi's scheme of development, has increased human greed boundless. Thirdly, degeneration of human values and erosion in ethics and probity in public life and morality have an all-pervasive impact on state, society and politics. Corruption in public life is more frequent not only in India but also in socialist countries like China. Fourthly, the strategy for planned change under a formal and statutory state structure and organized bureaucracy has led to the growth and development of institutional approach to development and nation-building and the situation has led to an increase in people's dependence on state intervention.

As a result of all these developments, over-bureaucratization, predominance of rules and regulations, undue formalism and preference for 'means' instead of 'ends' have become concomitant of the process of planned development in society, which can no longer tolerate a complete decentralized system as outlined in Gandhi's scheme of decentralization. In fact, our administrative culture based on the legacies of the British administration has retained its distrust of local governments since 1882.[51] Even after two decades of constitutionalization of panchayats and district planning in India, the activity mapping[52] and constitution of district planning committees in all the states are yet to be completed. It is doubtful if a modern state could accommodate Gandhian principles of decentralization completely in its policy framework.

In Gandhi's scheme of panchayats, there is no role of political parties but today it is an existing reality in our community life. Once Bryce observed that 'parties are inevitable' and representative government could not be worked out without them.[53] The Asoka Mehta Committee (1978) reiterated this position: 'Participation of political parties in Panchayati Raj elections would ensure clearer orientation towards development programme and facilitate healthier linkages with higher level political process.'[54] Today, political parties play the key role in the organization and functioning of the panchayati raj in almost all the states in India, and the experience is encouraging. Obviously, there is one major difficulty – local politics has lost its specificity and autonomy and has become an integral part of state and national politics in India, which reminds us of the state of affairs as once outlined by Cynthia Cockburn in her *The Local State* (1997). In such a situation, the Gandhian approach to decentralization and politics has lost much of its applicability. All these factors and findings reinforce the thesis that the propositions traced in the foundation of Gandhian doctrine of development and decentralization are not consistent with the present-day reality.

Conclusion

From the above account, it appears that Gandhi has over-emphasized the principles of local autonomy in his views on development and decentralization in a country like India, dominated by casteism, untouchability and other social vices that constitute the social hierarchy.[55] The concept of growth and development of *swaraj* and other political organizations in Gandhi's ideas is an autonomous movement from below to the top, which is unthinkable in the present political structure. Rather, the current trend is directly opposite. Unending greed and urge for capturing and retaining political power have led the political parties to adopt populist politics that has shaken the very foundation of confidence, self-reliance and individual dignity, though these are considered basic virtues in Gandhian politics.

Gandhi's philosophy of economic and political development is a product of political, social and economic conditions prevalent at that time, premeditated by an urgency to remove the negative and destructive impacts of British rule through application of indigenous methods of self-reliance and *swadeshi* based on non-violence and truth. Though Gandhi was conscious of existence and interplay of multiple factors, including inequality and injustice in Indian villages, he did not endorse the inevitability of class-struggle as a possible solution. Rather, he was anxious to bring in a space so that human beings are not modeled as instruments or mere cogs in the machine, but are involved in constructive activities in the village-centred Indian society.[56] Since the days of Gandhi, there have been unprecedented changes in all spheres of individual and polity with multifarious challenges besetting our society, which do not justify a blind adaptation of Gandhian economics and politics for solution of all such problems. No doubt, there will remain ample scope for academic debates on the relevance and applicability of his ideas in future, but in the present context, reinterpretation and adaptation with necessary modifications in the Gandhian approach may fit well into the domain of development discourse.

Notes

1. M.K. Gandhi, *Harijan*, 30 December 1939 and 18 January 1942; *Selected Works of Mahatma Gandhi*, Ahmedabad: Navajivan Publishing House, 1968.
2. *Young India*, 2 March 1922; *Selected Works of Mahatma Gandhi*, Ahmedabad: Navajivan Publishing House, 1968.
3. D.G. Tendulkar, *Mahatma: Life of Mohandas Karamchand Gandhi*, Vol. I, New Delhi: Publication Division, 1960, p. 185.
4. Louis Fischer, *The Life of Mahatma Gandhi*, New York: Mentor Books, 1950, p. 56.
5. Rajani Palme Dutt, *India Today*, England: Victor Gollancz, 1940 (original text reprint, July 1983), p. 629; and E.M.S. Namboodiripad, '125th Anniversary of Mahatma Gandhi', *Parichay*, Kolkata, 1995, p. 330. Also, Narahari Kaviraj, 'Mahatma Gandhi and Satyagraha', *Parichay*, West Bengal, Vol. XXXVII, Nos 2–4, January–February 1995, p. 24.
6. *Harijan*, 3 January 1946.
7. M.K. Gandhi, *An Autobiography*, Ahmedabad: Navajivan Publishing House, 1940, p. 365.
8. *Young India*, 2 July 1931; *Harijan*, 21 July 1940.
9. Tendulkar, op. cit., p. 161.
10. *Young India*, 2 March 1922.
11. M.K. Gandhi, 'A Letter to Jawaharlal Nehru', 5 October 1945; *Selected Letters*, Ahmedabad: Navajivan Publishing House, 1960.
12. *Young India*, 27 November 1924 and 18 June 1925.
13. Tendulkar, op. cit., p. 318.
14. M.K. Gandhi, *Sarvodaya*, Ahmedabad: Navajivan Publishing House, 1954, p. 74.
15. *Young India*, 2 July 1931.

16. *Harijan*, 9 March 1940.
17. *Harijan*, 2 January 1937.
18. 'A Letter to Pandit Nehru', *A Bunch of Old Letters*, Bombay: Navajivan Publishing House, 1958, pp. 506–507.
19. *Harijan*, 27 May 1939.
20. Sriman Narayan, *Gandhi: The Man and His Thought*, New Delhi: Publication Division, 1969, p. 40.
21. *Harijan*, 26 July 1942.
22. M.K. Gandhi, *Constructive Programme: Its Meaning and Place*, Ahmedabad: Navajivan Publishing House, 1991, pp. 1–30.
23. Jayaprakash Narayan, *Swaraj for the People*, Varanasi: Sarva Seva Sangh Prakashan, 1977, pp. 34–35.
24. M.K. Gandhi, *Constructive Programme*, op. cit., p. 19.
25. *Young India*, 28 May 1931.
26. M.K. Gandhi, *The Nation's Voice*, Ahmedabad: Navajivan Publishing House, 1974, p. 18.
27. *Harijan*, 18 January 1942 and 30 December 1939.
28. M.K. Gandhi, *Speeches and Writings of Mahatma Gandhi*, 4th edition, Madras: G.A. Natesan and Company, 1933, pp. 436–444.
29. *Harijan*, 16 November 1934 and 7 December 1934.
30. *Collective Works of Mahatma Gandhi*, Vol. XIII, New Delhi: Publication Division, 1958, p. 219 and 231.
31. *Young India*, 19 March 1931.
32. *Young India*, 3 August 1925.
33. *Harijan*, 28 July 1946.
34. *Harijan*, 26 July 1942.
35. *Harijan*, 18 January 1948.
36. *Harijan*, 18 January 1948.
37. *Harijan*, 28 July 1946.
38. M.K. Gandhi, *Constructive Programme*, op. cit.; also, Shriman Narayan, *Gandhian Constitution for Free India*, Allahabad: Kitabistan, 1946, pp. 68–69.
39. Shriman Narayan, *Gandhian Constitution for Free India*, Allahabad: Kitabistan, 1946, pp. 88–89 and 93–94.
40. Ibid., p. 88.
41. Sailesh Kumar Bandyopadhyay, *Gandhiji Gathankarma* (in Bengali), Kolkata: Mitra and Ghosh, 1977, p. 65.
42. Narayan, op. cit., pp. 98–100.

43. Rabindranath Tagore, *Towards Universal Man*, Delhi: Asia Publishing House, 1961, p. 304.
44. Karl Marx, 'The British Rule in India', in K. Marx and F. Engels, *The First Indian War of Independence 1857–1859*, Moscow: Progress Publishers, 1959, p. 19.
45. *Constitution Assembly Debates*, Vol. VII, New Delhi: Lok Sabha Publications, 1948–49, p. 39.
46. *Young India*, 21 August 1924.
47. *Young India*, 13 November 1924.
48. Nirmal Kumar Bose and P.H. Patwardhan, *Gandhi in Indian Politics*, Bombay: Lalvani Publishing House, 1967, p. 17.
49. Pyarelal, *Mahatma Gandhi: The Last Phase*, Vol. II, Ahmedabad: Navajivan Publishing House, 1956, p. 547.
50. C.V. Raghavulu and R. Ananda Rao, 'Gandhian Approach to Decentralization: Its Relevance', *Indian Journal of Public Administration*, Vol. XXIV, No. 3, 1978, p. 713.
51. George Mathew, *Panchayati Raj Update*, Vol. XX, No. 4, 2013, p. 6.
52. Kuldeep Mathur, *Panchayati Raj*, New Delhi: Oxford University Press, 2013, p. 78.
53. James Bryce, *Modern Democracies*, Vol. I, Calcutta: World Press, 1962, p. 134.
54. Recommendations of the *Committee on Panchayati Raj Institutions*, New Delhi: Government of India, Chapter IV: Elections, 1978.
55. Jayantanuja Bandyopadhyaya, *Social and Political Thought of Gandhi*, Howrah: Manuscript India, 1969, p. 123.
56. Amlan Datta, *Gandhi O Rabindranath: Byakti, Yukti, Samaj* (in Bengali), Kolkata: Ananda Publishers, 1978, p. 34.

CHAPTER 3

Tagore's Views on Decentralized Development

An Alternative Model

Kumkum Chattopadhyay

Since 1980s, a new wave has been gradually emerging in the sphere of development which, after its origin in Western liberal democracies, has come to influence the rest of the world in some way or the other. Margaret Thatcher of Great Britain and Ronald Reagan in the United States represented this paradigmatic shift, as both of them declared that the role of the government should be substantially reduced, and opportunities be created for full play of free market in economy. In this context, 'New Right' emerged as a baggage of diverse ideas.[1] Another concept that emerged during this period came to be known as Third System. According to this view, besides economic power (the transnational) and political power (the state), people's power is seen as a third kind, based on consciousness, organization and action. In other words, one could talk about three main actors: the Prince (First System), the Merchant (Second System) and the Citizen (Third System). Here, citizens constitute the third system when they do not seek either government or economic power. This was a trend which could be seen as a direct support for an alternative development model.[2] In this context, the concept of localization or localism became important in the face of globalization. This concept of localization or localism was distinctly different from the traditional concept of 'local'.

Following this trend, there has been a gradual search for tracing out the roots of development based on indigenous sources. India is no exception and it is found that a number of social and political thinkers in India had contributed to this field in the past. Rabindranath Tagore was one of the pioneers who gave constructive and relevant ideas in the sphere of socio-economic development. This article is an attempt to explore the ideas developed and experiments sponsored by Tagore in this context. Tagore was very much aware of the differences between the European and the Indian society. To his mind, India, due to her colonial heritage was trying to imitate the European model of development which, he feared, would not be a successful one. So, he prescribed his views for development of India.

Herein lies the relevance of the ideas of Rabindranath Tagore. An objective analysis of his works is sufficient to establish him as an alternative development thinker. He tried to think in terms of realities in India and realized that development could only be ensured through according due recognition to the tradition, nature and necessity of Indian society. This is evident from a brief review of his writings, novels and dramas as well as his correspondence. Since India was basically an agricultural society, he took direct initiative to improve agriculture by introducing scientific methods of cultivation based on *Samavayaneeti*. Besides, he had his own plan of rural reconstruction for development with special emphasis on decentralization. He also tried to introduce his own policy of educational development which was quite different from the contemporary one imposed by the British. This article also makes an attempt to understand his reflections on the cooperative principle, agriculture, rural reconstruction and education, which were the main pillars of development in the context of Indian society as visualized by Tagore. His concern for maintaining ecological balance also needs special mention in this connection.

Philosophy of Cooperative Principle

Samavayaneeti or cooperative principle constituted the essence of Tagore's development ideas. He had a firm conviction in the efficacy of this principle. He preached the principle, encouraged his fellow countrymen to implement it and even came forward to put it into practice. He earnestly tried to establish this principle based on logic. He pointed out that men were weak and small in the initial phase of evolution but were able to overcome the troubles created by larger and huge animals following the principles of unity. Thus, today, each and every man has become powerful because of the combination of physical and mental powers of a large number of their ancestors.[3]

Cooperation was an ideal to Rabindranath Tagore. He believed that it could be applied according to needs or situations in innumerable ways. As he was anxious about development in rural Bengal, he took the initiative of applying this principle in the villages. He had a vision for building up completely self-sufficient villages: 'The villagers must be educated, assisted and encouraged to establish primary schools, centres for training in arts and crafts, centres for religious activities, cooperative stores and banks ... Our main problem is how to build up model village communities.'[4] With this vision, Tagore became very enthusiastic about cooperative principles. He was convinced that wealth existed in the union of man and man, while separation was the cause of poverty. He did his best to convince his countrymen this simple fact.

Rabindranath Tagore tried to analyse Indian society both as a historian and as a sociologist. He observed that once upon a time, India used to experience a community-based life and during that period, the rich used to spend their wealth for public purposes such as digging of wells, establishment of temples and so on. This obviously proved their sense of charity and responsibility. But, that practice also debarred the village people from becoming aware of their immediate needs. As a result, they failed to develop themselves as self-sufficient and confident personalities. So, when the process of modernization started after the advent of the British and society was gradually being transformed following the migration of the rich from villages to cities and towns, these rural people became helpless since they had no power to believe that the means of their betterment had already existed in themselves. They were lacking in self-confidence. It was therefore necessary to restore confidence in them.[5] In his philosophy of cooperative principles, Tagore tried to establish the truth: 'we find bondage in separation and liberation in union'. Although he did not use the term 'social capital', yet he consciously tried to develop trust, norm and network within the boundary of a village so that people could learn to live collectively.

Agricultural Development

In 1890, Devendranath Tagore sent his son Rabindranath to look after their *zamindari* in East Bengal at *Shelaidah* and *Sahajadpur*. The experiences Tagore gathered during this period opened his eyes. He noticed that although agriculture was the primary and main source of living in society, the agricultural producers comprised the most neglected section in our country. Tagore came forward to rescue them not for their own sake but also for the sake of the society as a whole. He nullified a great many existing customs which were against the interests of the peasants. The policy followed and introduced by him satisfied the poor villagers who were his subjects, though officials at various levels of the *zamindari* system seriously got angry with him, since it was definitely a blow against their vested interests.[6] Naturally, Tagore had to face hurdles from every corner but, to some extent, he was successful in carrying on his programme. Thus, whenever we talk about alternative development in India, we have to go through his works – both theory and practice – because his ideas are relevant even today in this century.[7]

Tagore was very sceptical about the success of political movement. Once again he alarmed the political leaders about the priority of activities. No one paid any heed to his words. So, he came forward and assumed the responsibility himself. He was very disappointed with the boycott movement and burning of foreign clothes. To him, these negative and destructive approaches would not bring any solution. Rather, he looked at the sphere of agricultural development which he thought to be the most important area for developing a society. He realized that cultivation needed scientific methods and he sent his son Rathindrath along with Santosh Chandra Majumdar, son of his friend Srish Chandra Majumdar, to the Illinois University in USA in 1906. Next year, Negendranath Gangopadhyay, his youngest son-in-law, went to take lessons in agricultural science by Tagore's initiation.[8] During the recess in harvesting, Tagore tried to engage the villagers in small and cottage industries. He suggested a number of alternative occupations which they could perform during their recess such as fisheries, dairy farming, weaving of clothes, threshing sugarcane, etc. He collected different samples of local handicrafts. It was an attempt to encourage traditional local art, local culture and local handicraft.[9]

With a very scientific bent of mind, Tagore felt that soil needed special attention for agricultural development in any society. He was very keen on observing soil to understand differences from place to place. Elmhirst, being an expert on agriculture, brought the issue of soil conservation to the knowledge of our countrymen. Elmhirst was, probably, the most important figure in the rural reconstruction programme initiated by Tagore.[10]

Tagore believed that India could be proud of having a very rich natural reservoir of knowledge and felt that this knowledge could be scientifically utilized by combining it with modern inventions or discoveries. The fact that science and technology were gradually integrating the world was vividly perceived by him. So cultivation, to him, was no longer the exclusive responsibility of cultivators. He suggested that scientists and other educated people of the society should join hands with the producers.[11] Thus, the urban should embrace the rural and give whatever the latter needs.[12] His *Russiar Chithi* is a very valuable document in this respect.

Rabindranath Tagore was very serious about rescuing poor peasants from the control of the *zamindars* and moneylenders. At that moment, the idea of rural bank flashed through his mind and he established 'Patisar Krishi Bank' by collecting money from his friends as loan. But this bank used to suffer due to lack of funds and could not be managed successfully. In the meantime, Tagore won the Nobel Prize in 1913 and put a major part of the prize money in that bank. This gesture proves his generosity, benevolence and his genuine feeling for the poor peasants.[13] The concept of grain bank or *Dharmagola* used to exist in the society to serve poor peasants during famine. Tagore wanted to revitalize that practice. According to this concept, the surplus of crops was collected from every peasant and saved in *Dharmogola* to help the poor peasants, especially during famines or in case of personal crisis. Here originated the relevance of reconstruction. Tagore contemplated that a basic framework already existed in the society and the point was only to rearrange or reorganize it. He took the initiative and this practice became popular in many parts of rural Bengal.[14]

Rural Reconstruction

Tagore's concept of rural reconstruction plan was based upon an effective realization of the village needs and priorities which he gradually comprehended as he came in close contact with the villagers. His vision was to enable the villagers to help themselves and take up the leadership of the village on their own shoulders. This was a programme of self-help or self-assurance.[15] In order to implement his plan of rural reconstruction, he tried to combine the findings of science with local and cultural resources of the country, emphasizing the awakening of human capabilities. He was much assertive to point out that rural development should be viewed in the context of social and cultural development.[16] Tagore put much emphasis on bringing changes in values, tastes, attitudes, manners and outlook of the people. Accordingly, he tried to set in motion a new atmosphere through his songs, dramas, dances, poems and paintings. He considered cultural development as a corresponding and complementary process of rural development.[17] He was convinced that such transformation in culture would be accepted one day by the whole of India.

The Indigenous Society (Swadeshi Samaj)

'Swadeshi Samaj'[18] is a well-known essay by Tagore which was published in 1904. It contains the first comprehensive statement of his social philosophy. He analysed the causes of disintegration of Indian village life and made concrete suggestions for its reconstruction in this article.[19] As a sequel to the essay on 'Swadeshi Samaj', Tagore prepared a complete scheme to give practical effect to the ideas he had expressed in it. The whole scheme centred around the concept of rural reconstruction through organized efforts which could be seen in the form of a constitution.[20] Besides agricultural development through cooperative efforts, the revival of cottage industries to mitigate the poverty of the masses was emphasized. A very intimate relationship between the villagers and the rural workers, an honest attempt to bring harmonious relationship between the Hindus and the Muslims and the appointment of a people's representative as the leader of the society were the other features of the 'Swadeshi Samaj' as proposed by Tagore.[21] A constitution on 'Pallisamaj'[22] needs special mention here.

First phase of Rural Reconstruction: East Bengal Experiment

Tagore's estate in East Bengal included mainly three districts. *Birahimpur* – (headquarter *Shelaidah*), *Kaligram* – (headquarter *Patisar*) and *Sahajadpur,* the headquarter of which was named after the district. Rabindranath Tagore was completely different from his fellow *zamindars*. To quote L.S.S. O' Malley,

> It must not be imagined that a powerful landlord is always oppressive and uncharitable. A striking instance to the contrary is given in the Settlement Officer's account of the estate of Rabindranath Tagore, the Bengali poet, whose fame is worldwide. It is clear that to poetical genius, he adds practical and beneficial ideas of estate

management, which should be an example to the local Zemindars. Bengal District Gazetteers – Rajshahi, 1916.[23]

That was the beginning of his rural reconstruction programme. But even from that very moment, he had a holistic vision and he was very sincere, honest and determined to achieve his goal even in the formative phase. His programme included health, education, cottage industries, agriculture, fisheries, weaving, etc. In a word, an all-round development of a village was his ultimate objective which he considered necessary for building a self-sufficient and self-confident society. He introduced the experiment of tractor for cultivation, furnace for potteries and ceramics, a husking machine for paddies, which proved his scientific bent of mind.[24] The most remarkable innovation in this phase was the introduction of *Mandali* System at *Birahimpur,* which was basically a Hindu-dominated area. Here, he had to face resistance from all sides organized especially by the Hindus.[25] He concentrated on the Muslim-dominated *Kaligram.*[26]

A short history of the general welfare society of *Kaligram* may give us a hint about the nature of his programme. The tenants of the estate used to make an extra contribution at the rate of 3 pies for every rupee of the revenue paid. The funds thus realized were used to be spent on a fair and a religious festival. In 1312 B.S. (approximately 1905) at a meeting held in the memory of late Devendranath Tagore, the father of the poet, it was decided to establish an entrance school and a charitable dispensary and to raise a further contribution of 6 pies in addition to the original 3 pies per rupee for that purpose. This was the beginning of formation of the welfare fund at *Kaligram*. This name stood both for the fund and the body which organized it. To remove this anomaly, latter it was renamed as the General Welfare Society. The organization consisted of three branches at *Patisar, Ratwal* and *Kamta.* Instead of an entrance school, a minor one was established for the time being. A few years later, it was decided to do away with the original subscription of 3 pies earmarked for the fair and festival and to increase the total 'welfare levy' to 15 pies per rupee. Some 25 *pathsalas* (primary schools) spreading over the *pargana,* an English High School and a charitable dispensary at *Patisar* were financed from the fund in addition to some public works carried out every year.[27] In 1913, during a visit to the estate, Tagore advised that instead of spending most of the fund for a *Patisar* High School, it would be better to have a middle school and a charitable dispensary at each of the three branches and a *pathshala* in each village, while public works could be continued as before. This reorganization was carried out.[28] This decision of Tagore once more proved his holistic vision even in the pre-*Sriniketan* era.

Apart from the *pathsalas,* schools and charitable dispensaries, the society had substantial achievements to its credit in rural development activities. Mention may be made in particular of the dam at *Talimpur,* the embankments at *Kamta* and *Paroil, Debnagar-Saria road* and *Maskipur tank.* Besides, wells were dug up in many places.[29] But problems started to surface when peasant movements and other political forces began to operate more actively. The *raiyats* of *Kamta* division started an agitation against the welfare levy. Accordingly in *Paus,* 1346 B.S. (approximately 1940), this branch was closed down and all connections were dropped which had been started there.[30] The agricultural bank rendering very useful services for a long time to the cultivators was gradually winding up its business. The practice of settling disputes by arbitration, which greatly benefited people, had to be suspended after the Debt Settlement Act came into force, as this Act made arbitration by private bodies difficult, if not impossible.[31]

Sriniketan Experiment

The institution of *Sriniketan* was not an isolated experiment, but an integral part of Rabindranath Tagore's total educational and reconstruction work. At the same time, *Sriniketan* was certainly a product of his restlessness to do something for poverty-stricken rural India. He purchased the *Surul Kuthibari* at the cost of ₹ 10,000 in 1912 to implement his plan. But it still took one decade to start his programme due to two reasons: lack of funds and absence of a leader. In 1921, he met Leonard K. Elmhirst, a young agriculture graduate in the USA, who expressed his keen interest in Tagore's rural reconstruction programme and expressed his willingness to join the same. Tagore decided to entrust the task to Elmhirst, who had been acquainted with the conditions of Indian villages on some earlier occasions. Towards the end of 1921, Elmhirst came to *Santiniketan* and started work from *Surul Kuthibari* as a citadel of rural regeneration on 6 February 1922, after one year of *Visva-Bharati* being formally established as a university of unique type in 1921.[32]

Tagore and Elmhirst started giving shape to a complete scheme of rural reconstruction. From the very beginning, the Institute of *Sriniketan* was organized under a democratic *Karma Samity* (working committee), on which the representatives of total workers and many eminent men of the time came to serve. The most dedicated one in this venture was Kalimohan Ghosh. That was the beginning of *Sriniketan*.[33]

In this scheme of development, health received fore most priority in social welfare action-programmes which intended to carry out the anti-malaria schemes from preventive and curative angles. The village people were trained for cleaning the bushes and jungles, and filling up the pools of stagnant water with earth to prevent mosquitoes from breeding and as a curative measure, distribution of medicines for malarial fever among the villagers through door to door supply and dispensary at *Sriniketan* and in some other villages organized by the *Sriniketan* team of functionaries. The next set of work undertaken by the village people with active assistance of the team included road repairing, building of culverts and opening and repairing of drains for easy flow of water within the villages and crop fields. Since most of the rural population were farmers, various measures were adopted to augment the yield of agricultural production, through use of improved technology, good seeds and manures, arrangement of proper irrigation, offering cheap credit facility from cooperative credit societies and remunerative marketing of their produce. Elmhirst established a small laboratory to carry out experiments for improvement in production under particular soil and climatic conditions of the villages. Improved varieties of seeds of different crops, vegetables and horticulture plants were procured and distributed after imparting application of improved methods of cultivation to the villages. The lessons of new farm technology were imparted not only to the farmers around *Santiniketan–Sriniketan* campus of *Visva-Bharati*, but also to the farmers from different districts of Bengal and even from nearby provinces.[34]

A complete plan of rural reconstruction experiments with seeds, manures, rotation of crops, cattle and poultry farming was drawn up by 1928. A well-developed cooperative society was charged with the responsibilities of promoting programmes of health, education, agriculture and rural industries. The society maintained a grain bank, played as an arbitrator in local disputes and carried on educational propaganda through many attractive methods.[35]

Tagore was very conscious about environmental protection and his rural reconstruction programme was eco-friendly. He loved nature and could feel the worth of it. So, he was keen to firm up the programme of development in consonance with nature. He tried to make his *Sriniketan* experiment a complete one. So, he was conscious of including every aspect of 'reconstruction' in his programme. The organizations of *Siksha Satra, Lok Siksha Samsad, Siksha Charcha* and *Brati Balaka* proved his holistic vision in this context. He sought to integrate the traditional ideals of the past with the Western scientific genius.

Elmhirst started the Institute of Agriculture at *Sriniketan* which later came to be known as the Institute of Rural Reconstruction. Elmhirst became its first Director. Tagore once remarked that it was Elmhirst who developed this plan into a separate field of work.[36] Elmhirst proved himself in each aspect very successfully. His humane character has also been revealed in this context. He used to carry a 'first aid' box in order to serve the village people.[37] Tagore sincerely believed that socio-economic progress of India was necessary before achieving political freedom and the mission could only become successful if the villages of India became self-sufficient. *Sriniketan* came into existence in order to fulfill that purpose. Like Tagore, Elmhirst also used to believe that too much of dependence on government would destroy personal initiative and individual dignity. Both of them were against contemporary agitational politics and believed that social progress was inherent in the development of individual personality.

Rabindranath Tagore's idea of rural reconstruction was, no doubt, a path-breaking one, although it created much debate and attracted criticism from every corner of his contemporary society. But, Tagore was firm, for he had a very strong logic behind his concept and fortunately identified committed associates in his unique venture. He was sincere, honest and thoughtful, but a bit utopian. Yet, Tagore's model may be accepted as a micro model to be followed all over India, but the difficulty is to find a proper leader upon whom the success of such a project depends exclusively. Yet, such a programme, even if implemented partially, would benefit the society. Anybody interested in such type of programme should consult the scheme of Tagore as a pioneering one to throw light in the field of alternative development, with emphasis on human development.

Education and Development

Rabindranath Tagore was the first thinker to widen the definition of education and equated education with a total lifestyle of a human being. The establishment of *Brahmacharyashram* and the starting of *Visva-Bharati* – both were probably the most remarkable constructive achievements in Tagore's life. Keeping in mind these two incidents, his educational contributions can be classified mainly into three stages:

(a) Pre-Santiniketan stage,

(b) Post-Santiniketan and pre-Visva-Bharati stage, and

(c) Visva-Bharati stage.[38]

In a word, he tried to modernize Indian education perfectly in an Indian manner for wining a glorious place in the twentieth century world.

The methods of teaching introduced by Tagore were not exactly the imitation of ancient Indian traditional methods. Rather, he tried to remodel the contemporary British education policy in consonance with a system suitable for Indian society. Naturally, the system introduced by him had certain unique features.

He pointed out that Indian education policy was completely detached from the native soil and was then confined only to the upper layer of the society. It could not become helpful for India. The policy was also isolated from the soul of the country. In this context, Tagore tried to analyse the East-West concept very rationally with a sociological bent of mind. He noticed correctly that the different countries of Europe started the process of learning through Latin. Later, each country introduced learning through mother tongue. But there was some sort of unity among them so far as their source or origin was concerned. Moreover, all the countries were tied up by the bond of the same religion, i.e. Christianity. Thus, unity of learning and unity of religion laid the basis of Western civilization. The concept of eastern civilization was the opposite of West. It was not an integrated concept. Rather, it was a negative in relation to the West – it was basically non-European in nature and so it failed to develop any positive bond which the West implied. On the other hand, the nations or nationalities existing within the Eastern civilization were dissimilar, sometimes contradictory. For example, the Arabian culture and the Chinese culture were extremely opposite. The same was true about the contradictory cultures of the Hindus of India and Semitic races of western Asia. 'Under the compulsions of history, some areas may have had cultural exchanges but the mind of Asia never became a unified entity. So it is that, when we speak of Eastern civilization, we are thinking only of our own national civilization. That is why Asia, unlike Europe, has been unable to make a strong impact on the modern age.'[39] In the process of determining the education policy in India, this Western-Eastern dichotomy pointed out by Tagore should be taken into account.

Tagore expressed his views on every minute detail of education. Teaching should generate, according to him, a clear conception about the subject. If the basic concepts were not clear, the students could not be capable of reproduction.[40] Tagore used to think that one textbook needed a number of reference books.[41] In the scheme of education, the role of nature had been specifically emphasized by Tagore. A student should enjoy the learning process. With this idea, Tagore aimed at creating a joyful hermitage at *Santiniketan*. The children could enjoy freedom amidst the simple and enchanting loveliness of nature.

Tagore's another significant and useful proposal was to introduce mother tongue as the medium of instruction. But he was also conscious about the necessity of learning English. He proved his expertise as an English teacher. He not only suggested but also followed the teaching of English grammar in Bengali.[42] Tagore could feel that teaching through Bengali necessitated composition and compilation of an appropriate grammar book in Bengali. He realized that Bengali grammar should assume its own identity although it was indebted to Sanskrit. Thus, he laid the basis of Bengali language and popularized it as the medium of instruction.[43] As an educator, Tagore's interest in composing Bengali dictionary was no less important. As a writer, he contributed a lot to Bengali literature and language. In a word, he modernized Bengali language and brought a new style in Bengali literature by updating it without the help of any useful Bengali dictionary.

Tagore widened the area of education. He considered that the practice of any faculty is the other name of nurturing education. The purpose of education was to enrich the soul and mind of a person. So, he gave enough emphasis on music, dance, painting, etc. and introduced those faculties in his process of learning.[44] The school established by Tagore was a residential school. Here, both the students and the teachers collectively developed a lifestyle where both experienced common food and lodging, learning, sports and even gossiping or any kind of union. Thus, actually it was a family composed of teachers and students.[45] It is to be noted that night school was for the first time introduced by the students of Tagore's institution. Later, it was found that *Visva-Bharati* was the only university where rural reconstruction was incorporated in the curriculum.[46] The educational institution established by Rabindranath Tagore was maintained from his own pocket, financial assistance from his friends, donations and money collected through various performing programmes for a period of thirty years (1921–1951) without any help from the government.

Students' Organization

The system of *Chhatraswaraj* (self-rule of the students) was an important aspect of Tagore's constructive programme. By introducing the concept of *Chhatraswaraj*, he wanted to teach discipline and self-dependence along with the concept of active participation. This idea of *Chhatraswaraj* was not only an exceptional but also a revolutionary one which then aroused much criticism. In fact, how far the students could be able to properly utilize freedom was a debatable issue. Tagore also had to face strong opposition on the question of discipline because he transferred the responsibility of maintaining discipline to the students. He was proclaimed to be unpractical, guided by poetic whim.[47]

Ashram Sammilani was a committee of the students to carry on their programmes. The committee was treated as parliament of the students and all students were the members of that parliament. This parliament elected an executive committee which actually used to exercise power. Each *sammilani* had one secretary and even the captains used to obey him. The *sammilani* or parliament had the power to set rules and the executive committee used to supervise the implementation of rules. A court of justice was formed to give judgment on serious crimes. The secretary and the captains were the judges. A court used to function after dinner, maintaining its confidential nature.[48] The crimes used to vary from violation of rules to mimicry. But any sort of physical assault was not allowed as punishment. This students' union might be known as a Junior Republic.[49]

Tagore had a vision, the vision of proper upbringing of every child in order to develop a complete man, because the success or failure of any society was virtually dependent upon its members. His son, Rathindranath Tagore, recollects in *Pitrismriti,* a biography of his father, that the students came to *Santiniketan* from different environments, but used to carry on an exclusive impression, very unique and very original when they returned. This was the contribution of Tagore for extending education in order to lead the society towards progress.[50]

Protection of Environment

Environmental degradation is a serious problem of the day about which the present world is well aware of. Tagore, by his far-sightedness could feel that technological development was leading the world towards destruction. He was very conscious about the problem due to increase of population. In different writings and lectures, he warned people to become aware about protecting nature. His programme of rural reconstruction, his programme of education, his different essays, lectures, discussions and correspondences prove his sincerity in this sphere. His introduction to *The Robbery of the Soil,*[51] a lecture delivered by Elmhirst, is worth mentioning here. In his

'Japanyatri'[52], 'Bhumilakshmi'[53], 'Tapovan'[54] and in a number of essays, he expressed his anxiety about the conflict between man and nature. 'Muktodhara'[55] and 'Raktakarabi'[56] are important in this respect. He considered man as a part of nature and whenever and wherever this bond was loosened, whenever the issue became man versus nature, environmental balance was disturbed. He found that man had exploited nature from the very beginning of human civilization, thus damaging not only nature but also his own entity.

Tagore himself was always very careful about maintaining environmental balance. Besides his contributions in other spheres, his role as a conscious defender of environment is no less important, especially when this area has come to the limelight for the last thirty years in order to secure the earth from rapid decay. His total development programme was chalked out accordingly. In this venture, he always tried to avoid too much of mechanization, application of chemicals and technology. In order to save and protect the earth, it was necessary to become eco-friendly and Rabindranath Tagore was serious in this regard. The introduction of *halakarshana* (ploughing the fields) and *vriksharopana* (plantation) festivals establishes him as an environmental activist.

Conclusion

Rabindranath Tagore was always guided by an integrated approach to everything. In fact, it was his worldview. To him, this planet (earth) was a near and dear one. He treated human race as a part of nature. Any approach or programme of development proposed by Tagore had this approach of integrity and hence his plan of human development was meant for everyone. There were no distinctions on the basis of caste, class, race, language, religion and so on. Moreover, his concept and programme of development was also eco-friendly. He could envision that maintenance of ecological balance was a primary necessity for the sustenance of the earth. As human race is nothing but a species of this ecological system, any imbalance in ecology would bring disaster to the entire system, thus threatening the very existence of the human race. Similarly, any imbalance in development among human beings would also be unscientific for it would destroy the integrity existing among human beings throughout the world. So, his first aim was to develop the deprived while the mainstream development had always served the privileged. Tagore could properly realize the real implication of development and he wanted to arrange his programme of development with that intuition. His life was a journey to implement that premise of development with honesty and sincerity.

Tagore was both a humanist and a proponent of human development. With his knowledge and experience, he could contribute his own method for development of the country. In this aspect, he was exclusively original. Moreover, he asserted confidently that each society should follow its own method of development according to its nature. Instead of integration, he believed more in union, i.e. in the unity without sacrificing diversity. Human development was the basic theme in his philosophy. All these characteristics establish Tagore as an alternative development thinker. It is high time now to recognize him for his original contributions in the sphere of development studies and give him the honour for his far-sightedness and scientific outlook.

Notes

1. Mohit Bhattacharya, *Social Theory and Development Administration*, New Delhi: Jawahar Publishers and Distributors, 2002, p. 115.
2. Bjorn Hettne, *Development Theory and the Three Worlds*, Essex: Longman Scientific & Technical, 1992, pp. 165–166.
3. Rabindranath Tagore, *The Co-operative Principle*, Kolkata: Visva-Bharati, 1963, p. 27.
4. Ibid., p. 19.
5. Ibid., pp. 28–29.
6. Prabalkanti Hazra, *Sahitya O Sanskriti – Rabindrasankhya*, Kolkata: D.D. & Co., 1414 BS, p. 59.
7. Ibid.
8. Ibid., p. 61.
9. Ibid., p. 64.
10. Ibid., p. 66.
11. Rabindranath Tagore, 'Bhumilakshmi', in *Rabindra Rachanabali*, Centenary Volume, Kolkata: Government of West Bengal, 1368 BS, XII, p. 505.
12. Hazra, op. cit., pp. 67–68.
13. Ibid., p. 68.
14. Ibid., p. 14.
15. Sugata Dasgupta, *A Poet and a Plan*, London: Thacker Spink & Co. Pvt. Ltd., 1962, p. 22.
16. Ibid., p. 25.

17. Ibid., p. 26.
18. Rabindranath Tagore, 'Swadeshi Samaj', in *Rabindra Rachanabali*, Centenary Volume, Kolkata: Government of West Bengal, 1368 BS, XII, pp. 683–702.
19. Rabindranath Tagore, 'Swadeshi Samaj Prabandhapath', in *Rabindra Rachanabali*, Centenary Volume, Kolkata: Government of West Bengal, 1368 BS, XII, pp. 768–770.
20. Rabindranath Tagore, 'Swadeshi Samaj: Sanbidhan', in *Rabindra Rachanabali*, Centenary Volume, Kolkata: Government of West Bengal, 1368 BS, XII, pp. 774–778.
21. Rabindranath Tagore, 'Swadeshi Samaj Prabandhapath', op. cit.
22. Rabindranath Tagore, 'Pallisamaj: Sanbidhan', in *Rabindra Rachanabali*, Centenary Volume, Kolkata: Government of West Bengal, 1368 BS, XII, pp. 778–779.
23. Arunendu Bandyopadhyay, 'Santi-Sri Avenue', in *Paschimbanga*, Special Rabindra Sankhya, Kolkata: Government of West Bengal, 2007, pp. 16–17.
24. Ibid., p. 17.
25. Rabindranath Tagore, *Chithipatra*, Vol. 13, Kolkata: Visva-Bharati, 1992, p. 71.
26. Prasanta Kumar Paul, *Rabijibani*, Kolkata: Ananda Publishers Pvt. Ltd., 2004, p. 20.
27. Sudhir Sen, *Rabindranath Tagore on Rural Reconstruction*, Calcutta: Visva-Bharati, 1943, p. 121.
28. Ibid., p. 122.
29. Ibid.
30. Ibid.
31. Ibid., p. 123.
32. Arun Mukhopadhyay, 'Tagore's Sriniketan Experiment – Past and Present: An Assessment', *Occasional Paper No. 4*, New Delhi: Indian Association of Social Science Institution (IASSI), 1995, p. 4.
33. Dasgupta, op. cit., p. 17.
34. Mukhopadhyay, op. cit., pp. 5–6.
35. Dasgupta, op. cit.
36. Uma Dasgupta, 'Leonard Elmhirst', in *Sristi*, Special Issue, Sriniketan: Palli Samprasaran Kendra, Visva-Bharati, 2007, pp. 9–10.
37. Ibid., p. 14.
38. Satyendranath Roy, *Rabidranather Chintajagat: Sikshachinta*, Kolkata: Granthalaya Private Limited, 2002, p. 7.

39. Tagore, *The Co-operative Principles*, op. cit., p. 35.
40. Rabindranath Tagore, 'Sikshasamyasa', in *Rabindra Rachanabali*, Centenary Volume, Kolkata: Government of West Bengal, 1368 BS, XI, p. 561.
41. Rabindranath Tagore, 'Sikshar Herfer', in *Rabindra Rachanabali*, Centenary Volume, Kolkata: Government of West Bengal, 1368 BS, XI, p. 538.
42. Arun Kumar Mukhopadhyay, *Rabindra – Samiksha*, Kolkata: Dey's Publishing, 2005, p. 102.
43. Prabhat Kumar Mukhopadhyay, *Rabindrajibani*, Kolkata: Visva-Bharati Granthanvibhaga, 1406 BS, II, p. 28.
44. Hirendranath Dutta, *Santinikataner Ek Yuga*, Kolkata: Dey's Publishing, 1409 BS, p. 11.
45. Ibid., p. 6.
46. Ibid., p. 15.
47. Pramathanath Bisi, *Rabindranath O Santiniketan*, Kolkata: Visva-Bharati, 1353 BS, pp. 42–44.
48. Ibid., p. 44.
49. Prabhat Kumar Mukhopadhyay, *Santiniketan: Visva-Bharati*, Kolkata: Visva-Bharati Grantham Vibhag, 1407 BS, p. 49.
50. Rathindranath Tagore, *Pitrismriti*, Kolkata: Jijnasa, 1373 BS, p. 61.
51. Leonard K. Elmhirst, *Poet and Plowman*, Kolkata: Visva-Bharati, 2008, pp. 26–34.
52. Rabindranath Tagore, 'Japanyatri', in *Rabindra Rachanabali*, Centenary Volume, Kolkata: Government of West Bengal, 1368 BS, X, p. 480.
53. Rabindranath Tagore, 'Bhumilakshmi', in *Rabindra Rachanabali*, Centenary Volume, Kolkata: Government of West Bengal, 1368 BS, XIII, p. 506.
54. Rabindranath Tagore, 'Tapovan', in *Rabindra Rachanabali*, Centenary Volume, Kolkata: Government of West Bengal, 1368 BS, XI.
55. Rabindranath Tagore, 'Muktodhara', in *Rabindra Rachanabali*, *Centenary Volume*, Kolkata: Government of West Bengal, 1368 BS, VI.
56. Rabindranath Tagore, 'Raktakarabi', in *Rabindra Rachanabali*, Centenary Volume, Kolkata: Government of West Bengal, 1368 BS, VI.

II

Panchayati Raj in India: Experiences and Capacity Building

CHAPTER 4

Decentralizing for Development

Constitutional Perspective

Asok Kumar Mukhopadhyay

For the last two decades, 'development' has become a buzzword for everybody connected in any way with socio-economic changes in India. The political parties and politicians, academics engaged in social science research, bureaucrats at the central and state government departments exercising control over the processes of socio-economic change and non-government voluntary agencies, and journalists talk of 'development'. The perceptions about development are different to these groups of people, but the common point is that some sort of radical changes in economics and politics of the country are urgent in order to improve the living standard of the people and thereby strengthen the basis of polity.

The urgency has been felt since the 1970s when development efforts were sought to be institutionalized through new thinking on planning for development. Earlier, through bureaucracy a kind of vertical coordination was sought to be achieved between the state government and the district-level agencies of planning and development. But this arrangement did not bring in the desired fruits inasmuch as people's needs for socio-economic changes were not taken into account. There was no system of involving the different agencies and organizations connected with development activities at the level of localities and comprehensive areas. What passed for block-level planning was nothing more than coordination between different development programmes undertaken by different state government departments. Although the Balwantray Mehta Committee had talked of 'democratic decentralization' as early as 1957, there were no concrete constitutional and administrative changes for devolving powers, responsibilities and functionaries on to the elected panchayats. Rather, a number of development programmes and agencies like CADC, DPAP, IRDA, DRDA were created from time to time. None of these agencies and programmes was designed for introducing the development of these agencies and programmes were designed for introducing the development technique of 'planning from below'. These government agencies and also the panchayat bodies were supposed to be working for implementing the development schemes designed at the central government level.

The debate over decentralization for development started from three reports viz., the one by Asoka Mehta Committee on Panchayati Raj Institutions (1978) and the other two by Hanumantha Rao Committee on Decentralized Planning[1] and G.V.K. Rao Committee,[2] both in the mid-1980s. The debates and thinking generated by these bodies finally led to the 73rd and 74th Constitution Amendment Acts in 1992. The 73rd Amendment pertaining to panchayats came into effect on 25 April 1993 and the 74th Amendment pertaining to municipalities and municipal corporations came into effect on 1 June 1993.

The starting point of decentralizing for development has been Article 40 of the Constitution, which reads: 'The State shall take steps to organize village panchayats and endow them with such powers and authority as may be necessary to enable them to function as *units of self-government*' (italics added). This provision occurs in Part IV of the Constitution dealing with Directive Principles of State Policy. But the Constitution enjoined that there shall be no judicial remedy if these Directives are not observed by the State. Hence, no serious efforts were made till 1978 to organize the panchayats as units of 'self-government'.

After many experiments with panchayat and municipal administration in the 1970s and 1980s, it was found necessary to amend the Constitution with a view to giving these local government bodies a constitutional status, which they lacked for so long. Prior to these two constitutional amendments, local government was totally dependent, even for its life and existence, on the state government. Many panchayats and municipalities remained superseded for years together. The 73rd and 74th Constitution Amendments have amended Part IX of the Constitution and added Part IX-A, spread in Article 243 to

Article 243-ZG. In addition, two new Schedules (Eleventh Schedule pertaining to panchayats vide Article 243-G and Twelfth Schedule pertaining to municipalities and municipal corporations vide Article 243-W) have been added. Article 280 has been amended for extending the Finance Commission's jurisdiction to consider the recommendations of the State Finance Commission.

The main features of the 73rd and the 74th Amendments of the Constitution include:

(i) Directly elected local bodies and grassroots institutions like Gram Sabha;
(ii) Regular elections;
(iii) Reservation of seats and offices for women, SC, ST and, if the State government so decides, OBC;
(iv) State Election Commission;
(v) State Finance Commission;
(vi) District Planning Committee with four-fifths of members as people's representatives;
(vii) Metropolitan Planning Committee with two-thirds of members as people's representatives.
(viii) Specific permissible functional jurisdiction of panchayats in Eleventh Schedule having 29 items; and of municipalities in the Twelfth Schedule having 18 items.

Some state governments like West Bengal in their panchayat legislation have created new institutions like *Gram Sansad* and *Gram Unnayan Samiti* (Village Development Committee).[3]

Prior to the 73rd and 74th Amendments, there were two contradictory situations in Indian public administration. At the central level and at the state level, there was a vibrant democracy with Parliament and state legislatures enforcing accountability of the executive and demanding information through parliamentary interpellations and debates. However, the governmental organizations are so vast and complex, and they operate in such a cloak of secrecy and cover that the desired degree of transparency and accountability cannot be assured in all cases. But, by and large, on any major issue, political executive and, through them the bureaucracy, can be held accountable. But below the state level, there was a total authoritarian system run entirely by the bureaucracy.

On the other side, through enormous economic powers vested in the Union government, over the years there had been a tremendous accretion of powers at the Centre. Today, there is far too much power at the Centre, a great deal more than necessary in the states, and virtually none at the local level where the people live. This disjunction between power and the people was at the root of many ills of this polity. The central and the state governments were far removed from the masses. The bureaucratic district administration by its very nature got isolated from the people, dulling its sensitivity to the needs of the people. Hence, a fundamental change was called for. There was need for a third tier of representative governance at the district level and below to make democracy real to the rural and urban masses, where power would be exercised within the visibility of the people, and those who exercise power would be accountable to them. Downward accountability would make the system responsive. The present chasm between a few elected MPs and MLAs and the bureaucratic district administration, on the one hand, and the vast masses, on the other, was conveniently filled by the power-brokers, the middlemen, the vested interests. The power-brokers have established their vise-like grip only because democracy has not functioned at the grassroots.

The 73rd and 74th Constitution Amendments did bring about a third tier of representative governance at the district level and below. The 73rd Amendment has the potential of establishing at least the procedural part of good governance. The decentralized system of elected governance theoretically has certain inherent advantages.

One advantage is efficiency: decision-makers who live locally are likely to know more about local conditions, they should be able to match resources and needs more precisely. Another advantage is accountability: when decision-makers live and work in close contact with users, they are exposed to more effective scrutiny and are under greater pressure to deliver the goods. The third advantage is participation: there are more opportunities for local people to participate in planning services and to pay for them through local taxes. Experience shows that local government tends to give higher priority to human development than the central government does. In India, the last point has a greater significance because of reservation of not less than one-third seats and elected offices for women and for SCs, STs and OBCs in proportion of their numbers to the total population. Adequate representation of women and Dalits is going to make a qualitative change in the functioning of panchayats and municipal bodies. The usual male chauvinistic cynicism that women are mere proxies is no longer acceptable. There may be some cases of such proxy functioning but once women taste power, they would assert their independence as is found in actual experience. The other fear is that in the absence of land reform and with the existing inegalitarian asset and wealth distribution, it might empower the powerful. While not discounting the possibility, with regular elections and performance audit by the electorate, the existing powerful would lose power and the transfer of power would take place.

It is not suggested that panchayats or the municipalities provide the panacea for all the evils of misgovernance. The point is that they have the potential for good governance at the local level provided they are institutionally, legally and financially supported by the existing power structure in the society.

The 73rd Amendment defines panchayats as institutions of *self government*. Article 243-G, which empowers the state legislature to endow powers and authority to panchayats, clearly states that such endowment should 'enable them to function as institution of self-government'. Unfortunately, this concept of self-government with its concomitant attributes are either not fully understood or very dimly appreciated. This basic ideology has been largely ignored in the recent state legislations. Panchayats still fall short of being genuine institutions of participatory self-government. Panchayats cannot develop as genuine units of self-government without a drastic reduction and restructuring of central and state government apparatus, especially in respect of items in the Eleventh Schedule. Stripping this enormous administrative structure of its overburden and shedding the excessive concentration of power at higher levels are essential prerequisites for the empowerment of panchayats. The central government should think in terms of reducing its own size and powers, and the principles accepted for restructuring of the central government should apply *mutatis mutandis* to state governments.

Some of the state legislations on panchayats have made a mockery of allocation of powers and authority to different tiers of panchayats. Some legislations have just reprinted the Eleventh Schedule for each tier; some others have given the authority to the state executive to delegate such powers and authority to different tiers as it thinks best; in one or two cases, a serious exercise has been made in this regard. But actual devolution of financial, executive and legal authority and power to make the panchayats genuine institutions of self-government is yet to take place. The basic principle of allocation of powers and functions among the Centre, state and local levels should be that what can be done at the lower level must necessarily be done at that level and not by higher bodies. In a more restrictive way, the Centre and the state should exercise only residual powers in respect of items included in the Eleventh Schedule.

The Eleventh Schedule really indicates the floor. The State can devolve much more. For example, at lower tiers of government, the functions to resolve disputes of both civil and criminal nature should be given to the elected bodies.

The need for decentralized planning cannot be overemphasized. District-level schemes should be sponsored by the ZP/PS/GP; these schemes should not be handed over to them from above. Panchayats at these levels should have a reasonable percentage of Plan funds and other financial resources, which should be totally untied so that they can use these resources on the basis of their own priorities and choice. There are a large number of central and state laws, regulations and subordinate legalization which militate against the required devolution of powers and functions to the panchayats. The Law Commission or a similar body of experts should be entrusted to do this job urgently.

The 73rd Amendment has given a constitutional duty to the panchayats for the 'preparation of plans for economic development and social justice'.[4] The point to note is that the panchayats cannot prepare any plan for economic development which does not ensure social justice. The concept of economic development through social justice has got constitutional recognition only in respect of the panchayats.

The 73rd Amendment does provide a fine format for good governance for the rural masses, but it is doubtful how it is going to develop. Concerted popular movement is necessary for empowerment of the panchayats because the entrenched interests would not like to part with their existing powers. International experience also indicates that. The Human Development Report of 1996 comments: 'But a more general brake on decentralization is that central government has been reluctant to release to the local level either funds or decision-making power.'[5]

The national conference of the heads of panchayats held on 5 and 6 April 2002 adopted a 15-point National Declaration for Local Self-governance seeking to give more powers to the local bodies. There was a consensus that the 73rd Amendment, although historic and momentous, failed to meet the objectives of democratic decentralization of governance power. The panchayats suffer from inadequate powers and funds. They have responsibilities for supplying drinking water, primary education and health care but no commensurate funds.

Hence, there is a case for amending the Constitution again. Panchayats may be given incentive grants for better performance on the line of the scheme meant for the states.

At the end, it may be noted that India's political leadership across party lines has not been able to take a firm decision about what ought to be the regulative ideal of the country's governmental system viz., representative democracy or pluralist democracy or populist democracy. It appears that the overall consensus is for making the governmental system a mix of all three types, and that democratic decentralization attempted so far has been essentially of a halting and hesitant type. People are yet to be meaningfully involved in local-level planning and governance as the decision-takers in choosing their path of development, exercising discretion in fixing priorities of development programmes, and ensuring comprehensive and effective accountability of the functionaries in local democracy. The issue is finally connected not only with the nature of economics and politics, but also with sociology, and by no means, with constitutional change and governmental innovation. Decentralizing for development is no mere political or electoral slogan, nor is it an administrative or management technique only. This concept represents a new social philosophy which helps realising the essence of democratic governance.

Notes

1. Government of India, *Report of the Working Group on District Planning*, New Delhi: Planning Commission, 1984.
2. Government of India, *Report of the Committee to Review the Existing Administrative Arrangements for Rural Development and Poverty Alleviation Programmes* (CAARD), New Delhi: Department of Rural Development, 1985.

   Note: Summary and Recommendations of both the Reports (1984 and 1985) are available in Anil Kumar Jana, *Administering District Plans in India: Issues, Constraints and Choices*, New Delhi: Concept Publishing Company, 2004, Appendices I and II.
3. Government of West Bengal, The West Bengal Panchayat Act, 1973 (As Amended), Kolkata: Department of Law, Section 16A.
4. *The Constitution of India*, New Delhi: Ministry of Law and Justice, Article 243G.
5. *Human Development Report 1996*, New Delhi: Oxford University Press, 1996, p. 74.

CHAPTER 5

Local Governance in Indian Federal System

Where the Shoe Pinches

Prabhat Kumar Datta

The idea of forming a federal form of government in India became an issue of debate and discussion during the freedom movement in the early years of the last century. The idea gathered considerable momentum when the Lucknow Pact was signed by the Indian National Congress (INC) and the Muslim League (ML) in 1916. Two contradictory pulls had starting becoming active since then. On the one hand, there was the Indian National Congress fighting for a high dose of centralization and on the other hand, the Muslim League working for best possible decentralization.[1] In this 'unitary versus federal' controversy, the issue of demarcation of powers figured prominently and the Congress and the League leaders differed sharply on the question of which tier of the government would be exercising the residual powers. All Parties Conference headed by Motilal Nehru, the Round Table Conferences and all the subsequent negotiations culminating in the British Cabinet Missions came to grips with the question of demarcation of powers between the Union and the states. The Constituent Assembly which was convened in 1946 debated the issue for quite some time out of which emerged the federal constitution. It was included in the 1946 formula, which was a sort of a compromise between the INC and the ML, that the Centre should have powers only over foreign affairs, defence and communications.[2]

Congress Perception of Federalism

This formula was eventually rejected by the Muslim League, which opted for a sovereign state. It was expected that Muslim-majority provinces could achieve greater gains out of it. With the partition of the country in 1947, the prime motive of the Congress for the stress on provincial autonomy seemed to have lost its force. Immediately after Partition, Nehru observed that the need of the hour was a strong Centre with a federal structure. To quote, '... it would be injurious to the interests of the country to provide for a weak central authority which would be incapable of ensuring peace, co-ordinating vital matters of common concern and speaking effectively for the whole country in the international sphere. At the same time, we are quite clear in our minds that there are many matters in which sole authority must rest with unit, and that to frame our Constitution on the basis of a unitary state would be a retrograde step, both politically and administratively.'[3] This unusual situation where the League did not find any reason to put pressure on the framers of the Constitution to opt for the structure already arrived at, provided necessary objective conditions for the Congress to move away from its earlier position. As a result, 'the superficial federal structure remained', as Namboodiripad comments, but 'it was hedged in by innumerable provisions which it could make it possible for strong ruling party dominant at the Centre to make inroads into the powers of the federating units and transform the Constitution into a unitary one, while it appeared to be federal.'[4]

Functioning of the Federal System

The federal system of post-colonial India is patterned broadly on the Government of India Act, 1935. India had to opt for a federal system with a strong Centre, as it was argued, to avoid repetition of traumatic consequences of Partition and in the interest of speedy socio-economic development. Subsequently, the logic of a strong Centre shaped the Congress politics and the scheme of central planning was worked out in such a way as to make the Union much stronger and correspondingly the states weaker than the Constitution-makers ever visualized. In a federal form of government, the Union and the states are required to share the burden of governing the country with states acting as the vital links with people. This role of the state got eroded following intensification of centralization in subsequent years facilitated by the uninterrupted one-party rule of the Congress from 1950 – 1967. And whatever differences or conflicts arose between the Centre and states, they came to be resolved not as governments but between two wings of the same political party. This process was facilitated by the fact that Prime Minister Nehru happened to wield personal authority that overshadowed the chief ministers of almost all states.

The hegemonic rule of the Congress suffered a serious setback in 1967, but it could not effectively arrest the processes of centralization. It is, however, true that state autonomy movements gathered momentum in later years following the installation of non-Congress governments in many states, but the return of Congress to power could not produce desired results. There is no denying the fact that over the years, the states have been enfeebled to play the role of a partner in governance effectively. They have been reduced to looking to the Union for funds because of highly unequal financial relations and for the central forces to deal with the law and order problem of the states, which assumed an alarming turn in early 1970s. The 42nd Amendment of the Constitution sought to give constitutional sanction to the measures helping the so-called federal Constitution turn into a unitary one. It had enhanced the authority of the central government by transferring education from the state list to concurrent list and empowering the Centre to deploy its forces like Central Reserve Police Force and Border Security Force unilaterally in any state. But things did not move in the desired direction because the Congress government was thrown out of power in the general elections of March 1977.

Article 356 continued to be a strong threat to the states ruled by the Opposition parties before the installation of a coalition government at the Centre in 1977 because its misuse for political purposes a number of times created a genuine concern for the states. The recent use of Article 355 in the name of protecting the states against internal disturbances has been a new weapon in the hands of the Centre to oversee law and order situation in the states although it belongs essentially to the constitutionally mandated domain of the states. Because of the centre's financial clout and constitutional authority to intervene, the states have been reduced to feeble partners in the governance of the country.

The Marxists would, however, point out that the compelling reason behind increasing centralization has been the role of the bourgeoisie, who wanted a very strong Centre. That the Indian bourgeoisie was not in favour of decentralized polity, became evident from the speech delivered by the president of the Federation of Indian Chambers of Commerce and Industries in India in 1969. He observed that India had made two mistakes, namely, the formation of linguistic states and adoption of the federal Constitution.[5] Clearly, the ruling elites cannot accept even limited decentralization, the conditions of which were created by the formation of linguistic states and very weak units of federation established by the Constitution.

Incidentally, the need for effective decentralized polity in India became very strongly felt after the re-organization of the country in 1950s in accordance with recommendations of the States Re-organization Commission (SRC). Interestingly, the process of the formation of the linguistic states was accompanied by the drive towards centralization. The people at large and the ruling class who took over the reins of administration of the new states were happy with formation of new states. But they became more and more subjected to the overall control exercised by the Centre.

Demand for Review of Centre-State Relations

After 1967, resistance to this trend of centralization increased. Regional political parties like Dravida Munnetra Kazagham (DMK) in Tamil Nadu and the Akali Dal in Punjab joined the other Opposition parties to demand a review of existing federal relations. The issue gathered public attention. The Rajamannar Committee constituted by the DMK government, *inter alia,* proposed a repeal of Articles 356 and 357. It also recommended deletion of Articles 256 and 257 relating to the issue of directions by the states and suggested that the issue of directions should be preceded by the consultation and approval of the Inter-State Council.[6] The first non-Congress government in the country led by E.M.S. Namboodiripad in Kerala had also upheld the cause of strong states along with a strong Centre for which it had prepared a document.

Strikingly, the Centre had taken steps for the enactment of the Disturbed Area (Special Courts) Amendment Bill which sought to empower it to set up special courts for speedy trial of offences in the disturbed areas. It was considered as an encroachment on the jurisdiction of the states because law and order is a state subject. This tradition continued unabated until the era of coalition politics began at the Centre. Coalition politics has not been able to bring about any remarkable change in the scenario because the Opposition parties which demand a strong Centre and strong states were yet to emerge as so effective as to ensure it. It may be recalled that in 1980s, the Opposition parties came together for re-texturing the federal polity around the principle of autonomy. In the wake of the ever-growing demand for re-examination of the Centre-state relations, the central government led by Mrs Indira Gandhi was almost compelled to constitute the Sarkaria Commission, which was entrusted with the job of probing into the central issues of Centre-state relationship.

Emergence of Third Layer in Governance

Given this backdrop, this paper seeks to focus on the rise of a third layer in India's inter-governmental structures generally known as the village local self-government through the amendment of the Constitution in 1992. It needs to be emphasized that the Constitution of India, as adopted in 1949, did not envisage any third stratum except providing for the state list in the Eleventh Schedule. It may be recalled that it was M.K. Gandhi who favoured strong Panchayati Raj Institutions which would have democratic bases of their own and be invested with powers so that villagers could experience real *swaraj.* There is, however, Article 40 in the Directive Principles of State Policy in the Constitution requiring the state to organize village panchayats as units of self-government. Significantly, the Article conceptualizes Panchayati Raj Institutions as units of self-government and reads, 'the State shall take steps to organize village panchayats and endow them with such powers and authority as may be necessary to enable them to function as units of self-government.'

The first generation panchayati raj institutions in India began following the recommendations of the Balwantray Mehta Committee Report.[7] The Committee, which recommended a non-political three-tier panchayati raj system, was guided by the basic consideration of ensuring people's participation in the implementation of development programmes, which was expected to unleash the process of change and growth. It seems that the constitutional perception of panchayats was not reflected in the design of the first generation panchayati raj and the Committee was largely guided by the administrative and developmental considerations. The Asoka Mehta Committee's dominant thinking, which was branded as a new approach, centred round the functional necessity for decentralization of administration as it recommended two-tier panchayats, one at the village and the other at the block level, although it stood for participation of the political parties in panchayats. The committee had also realized the need for considering the question of Centre-state relations as a necessary pre-condition for strengthening the local government.

Constitutionalization of Local Government

The 73rd and 74th Constitutional Amendments in 1992 marked a definite watershed in the history of local self-government in post-colonial India. They define local self-government as institutions of self-government. In Articles 243G and 243H, the term 'self-government' is used, which means the autonomy of the government without outside interference. It may be recalled that the village community in ancient India enjoyed autonomy in terms of organization, functions, functionaries and finances. Every village community had the freedom to develop and set up its own institutions of governance. An institution of self-government must have, at the minimum, the following:

- The delineation of functional areas where it is responsible. The listing of 29 subjects in the Eleventh Schedule of the Constitution may be said to have done it, though very feebly.
- Wherewithal to carry out its assigned tasks. This implies that PRIs should not be required to go with a begging bowl to the state or central government, and funds available to them should match their responsibilities. The Amendments have dealt with this issue by providing for the State Finance Commissions.
- PRIs should be able to decide how much of bureaucracy they want and should be able to recruit their own personnel. There is no constitutional mandate in this regard.

The 73rd Amendment makes it mandatory for every state to constitute three-tier panchayats. It is also laid down that the state legislatures may, by law, vest rural local bodies with powers and functions and responsibilities under entry 5 of List II – State List of the Seventh Schedule of the Constitution.

The Eleventh Schedule does not list subjects or functions but only matters, as T.N. Srivastava points out.[8] There is no mandate that rural local bodies would perform these functions or these would be transferred to rural local bodies or the schemes related to them would be entrusted to them for implementation. The legislature of a state is required to endow these bodies with such functions as may be necessary to enable them to function as institutions of self-government. Such law may contain provisions for devolution of powers and responsibilities, subject to such conditions as may be specified therein for the preparation of plans for economic development and social justice and for the implementation of schemes as may be entrusted to them, including those mentioned in the Eleventh and Twelfth Schedule. The state legislature is thus the sole determinant of self-government. The repeated usage of the word 'may' in the Article fails to make it mandatory on the part of the state government to implement these provisions, thus leaving the scope of power-sharing with the state government solely at the disposal of the political leadership at the state level. Presumably, Parliament was compelled to use the word 'may' because some of the items come under the purview of the state list. It is also a clear indication that the government lacked genuine will to create a vibrant third layer in the structure of governance of the country. It is also indicative of the fact that it is not possible to strengthen the process of decentralization in India without overhauling the existing arrangements of Centre-state relationship.

Thus panchayats cannot enjoy full autonomy as they are set within the states and form part of the State List. Nor can the states for that matter, as they are placed within the Indian Union. What the Seventy Third Amendment has done, as Mukerjee[9] thinks, is to constitutionalize three strata of government. Therefore, he continues, there will now be a five-storeyed pyramid of governments rising from the village panchayats at the base to the Union at the apex.

The lack of effective support for local government system in the villages seems to be evident from the change of words in the amendment of the Constitution. Article 40 of the Constitution in the Directive Principles of State Policy conceives of panchayats 'as units of self-government'. The Seventy Third Amendment substituted the word 'unit' with 'institutions'. That the word 'unit' is stronger than institutions needs no explanation. It is wrong to believe that the substitution has no practical significance and has been done without any purpose. In fact, it seems to weaken the constitutional base of the PRIs in India. It may be recalled that the inclusion of these words in the Constitution was done after a protracted debate. The Draft Constitution did not mention any thing about panchayats. Gandhi was alive. He reacted, to quote, by saying, 'It is certainly an omission calling for immediate attention if our independence is to reflect the people's voice.'[10] Ambedkar defended it, saying that 'villages are sinks of localism, ignorance and narrow-mindedness and as such cannot be starting point of India's democracy'.[11] His speech triggered a serious debate and the Assembly members had to work hard to find suitable words. The words 'units of self-government' were incorporated following the suggestion of K. Santhanam. Significantly, those who drafted the Bill leading to the Seventy Third Amendment Act did not explain why they had substituted these words with 'institutions' of self-government.

The Amendment Act provides for a schedule to indicate which functions have to be transferred to the PRIs. There are lists for the two tiers of the Government in India. Then thus the question that arises is why a Schedule for the third layer? Presumably, the architects of the Seventy Third Amendment Act had realized that providing a list would have required re-examination of the whole gamut of Centre-state relations about which there is reluctance on the part of the Indian state. This implies that the Indian state was not genuinely serious to strengthen the third stratum although it was created through an amendment of the constitution.

Devolution in State Acts

The 73rd Amendment of the Constitution of India stipulates the transfer of powers and functions to Panchayati Raj Institutions as a part of the decentralization process. The state governments were supposed to transfer 29 subjects listed in the Eleventh Schedule of the Constitution. While the states like Kerala, Karnataka and West Bengal have carved out a clear route of devolution to PRIs, other states like Rajasthan, Maharashtra, Gujarat and Bihar have variations in their initiatives in this regard. States like Haryana and Uttar Pradesh have still to set the ball rolling. Most states have not yet devolved all the 29 functions. On an average, 21.3 out of 29 functions have been devolved.

A close scrutiny of the Acts in different states tends to indicate that except in a few states, clear functional mapping for the different tiers does not exist. There are states like UP where departmental heads at the district level could function independently of the PRIs.

More recently, however, the Government of India decided in favour of undertaking activity mapping to ensure effective devolution of functions (as listed in Schedule XI) to all the three tiers of the PRIs. It is a healthy initiative and meaningful exercise as it involves breaking up of activities into smaller units and assigning them to specific tiers within the system to enable a more effective delivery of public services and a better quality of life for the citizens. On an average, the states have carried out activity mapping only in 17.6 out of 29 functions.

Transfer of Funds

The district tiers of panchayats do not have any powers to levy taxes, duties, tolls or fees on their own and are dependent on the state governments for meeting their running expenses. No indication of the size of funds that would flow to the districts is given by the central or state governments, making decentralized planning a mockery. Most funds flow to the districts as a part of the centrally-sponsored schemes or central sector or state plan schemes, the size of which is also not known. In any case, these are tied funds leaving little scope for planning. There are, however, some exceptions. For example, Kerala transfers a significant portion of the plan funds to the village panchayats through budgetary allocations.

Panchayats continue to be almost fully financially dependent on the Centre or the states for funds. The State Finance Commissions (SFC) have been given the powers to make recommendations for assignment and sharing of taxes, duties, tolls and fees but little work has been done by any SFCs. They have by and large concentrated on formalizing the existing level of transfer without evolving a suitable formula for this purpose. Referring to the role of the SFCs, the mid-term appraisal of the Ninth Plan pointed out, 'more buoyant taxes like sales tax and excise are kept out of the purview of the PRIs, Plan'. All SFCs have put great emphasis on internal revenue mobilization but none has suggested any effective mechanism for PRIs to generate their revenue. In fact, given the constitutional allocation of the domain of taxing powers between the Centre and the states, there is really nothing much to do in this regard by the SFC. This also underscores the need for another round of amendments in order to facilitate the process of decentralization. The state governments have also been slow and hesitant in accepting the recommendations where they are useful in terms of improving the revenue generation capacity of the local bodies. Only two states – Karnataka and Sikkim – have devolved funds to the panchayats for the 29 subjects.

It may be mentioned that the Task Force constituted by the Government of India, a fallout of a conference of panchayat ministers of different states held in June in 2001, made it clear that there should be district-wise and panchayat-wise allocation of funds in the annual budgets of the states and that the state governments should provide a certain percentage of their grants as untied grants. It was recommended that the gram panchayats should get 70 of the untied grants while the district and intermediate panchayats should share the remaining 30 per cent. There are scholars who feel that SFCs are just ornamental arrangements because the resource base of the PRIs is very weak. There is need for recasting the Centre-state financial relations in order first to widen the resource base of the PRIs. It is true that there are political implications of imposition of taxes at the local level, which lead to reluctance on the part of the local government to raise resources through taxes. But this calls for exploring other ways of resource mobilization with lesser political implications.

Transfer of Functionaries

To function effectively as institutions of self-government, the PRIs need to have the power to recruit and control staff required for managing functions. The state governments still have retained for themselves the powers for inspection, inquiring into the affairs of the panchayats, suspension of panchayat resolutions and issuing directions. Besides, in most states, the key functionaries, namely the secretaries and executive officers at all the three levels of panchayats, are state government employees who are appointed, transferred and controlled by the state government. Being under the direct control of the state administrative hierarchy, they are often reluctant to work under the administrative control of the elected panchayats. Kerala is the only state which has completely transferred the control of functionaries to panchayats.

Rural local bodies do not have any staff even for maintenance functions, which is their basic domain. Even the maintenance and development functions are performed by the line departments. These departments have complete control over the village level staff and the panchayats do not have anything worthwhile to do with them. The departmental staff implement the programme without any knowledge or involvement of panchayats. In our study on village-based planning, we have seen how the line department is reluctant to co-operate with PRIs. In Odisha, the doctors sat in demonstration when their services were transferred to the PRIs.

Kerala is the only state which has completely transferred the control of functionaries to panchayats. More than 100 officials have been devolved to district panchayats. Similarly, Maharashtra has transferred functionaries to different tiers of panchayats. The conference of state panchayat ministers held in Kolkata resolved to evolve a cadre of functionaries so that the necessary talent and skills are continually available to panchayats at all levels for effective discharge of their functions. The local bodies do not have the power to create any posts or regulate their remuneration. When the state creates posts, it is done in the prevailing pay structure of the state, which has nothing to do with the paying capacity of a panchayat. No local body has any freedom on this account.

The conformity legislations in most states have not significantly alerted the functional domains of the gram panchayats across the country. A study of 15 states showed that in cases of higher levels of panchayats, previous provisions were repeated wherever earlier Acts had existed and also no additional grant of powers to administrative staff was made to them to enable them to implement their given responsibilities. On the other hand, funds and staff are retained by the line departments of the government which continue to function, as before, independently of panchayats.[12]

The Amendments do not create any new set of institutions but recognize afresh the concept and role of the local bodies as institutions of self-government and instruments of planning for economic development and social justice. The inclusion of two new Schedules added a new dimension to it because it was felt that these institutions would now be entrusted with implementation of schemes on subjects included therein. But this has not happened as is evident from the MPLAD Scheme.

Unusual Developments

The MP Local Area Development Scheme was launched immediately after the Amendment in 1992. Under this scheme, a sum of ₹ 1,580 crore per year is placed at the disposal of the Members of Parliament. The MPs are allowed to spend the money to undertake local area development schemes without consulting the panchayats. It has serious implications for PRIs as the third layers of Government in India because the constitutionally mandated local government institutions are being bypassed. Under the scheme, each MP can suggest to the district collector works worth up to ₹ 2 crore in a year. The Ministry releases the funds directly to the collectors, who get the works done on the advice of the MP concerned. Interestingly, some state governments have also started giving funds to their MLAs. Several municipalities in Rajasthan and Delhi have also been following this model. This is a dangerous trend and has an adverse impact on the functioning of PRIs. The central government has given an illustrative list of 28 items. There is also a list of works not permissible such as raising of memorials, building of places of worship and the like.

One may refer to the report of the Comptroller and Auditor General (2001) to present the picture of what is happening on the ground. The report showed that the scheme was plagued not only by the inadequacy of funds, but also by the increasing underutilization, misuse and diversion of money earmarked for the projects. The report noted that 64 per cent of the released amount could be spent. Similar have been the findings of the sample study of audit in 106 constituencies where it was found that 31 per cent of the total money was, in fact, not spent at all. The guidelines seem to have been observed more in their breach. In Nagaland, for example, the money was spent for building roads connecting the church. In Odisha, temples were built, in Madhya Pradesh money was spent for building housing complex for the police officials.

The overall picture that emerges is that a large share of MPLAD funds is spent in a top-down manner without taking into consideration people's needs as the PRIs have been bypassed. Beneficiaries also alleged that they were paid much less than the specified minimum wages in employment works under the scheme and an overwhelming number (62%) agreed that the quality of assets created was either bad or very bad. One may argue that things would have been better if the money would have been spent through panchayats. It is true that it has nothing to do with the emergence of the PRIs as the third layer but it speaks of what happens when the grassroots democratic institutions are neglected. It shows how the MPLAD scheme is adversely affecting the process of rural development.[13]

What causes serious concern in the context of local self-government as the third layer in our federal structure is that most of the schemes being funded and executed form part of the Eleventh and Twelfth Schedules to the Constitution, which define the functional domain of the panchayats and municipalities. The guidelines authorizing the MPs to exercise their personal choice and decision in funding and executing the scheme lead to usurpation of the power and responsibilities of the local bodies which have been created by them through an amendment of the Constitution. It has been argued that in many instances, the choice of schemes and amounts expected can significantly alter or distort local priorities as may be decided or desired by the local bodies. Having considered the problems, the Administrative Reforms Committee (ARC) in its successive reports has recommended the abolition of the scheme. The matter was hotly debated. As most of the MPs openly expressed their unwillingness on the floor of Parliament to give up the scheme, it was finally decided to continue the scheme but with new and stringent safeguards.

New guidelines framed in the middle of November 2005 have complicated the situation. Several legal and constitutional experts have dubbed the new guidelines as *'unconstitutional'* on the ground that they defy and distort some of the basic features of the Constitution such as public audit. For instance, the attempt to do away with CAG audit of the scheme accounts, as stated in the guidelines, is actually an attempt to disempower Parliament in exercising control over public expenditure. It shows how disrespectful the political leaders are to the fundamental pillar of Indian democracy. Those who do not want Parliament to exercise financial control over public funds cannot be expected to allow social audit at the level of the villages. The way the ruling coalition at the Centre stood in the way of formation of the Joint Parliamentary Committee to examine the telecom scam indicates the attitude of the Indian ruling classes to democracy in general, not to speak of grassroots democracy.

There are many Acts which contradict the constitutional status and mandate of the PRIs. But no state government except Kerala has cared to examine the matter thoroughly. This is very important because as the Kerala experience shows, in states there are Acts which impede the functioning of the panchayats, as they contradict the provisions of some of the existing laws, rules and orders. Autonomy to act within the domain is further constrained by the continued existence of the administrative departments at the district level and below over which the PRIs have no control in most of the states. In our recent study on the functioning of the gram unnayan samitis in West Bengal, we observed that the functionaries of the line departments do not extend necessary cooperation to the PRIs. It may be recalled that in Odisha the services of the doctors in the rural hospitals were placed under the PRIs. The doctors went on strike asserting that they would not work under the PRIs.

Rise of Parallel Bodies

Broadly speaking, the functions performed by the parallel bodies can be classified as ensuring user/beneficiary participation, convergence of programmes and promoting/ensuring efficiency. While these are the basic functions of the PRIs, the matters like irrigation, watershed management and development and minor forest produce come under the purview of the Eleventh Schedule, which lays down the functions of the PRIs. The gram vikas samiti in Haryana and the vigilance committee in Himachal Pradesh encroach upon the statutory functions of the panchayat bodies as spelt out in the Panchayat Acts of the respective states. There are programmes like Janmabhoomi in AP and Gokulgram in Gujarat where the state governments deal directly with the village community without the involvement of panchayats. They are not programmes under the MPLAD but the panchayats are bypassed by the state governments. It seems that the state governments are not serious about democratic decentralization. The Janmabhoomi (JB) programme tends to mobilize local people, the entire state administrative machinery and draws upon all the existing central and state government schemes as resource for development work and thus, substitutes the functions of the gram panchayat. Although the sarpanch is to preside over the Janmabhoomi gram sabha, the real player is the officer.

The district rural development agencies, which handle crores of rupees, should have disappeared from the scene following the Seventy Third Amendment of the Constitution. But no such signs are visible. The debate is going on in some states. The DRDAs have been constituted as late as in 2002. Some state governments have refused to comply with the central government guidelines to ensure that the district rural development agencies get merged with the zilla parishads and the central government has failed to enforce it. The general reaction against the parallel bodies is that they represent processes external to the constitutionally mandated role of panchayats and enable bureaucracies to override democratic bodies. Thus, they pose serious threats to the effective functioning of local self-governing institutions.

Delicate democratic decentralized plant like panchayats cannot grow in Indian villages without active support of the political leaders as is evident from the experience of the decline of the first generation panchayati raj. It may be recalled that the first generation panchayats in India started functioning with a lot of fanfare but declined due to cooling off of political enthusiasm. Scholars have shown that it was because the authority of the higher level political leadership came under challenge following the rise of panchayati raj. One may argue that political leaders showed their interest to re-legitimize their authority in a period of crisis and compulsion of neo-liberal policy of the state. This might have prompted them to create an impression in the minds of the people that they are for decentralization. Decentralization is also required to be promoted to meet the needs of neo-liberal regime, but this decentralization is not devolution but decentralization with central control as the colonial rulers did in the past.

Centrally-Sponsored Schemes

The launching of a large number of programmes and centrally-sponsored schemes (more than 200 currently) sponsored by different Union ministries has posed a serious challenge to democratic decentralization. Many of the subjects they deal with are either included in the State List or in the 11th and 12th Schedules. The share of the CSSs in the plan budget of the federal government has shot up to 70 per cent against less than 30 per cent in the early 1980s, which goes against the very spirit of decentralization initiated through major constitutional amendments.

Besides the centrally-sponsored schemes (CSS), there are also 26 sectoral programmes falling under the 29 subjects of the 11th Schedule which the central ministries handle. The schemes are drawn up at the Centre and implemented at the local level. The association of local bodies with the implementation processes does not really serve the purpose because the implementing bodies only implement according to the rules laid down elsewhere. The local government has to accept them because the Centre has got the financial clout.

The adverse implications of the centrally-sponsored schemes for the federal system in India can be understood with reference to schemes under JNNURM. The central government launched the Jawaharlal Nehru Urban Renewal Mission on 3 December 2005 to create 'economically productive, efficient, equitable and responsive cities'. It focuses on four major things: improvement and augmentation of the economic and social infrastructure of the cities, ensuring basic services to the urban poor including security of tenure at affordable prices, initiation of wide-ranging urban sector reforms with the objective of eliminating legal, institutional and financial constraints which may stand in the way strengthening of municipal governance in terms of the provisions of the 74th Amendment of the Constitution. JNNURM is a project-based programme. Thus, a detailed project report (DPR) has to be prepared. There is a procedure for scrutinizing the DPRs. The financing of the projects is done by the central government, state government and the ULBs. There are detailed guidelines in this regard.

The release of the central grant is linked to the assessment of implementation of reforms agenda as per mutually agreed roadmap. This is done through a memorandum of agreement which joins the legs and binds the parties. It has two sub-missions – sub-mission for urban infrastructure and governance and sub-mission for basic services to the urban poor.

The programme talks of two kinds of reforms – mandatory and optional. One set of mandatory reforms includes adoption of the modern accrual based double entry system of accounting, reform of property tax with efficiency of collection to reach at least 85 per cent within the next seven years, levy of reasonable water with objective of full cost recovery of O&M or recurring costs, internal earmarking within local bodies for basic services to the urban poor, provision of basic services to the urban poor including security of tenure at affordable prices, improved housing, water supply and sanitation. All these reforms have to be undertaken by the ULBs/parastatal bodies for which they have to enter into an agreement with the government.

The question that one can raise without raising doubt about the usefulness of the reforms is that these reforms are imposed on the urban local bodies by the Centre. These local bodies are now institutions of self-government in terms of the Seventy Fourth Amendment. It may also be mentioned that urban local bodies are not left with any effective option because following the creation of this body, all the major centrally-sponsored programmes are brought under the Mission. A local body which refuses to accept the projects under the Mission will virtually be deprived of all central funds for urban development. The central government did not even think of discussing the issue on the floor of the Parliament, not to speak of consulting the local bodies. It should have been discussed in detail because it reflects a paradigmatic shift in the policy of urban development. Significantly, one of the declared objectives of the Mission is to strengthen the Seventy Fourth Amendment of the Constitution.

There is another set of mandatory reforms to be carried out by the state governments. These reforms include:

- Implementation of decentralization measures as envisaged in the Seventy Third Amendment of the Constitution.
- Repeal of urban land ceiling and regulation Act.
- Reform of rent control laws, balancing the interests of land owners and tenants.
- Rationalization of stamp duty to bring it down to not more than 5 per cent.
- Enactment of public disclosure law to ensure preparation of medium-level fiscal plans of the ULBs and parastatals and release of quarterly information to all stakeholders.

The reforms programme smacks of neo-liberal policy shift of the Indian state as is evident from the reforms like repeal of land ceiling laws. Some of these reforms impinge on the autonomy of the states. The state governments are asked to implement these reforms without taking their observations into account. The Constitution has provided for a consultation apparatus in the form of Inter-State Council. This matter could have been discussed in that forum in order to elicit reactions of the state governments. Secondly, the reduction of the stamp duty would cost the state exchequer heavily. There is no proposal about alternatives to compensate that loss.

This group of critics apprehends that the provision of JNNURM may pressure the state governments to adopt the model municipal law for the country which has been drafted by the Government of India. Given the country's size and diversity, such an action would be disastrous for the country. A local government in a liberal democratic set-up, has to depend on grassroots and to reflect local will. It may be recalled that this was the idea conceived by J.S. Mill, Tocqueville and Bryce. In the Indian context, Ripon had sought to develop it long back in 1882. Any attempt to develop and implement a uniform pattern of local government throughout the country goes not only against the very spirit of Western concept of local government, but also against the tradition of local self-government in India.

Decentralized District Planning

Another important area where the state governments have shown scant regard for constitutional provisions is the area of district planning. The constitutional Amendment requires the state governments to constitute the District Planning Committees (DPCs) to facilitate decentralized planning. The states took more than a decade to constitute DPCs. There are still states like Jharkhand and Uttarakhand which have not yet formed DPCs because the elections to PRIs are still to be held.

There is a peculiar situation in some where they are in place. Mention may be made of Gujarat, Himachal Pradesh, Odisha, where the chairperson of the DPC is the minister, which goes against the very spirit of the constitution of the DPC. There are also states where the DPCs are headed by the bureaucrats, which also works against the basic philosophy of the DPC. The Centre has not intervened to compel the state governments to constitute the DPCs. This raises a question: who will enforce the implementation of the Amendment of the Constitution? The Centre has financial clout. It could have threatened the states of dire consequences even to the extent of non-release of central funds to ensure compliance of the constitutional provisions. Thus, this silence or inaction of the Centre raises doubts about its genuine interest in decentralization through panchayati raj.

Conclusion

It is evident from the above discussion that PRIs are still to emerge as the third stratum, as claimed by Indira Rajaraman, in India's federal system. Incidentally, the Ninth Plan pleaded for greater decentralization and referred to the concept of cooperative federalism whereby much greater freedom would be given to states to determine not only their own priorities but also the modalities of public intervention and provision of public goods and services. This concept also embodies a higher degree of dialogue and coordination between states. But the discussion above clearly shows that the scope of dialogue between the Centre and the states, not to speak of the local and central government, is getting reduced as a result of the introduction of a new set of schemes.

It may be recalled that Nineties, which saw the rise of the constitionalized panchayats, were swept by the wave of decentralization promoted by the international donors and it came in the wake of liberalization. It was not a product of pressure from below but a culmination of the compulsion which was created in the 1970s. One may, however, hope that the new social movements which are gathering momentum in different parts of India may help in generating pressure from below to strengthen the local government as a step towards its being a genuine third stratum in future.

Notes

1. Prabhat Datta, *Politics of Region and Religion in India*, New Delhi: Uppal Publishing House, 1991, p. 46.
2. See editorial introduction in K. Mathew Kurian and P.N. Varughese (eds), *Centre-State Relations in India*, New Delhi: Macmillan, 1981, p. 4.
3. Jawarharlal Nehru in the Constituent Assembly, 5 July 1947.
4. E.M.S. Namboodiripad, 'National Political Background of Indian Federalism', in K. Mathew Kurian and P.N. Varughese (eds), *Centre-State Relations in India*, New Delhi: Macmillan, 1981, p. 4.
5. Federation of the Indian Chambers of Commerce, Proceedings of the Forty Second Annual Session, 14–17 March 1969, p. 43.
6. See extracts in Kurian and Varughese, op. cit.
7. Prabhat Datta, *The Second Generation Panchayats in India*, Calcutta: Calcutta Book House, 1992.
8. T.N. Srivastava, 'Local Self-Government and the Constitution', *Economic and Political Weekly*, Vol. 37, No. 30, 27 July 2002.
9. Nirmal Mukerjee, 'The Third Stratum', in *Renewing Local Self-Government in Rural India*, New Delhi: Department of Rural Development, Government of India, 1994.
10. *Harijan*, 21 December 1947.
11. Association of Voluntary Agencies for Rural Development, *Panchayati Raj as the Basis of Indian Polity*, New Delhi: AVARD, 1966, p. 15.
12. *Panchayati Raj Update*, December 2001.
13. Prabhat Datta, 'Democratic Decentralization through Panchayati Raj in Contemporary India: The Changes and Challenges', *Heidelberg Papers in South Asia and Comparative Politics, Working Paper 49*, Germany: Heidelberg University, 2009.

CHAPTER 6

Participatory Democracy and Panchayats in India

Problems and Prospects

Budh Bahadur Lama

Participatory democracy is a process of collective decision-making that combines elements from both direct and representative democracy. Citizens have the power to decide on policy proposals and politicians assume the task of implementation of such policies. The electorate can monitor politicians' performance simply by comparing citizens' proposals with the policies actually implemented. As a result, the discretion of politicians is severely controlled. In this system, the extent to which citizens can affect policy and determine social priorities is directly aligned with the degree to which they choose to involve themselves in the process.[1] According to UNDP, 'participation means that people are closely involved in economic, social, cultural and political processes that affect their lives'.[2] Therefore, participation is a process by which people may influence the direction and execution of a development programme to enhance prosperity in terms of income, personal growth, self-reliance or other values that they cherish in a democratic society. The objective of this paper is to examine the nature of participatory democracy as an alternative form of governance for representative democracy at the grassroots level in the first section, and to highlight the nature of relationship between participatory democracy and gram panchayats in India, which are meant for enhancing popular participation at the village level. It also attempts to present the historical evolution of panchayats along with its practical experiences after the Seventy Third Amendment Act with a focus on the problems and prospects of PRIs in India.

Participatory Democracy: A Conceptual Framework

Participation is at the core of democracy since time memorial. Since the beginning of the ancient Greek democracy around 550 BC, people's participation in determining decisions affecting their own lives has been considered as one of the major characteristics of the Athenian system of governance. However, the concept of democracy has evolved into various forms in different times and contexts. The dynamic nature of democracy has also affected the form and character of participation and as the concept has also been reconceptualized, so also has been the case of participation. Athenian democracy was built on the concept of direct participation 'in which the people governed directly rather than through the medium of elections and representative institutions'.[3] In due course, other forms of democratic governance emerged such as liberal democracy, representative democracy, elitist democracy, pluralist democracy and popular democracy. Accordingly, direct participation of people in governance came to be replaced by indirect participation through representation being actualized either through the political leaders or interest groups. With the advent of the concept of nation-state, the exercise of direct participation in a modern state became unattainable and therefore, representation had to be followed in order to make democracy attainable. This is how representative democracy came into being in the modern era and started operating in different nation-states.

However, in course of time, the functioning of representative democracy was derailed and directed towards personal gains and benefits, which caused disappointment in the society and people began to look for an alternative form of governance. In order to protect the established order, the trend towards limiting popular participation began to emerge. But the concept of direct participation of people in decision-making earned a general acceptance in the society which needed to be contextualized in order to make modern democracy successful. It is in this context that another variant of democracy known as 'participatory democracy' emerged in an attempt to reinforce people's power to determine their own fate and to correct representative democracy whenever it becomes 'misrepresentative'.

Over the last three decades or so, there has been a revival of interest in popular participation and it has in fact turned out to be a key feature of what is known as the 'new democratic theory.'[4] Participatory democracy is an integral part of this theory. The new democratic theory offers a critique to both traditional or classical democratic theory and modern democratic theory. The core of the critique is the weakness of liberal democracy, representative democracy, elitist democracy, pluralist democracy and the like. This weakness is being taken as a roadmap to building up of the new democratic theory' on the principle of enhancing full participation of the people in decision-making in the state and in other spheres. The theory distinguishes itself from the rest on the role of 'people'. According to traditional or classical democratic theory, 'the people are given a negative role, that is, the people are involved in little more than rather passively choosing between options presented to them'. This is based on the idea that the elected representatives have a greater knowledge – and more wisdom – than their constituents and thus they should accordingly have considerable autonomy in making political decisions.[5]

In contrast, under participatory democracy, the people are given a positive role by actually initiating the policies. In this regard, the representatives are largely considered as messengers or delegates conveying the decisions of their constituents. According to Holden, participatory democracy is a 'form of direct democracy and representation is only merely used as a device to deal with the problem of scale.'[6] This is shaped on the principle of popular participation in which 'the people do not merely register their views on what is done or proposed by the government or representative; rather, they will also conceive to participate in the process of government themselves. Pateman claims that under participatory democracy, participation is so important that a system of representation is only somewhat regretfully accepted as a necessary modification of or supplement to direct participation by the people.[7] Most of the participatory theorists derived the idea from the work of Rousseau, when argued that 'sovereignty, for the same reason as makes it inalienable, cannot be represented ... Legislation was to be directly enacted by the assembled people ... Every law the people has not ratified in person is *null and void is in fact not a law*.'[8] Participatory democracy is, therefore, a reaction to the deficiencies resulted from other types of democracy which lay much emphasis on representation. It strives to bring about greater democratization through participation and intends to create opportunities for all members of a political group to make meaningful contributions in decision-making, and seeks to broaden the range of people who have access to such opportunities. One of the unique features as pointed out by Cook and Morgan is that participatory democracy calls for restructuring of the whole political system and not just one aspect of polity or society. 'Indeed, it is this demand for a change in the political system itself that is critical in participatory democracy.'[9]

One of the common forms of participatory democracy is indeed direct democracy, which is exercised through various ways in modern times. They include such methods as holding referenda, recalls, initiatives, and citizen assemblies for collective decision-making. People can hold a binding referendum on whether or not a certain law should be scrapped. This tends to give a veto on government legislation. Recalls entail the practice in which the people have the right to recall elected officials by petition and referendum. Similarly, citizens' initiatives are being put to a referendum rather than just relying on the elected representatives. Switzerland represents this type of direct democracy. In addition, there are other methods that are used to promote people's participation in representative institutions. Parliamentary public hearings held at the committee level can be regarded as tools to enrich the quality of legislation through people's participation. Also, the civil society organizations, which include various interest and pressure groups, are used as instruments to foster people's participation along other representative institutions and processes.

However, the role of the interest and pressure groups in enhancing people's participation is somewhat challenged by the participatory theorists, who accuse powerful interest groups of blocking the people from their government and for pursuing their own agenda. In most cases, it is observed that the institutions and processes of representative democracy have failed to represent people's interests and demands. Therefore, participatory democracy is indeed a situational necessity to uphold popular sovereignty in the present context of governance in South Asia in general and in India, in particular. Rajni Kothari[10] makes a powerful critique of prevailing democratic theory and practice in the changing global as well as Indian context and concludes that democracy has failed to achieve its objective of human emancipation. He argues that the model for democracy should be reshaped into a decentralized, participatory and emancipatory democracy. He quotes, 'I have found myself getting increasingly concerned with the failure of democracy – not just as a political system, but of the democratic idea itself – in fulfilling the basic task of reaching out to people, especially those residing in the lower reaches of the social order. I began to feel increasingly uneasy with the recent democratic developments.' Following Kothari's arguments on democracy, we may conclude that a successful democracy means greater involvement or participation of people in the political system. Hence, in India, panchayats and municipalities have been established in rural and urban areas, respectively, for enhancing people's participation in governance.

Participatory Democracy and Panchayats

During the past twenty years or so, there has been an increasing upsurge towards promoting democratic decentralization and participatory democracy in the world in general and in South Asia in particular. International development agencies, UN institutions and their allied agencies and the governments of various South Asian countries have consistently attempted to focus on these issues and to bring them into practice. It is claimed that a representative democracy to a large extent provides space for people's participation in the process of governance and hence the question of participatory governance through grassroots institutions has gained prominence over the years. Democratic decentralization as an approach is meant for extending and enriching local democracy. India as the largest democracy of the world has taken initiatives for extending democracy to the doorsteps of the people on the principles of democratic decentralization. Urban and rural local representative bodies have been looking after the local affairs of India. The idea of participatory democracy has been strengthened in India by guaranteeing a constitutional status to the gram panchayats. One of the most important provisions of the Seventy Third Amendment Act is setting up of *gram sabha* at the lower tier of panchayats, known as gram panchayat with the citizens of the locality concerned to ensure their direct participation.

In India, due to large geographical location and huge population, there is no opportunity to think of a participatory democracy in place of representative democracy. Hence, an attempt has been made to operationalize the system of representative democracy with a vision of people's direct participation at least at the grassroots level. The constitutional Amendment has paved the way for rural people to participate directly in grassroots governance to initiate and determine the policies which affect their lives directly. Following the Amendment Act, the rural people through their elected panchayats and gram sabha may exercise direct control over their representatives and the elected representatives are treated as delegates of the people. The ultimate power to make decisions thus lies in the hands of the people in a way. The rationale behind participatory democracy is to bring back the sovereign power from the representatives to the hands of the people. People themselves constitute a tier of government to govern on the basis of their common interest and needs in a democratic manner. The main purpose of introducing gram sabhas at the grassroots level of the panchayats is to make them the 'watchdog' of all social service institutions at the village level,[11] so as to reinforcing the practice of participatory democracy in the form of panchayats in India. It justifies the claim that there is a close relationship between participatory democracy and gram panchayats in India. People's participation is one of the main ingredients of democracy and only through it responsiveness of elected representatives may be proved and people could be close to the government.[12]

Evolution of Panchayats

Panchayats have been a vibrant and dynamic identity in the Indian villages since time immemorial. It continued to exist with bureaucratic support in the colonial period, though with limited power, authority and activities. Various attempts have been made to bring it in the democratic process of the country after Independence without much satisfactory results.

History tells us that local self-government, in one form or another, has been in existence in the sub-continent for centuries. In ancient times, panchayati raj system prevailed during the Chola period. In fact, Rippon's Resolution of 1881 and 1882 can be taken to be the origin of modern local self-government in India.

During freedom movement and particularly in the non-cooperation era, there was a strong urge for establishment of these local bodies after independence. Panchayati raj was viewed to be the attainment of *village swaraj* in Gandhi's ideas. 'India lives in her villages,' Gandhi opined and stressed that 'Indian independence must begin at the bottom' and only in this way democracy could be meaningful which could not be actualized through some leaders sitting at the Centre. He strongly believed in decentralization and pleaded for devolution of powers to the localities and villages.[13] Though B.R. Ambedkar strongly opposed the inclusion of provisions for panchayats in the Constitution, he was finally compelled to accommodate the provisions for panchayats in the Constitution through incorporating it in the Directive Principles of State Policy.

The first organized effort to ensure development and management of administration of rural India was made through the Community Development Programme (CDP) in 1952 and National Extension Service (NES) in 1953. The programme was based on an integrated approach to the various aspects of rural development. The objectives were to promote self-help and self-reliance among rural people, to generate a process of integrated social, economic and cultural change with the aim of transforming social and political life of the villagers. CDP was launched in 55 selected blocks. The provisions for appointing Block Development Officers (BDO) and Village Level Workers (VLW) were made under CDP. NES blocks were earmarked as the lowest unit of development of administration. But both the programmes had a cardinal problem that they were fully bureaucracy dependent and devoid of popular participation.

The shortcoming prompted the government to appoint a committee headed by Balwantray Mehta in 1957. The committee recommended a three-tier system of panchayats from village to the district level – Gram Panchayat at the village level, Panchayat Samiti at the block level and Zilla Parishad at the district level. Following the recommendations, panchayati raj was launched on 2 October 1957 in Nagaur district of Rajasthan. Andhra Pradesh and many state governments followed Rajasthan. Yet, by the mid-sixties, the hype to strengthen the panchayati raj system gave way to a growing tendency of centralization and the PRIs descended to ground zero. In 1977, the Janata Government tried to revive the PRIs. Accordingly, a committee headed by Asoka Mehta was appointed to review the working of the PRIs. The committee suggested a minor change in the existing system. The three-tier system of PRIs was to be replaced by a two-tier one, i.e. Zilla Parishad at the district level and Mandal Panchayat (consisting of a number of villages) below it. In addition, the committee also recommended the creation of Nyaya Panchayat. However, owing to the disintegration of the Janata Government in 1980, the recommendations of the Asoka Mehta Committee could not be implemented though some experiments were carried out in West Bengal, Kerala and Karnataka to revive and strengthen the existing system through further decentralization and people's participation. But during the next five years or so, no steady progress was made. One committee under the chairmanship of G.V.K. Rao reported in 1985, suggesting appropriate improvement in the representative character and strengthening of the capability of the people's representatives and administrative personnel in the PRIs, while the L.M. Singhvi Committee recommended constitutional status for panchayati raj in 1986. In July–August 1989, the then Congress government introduced the 64th Constitutional Amendment Bill with a view to streamlining panchayati raj. However, the Bill was defeated in Rajya Sabha. V.P. Singh government also tried to push a Bill in 1990 but it lapsed with the dissolution of Lok Sabha.

At last, the central (P.V. Narasimha Rao's) government enacted the Seventy Third Constitutional Amendment, which was passed in Parliament on 23 December 1992 and became effective on 24 April 1993. This Act has added Part-IX to the Constitution of India, and has given a practical shape to Article 40 of the Constitution, according a constitutional status to the Panchayati Raj Institutions. The Amendment ensures a three-tier structure at the zilla, block and village levels, an election commission to hold elections periodically, a state level finance commission to find out ways and means to increase resources for local bodies, reservation of one-third of seats in all respects of the three tiers for women, reservation of seats for SCs/STs in proportion to their population in all the positions of the three tiers, establishment of gram sabha for enhancing people's participation for their own development, and establishment of planning committee for local bodies and an earmarked list of 29 items under 11th Schedule.

Before the Seventy Third Amendment, panchayati raj system was not effective in the way it should have been. Its powers were limited. Undoubtedly, the credit to initiate constitutional recognition to panchayat as a 'third tier of governance'[14] should go to former Prime Minister, late Rajiv Gandhi, who strongly believed in strengthening panchayats through the constitutional status. As D. Bandyopadhyay rightly comments, 'Against this thumb-nail historical sketch of panchayats in India, it is a bit riddle why and how Rajiv Gandhi – a totally apolitical person to begin with – did realize, appreciate and with single-minded devotion and determination activate an ancient and currently defunct system of governance at the local level – the

Panchayats.'[15] In addition, we also access the provisions of the panchayats (Extension to the Scheduled Areas) Act, 1996 (PESA) which came into force on 24 December 1996. The Act extends panchayats to the tribal areas of 10 states, namely Andhra Pradesh, Bihar, Jharkhand, Gujarat, Himachal Pradesh, Maharashtra, Madhya Pradesh, Chhattisgarh, Odisha and Rajasthan. It intends to enable tribal societies to assume control over their destiny and to preserve and conserve their traditional rights over natural resources.

Now, the world's most populous democracy has constitutionally mandated 2,32,332 village panchayats, 6,000 intermediate panchayats and 534 zilla panchayats. The three tiers of these elected bodies consist of as many as 27,75,858 village panchayat members, 1,44,491 members of intermediate panchayats and 15,067 members of zilla panchayats. This is the broadest representative base which exists in any country of the world (India Panchayati Raj Report, 2001, NIRD). The, political and democratic implications of these figures can be gauged from the fact that more than fifty per cent of these grassroots representatives are from the downtrodden and marginalized sections of the society, namely women (one-third of the total), the SCs, STs and OBCs (as per their proportion of the population). This kind of constitutional provision has created a scope for accomplishing development with social justice, which is the mandate of the new panchayat raj system. The new system brings all those who are interested to have their voices heard in decision-making through participation in Panchayati Raj Institutions. The whole system is directed towards bringing 'social justice' and 'empowerment' to the weaker sections on which the development initiative has to be built upon for achieving overall human development and welfare of the society.

Gram Panchayats: Problems and Prospects

Gram Sabha means a body consisting of persons registered in the electoral rolls relating to a village comprised within the area of panchayat at the village level. The gram sabha is really the keystone of the whole system of democratic decentralization. It is direct democracy at the grassroots level. Legal empowerment of the gram sabha had already been completed almost in all the states Acts immediately after the constitutional Amendment Act, 1992. It is in fact the 'watchdog' of the working of the panchayats. It may control the panchayats becoming irresponsible and unaccountable to the people if the gram sabha becomes free to perform its actual role in practice. Gandhiji remarked, 'True democracy could not be worked by some persons sitting at the top. It had to be worked from below by the people of every village.'[16] The greater the power of gram sabha, the better it is for the people. J.P. Narayan rightly comments: 'Let us not have only representative government from the village up to Delhi. One place at least, let there be direct government, a direct democracy. The relationship between Panchayat and Gram Sabha should be that of Cabinet and Assembly.'[17] It was really the concept of Gandhiji's 'swarajya' – democracy at the grassroots level.

The importance of grassroots level organizations has always been recognized by both the academics and the political personalities. Even Nehru himself observed that 'local self-government was and must be the basis of any true system of democracy. People had got into the habit of thinking of democracy at the top and not so much below. Democracy at the top could not be a success unless it was built on this foundation below'.[18] The term 'people's participation' has several connotations. It refers to the idea that people have the right to decide their own needs, and can be interpreted in two ways. Firstly, it means people's involvement and engagement in the development projects during all its phases, including planning, implementation, monitoring and evaluation. Secondly, it means group action in the form of Self-Help Groups (SHG), Social Action Groups (SAG), Non-Governmental Organizations (NGO), etc. People's participation through gram sabha comes under the first definition. Nowadays, community participation is more commonly used instead of people's participation. During 1990s, after the implementation of the Amendment Act, its meaning has changed further. Now it not only means people's participation in decision-making but also in its implementation, monitoring and evaluation.

Sustainable rural development can only be brought about through an active involvement of people and community in management of local affairs. Active people's participation is the prerequisite condition for successful implementation of rural development programmes. The gram sabha is an institution which can bestow collective strength on the poor and the deprived, who in turn gain self-confidence to stand on their own and regain the spirit of self-reliance and human dignity. But the role of the gram sabha is being gradually reduced day by day. It is never treated as the assembly of the panchayat. Rather, it is considered merely as an advisory body. Under the Act, a gram sabha may exercise such powers and perform such functions at the village level as the legislature of a state may provide by law. Thus, the ball is in the state legislature's court, which for all practical purpose means the state government. The members of gram sabha have nothing to do except constituting the sabha. The state government dominates, and gram sabhas face a perpetual situation of dependency and uncertainty by which the importance of the concept of people's participation gets blurred.

Participation cannot be imposed on people from above; it should be voluntary and based on the 'will' to participate. By participation, we mean direct involvement of people and not indirect involvement through their representatives. This is because of the existing socio-economic and political structure of the society in most of the developing countries. In most cases, the representatives of the people are likely to represent the rich, rather than the interest of the poor majority. Moreover, in such a large country like ours, direct participation of the people is possible only at the local level. This is also in consonance with the assumptions that an equitable sharing of the benefits of development by the poor is possible only when there is equitable participation by them in the process of development. By doing so, people can influence the decisions at the higher levels through their joint efforts and common voice. This may be termed the 'bottom-up approach to integrated rural development'. In other words, people's participation or involvement can better be understood as participation in decision-making; participation in implementation of programmes and projects; participation in monitoring and evaluation of programmes and projects and participation in sharing the benefits of development.

Presently, there is no actual participation of the rural poor in any kind of decision-making at the village, block, and district levels. The government planning is defective as the normal procedure is that the guidelines for resource utilization, budget allocation to different sectors and regions and the programmes and projects for area development are prepared by central government. However, direct participation of the poor in decision-making is possible only at the village level. Even at the village level, discussion regarding community development projects such as drinking water, social construction, etc. is confined to a small caucus of so-called village elites. D. Bandyopadhyay strongly criticises the government's initiative of the concept of gram unnayan samiti (village development committee) in West Bengal. He argues that the government has created numerous tiers of non-functional panchayati raj bodies without giving adequate resources, functions and functionaries to the panchayats.'[19] These schemes must be discussed freely in the open assemblies in presence of all the villagers so that poor sections have some say in the decision-making and execution of these schemes.

The legislative empowerment of the gram sabha in India is a political development of utmost importance because it marks the clearest break from the most dominant political orthodoxy of this century. The faith in gram sabha is based on the belief that the objective conditions of the poor are directly involved in the process of formulation and implementation of decisions affecting their lives.[20] At least two meetings of gram sabha should be held in a year. More specifically, most of the SC representatives are facing the problem of non-cooperation from the official and upper castes/dominant sections of their gram panchayats. These problems have not only been obstructing developmental works but also prohibiting elected representatives from participating in the panchayats. These problems exist everywhere across the country though in different levels of intensity.[21]

On the basis of the above, it may be said that the panchayats at village, block, and district levels are close to the masses and provide ample opportunities to local people to solve their problems collectively in a participatory manner and thereby strengthen the process of human development. The successful experiment of participatory planning through mobilization of several thousands of people in the implementation of the Ninth Five Year Plan in Kerala is a unique example of this and became a household name across the country. Similar sorts of experiments have to be initiated in other states also for making panchayats the effective vehicle for fulfilling expectations and aspirations of the people. The state government transferred nearly all the powers previously exercised by gram panchayats to gram sabhas through the introduction of 'Gram Swaraj' on 26 January 2001. It has thus transformed representative democracy at the grassroots into direct democracy. More than 60 countries world-wide have experimented with some sort of democratic decentralization during the last 15 years or so. But evidence currently available indicates that none has gone in for direct democracy at the local level to the extent that West Bengal did. Gram sansad and village development council at the constituency level of village panchayats have been made mandatory and they function on principles of participatory democracy in West Bengal at the grassroots level. Gram sabha or people's forum has always been an integral part of the concept of a gram panchayat.

The significance of gram sabha or gram sansad has not as yet rubbed upon the villagers. Their eyes are still focused on the gram panchayat as the hub of all activity. Not only this, even panchayat officials and the local elites have paid little interest in the functioning of the gram sabha. After *Gram Swaraj (*26 January 2001), all the powers are transferred to gram sabhas instead of gram panchayats. At gram sabha, various committees are formed to look into different issues. A *Gram Kosh* is also constituted which will include both cash and kind. Conceptually, the gram swaraj reflects a form of direct democracy where the people are directly held accountable and responsible to deal with all local issues. Though it is the beginning of an experiment, the evidence suggests that it has all the potential to perform the roles assigned to it, provided the people at local level are made aware and understand the multifaceted role of gram sabha.

To make panchayats viable and effective, three hurdles have to be overcome. First, the domination of the bureaucracy over the Panchayati Raj Institutions (PRIs), the agent for implementation of all major programmes (CDP or IRDP, etc.) and other various parallel bodies such as the District Rural Development Agency (DRDA) have grossly undermined the importance of the PRIs. Either they have to be disbanded or made accountable to the PRIs. Secondly, lack of adequate financial resources to carry out the functions hinders the effectiveness of the elected bodies. Grant-in-aid is the major component of the PRIs' revenue. This needs to be supplemented with adequate collection of taxes by the PRIs and a mandatory transfer of some of the state government's revenues on the recommendation of the state finance commission duly established for the purpose. The last hurdle is related to the lack of training programmes for the participants of the PRIs. Without proper training, they lack the direction and awareness about proper functioning of the Panchayati Raj Institutions.

Conclusion

To conclude, admitting that the PRIs in India are weak and assuming that it will not be smooth sailing for them even after the Amendment, they have an important role to play in India's development. However, the PRIs have several achievements to their credit. These institutions have enhanced the political consciousness of the people and initiated a process of democratic seed drilling in Indian soil. The government should attempt now gradually to delimit the role of bureaucracy, promote local leadership, remove structural deficiencies and encourage PRIs to strengthen their financial resources, bring in effective coordination among these institutions and between PRIs and the department of the state governments and give them effective powers in relation to planning and implementation. To realize a viable and successful panchayati raj, the system needs direct involvement of people in all its affairs.

Notes

1. Inspired by earlier thinkers like Rousseau and J.S. Mill, the first theoretical formulations of participatory democracy have been made by Carole Pateman, *Participation and Democratic Theory*, London: Cambridge University Press, 1970; and C.B. Macpherson, *The Life and Time of Liberal Democracy*, New York: Oxford University Press, 1977. An excellent discussion of the main features of this model of democracy can be found in David Held, *Models of Democracy*, Cambridge: Polity Press, 1987.
2. UNDP, *Human Development Report 1993*, New Delhi: Oxford University Press, 1993, p. 21.
3. Barry Holden, *The Nature of Democracy*, Great Britain: Thomas Nelson and Sons, 1974, p. 5.
4. K.A. Megill, 'Preface', *The New Democratic Theory*, London: The University of Michigan Press, 1970.
5. Holden, op. cit., p. 69.
6. Ibid., p. 70.
7. Carole Pateman, *Participation and Democratic Theory*, London: Cambridge University Press, 1970.
8. Ibid.
9. Terence E. Cook and Patrick M. Morgan, *Participatory Democracy*, New York: Harper & Row, 1970.
10. Rajni Kothari, 'Preface', *Rethinking Democracy*, New Delhi: Orient Longman Private Limited, 2005.
11. R.P. Joshi and G.S. Narwani, *Panchayat Raj in India: Emerging Trends Across the States*, Jaipur: Rawat Publications, 2002.
12. Ibid., p. 118.
13. R.P. Joshi (ed.), *Constitutionalization of Panchayati Raj: A Reassessment*, Jaipur: Rawat Publications, 1999.
14. M. Aslam, *Panchayati Raj in India*, New Delhi: National Book Trust, 2007, p. 36.

15. D. Bandopadhyay, 'Panchayats and Democracy: Elites versus Dalits', in *New Issues in Panchayati Raj: Report on the Task Force on Panchayati Raj*, Rajiv Gandhi Foundation, New Delhi: Concept Publishing Company, 2004.
16. Joshi, op. cit., p. 100.
17. Mahipal, 'Effectiveness of Gram Sabha', *National Herald*, New Delhi, April 2000.
18. S.P. Jain, 'The Gram Sabha: Gateway to Grassroots Democracy', *Journal of Rural Development*, NIRD, Vol. 16, No. 4, 1997, pp. 566–567.
19. D. Bandopadhyay, 'The Caucus and Masses: West Bengal Panchayat (Amendment) Act 2003', *Economic and Political Weekly*, Vol. 38, No. 46, 15 November 2003.
20. Yatindra Singh Sisodia, 'People's Participation in Gram Sabha', *Kurukshetra*, May 2006, p. 35.
21. Mahipal, 'Panchayat Raj and Development', *Yojana*, August 2004, p. 51.

CHAPTER 7

Role of Panchayati Raj Institutions in Rural Development

West Bengal in Retrospect

Apurba Kumar Mukhopadhyay

That India is not a poor country but a country of the poor is common knowledge. If it were so during the colonial era, it has not changed for the better since Independence. More intriguing, perhaps, is the fact that while the poor count in large number, they hardly count in shaping policies and programmes aimed at reshaping their destiny, in the world's largest democracy even after 66 years of independence. The reason is not far to seek. The poor in India are administered by their chosen people, democratically elected, from New Delhi primarily and only marginally from the provincial capitals. As a result, resources earmarked for their development and welfare hardly percolate down to the grassroots level, used up as those are in course of the long journey from the top downward. The Indian State funnily enough understood this simple truth after 42 years of the functioning of the country's democratic Constitution and came up with the two Amendment Acts, the Seventy Third and the Seventy Fourth, in December, 1992. This legislative initiative was the first official acknowledgement of the need to decentre and decentralize both the state's power and resources through creation of local states in the form of PRIs in rural India. The political context of this belated realization requires critical interrogation and will engage us in the following section.

I

A complementary relationship is assumed between globalization and decentralization – two apparently incompatible phenomena. In the perception of the global lending and donor agencies, the fund-bank prescription, to be more precise, thinking in global terms must be followed by acting locally.[1] With the dismantling of the modern nation-state as an economic agent, particularly in the beleaguered Third World, the shocks generated by the global market forces amongst the marginalized nation and the marginal men and women therein, have to be absorbed by local or sub-national systems of governance. We may turn toward Joseph Stiglitz, the Nobel laureate and former chief economist of the World Bank, for an ideological justification of decentralization, He says, 'When workers are deprived of the opportunity to *meaningful* participation in the community by working – when, through no fault of their own, they simply cannot find work – they lose self-esteem. Welfare is no substitute for work; and in any case, many developing countries lack even an adequate social safety net, so that the adverse consequences of unemployment are truly dire.' In such a desperate situation fraught with a whole series of disruptive social consequences, the remedy lies in 'open, transparent and participatory process' of development through adjustment. In the not so friendly ambience of globalization, according to Stiglitz, 'if individuals believe that they have had *meaningful* (emphasis original) participation in the decisions that are affecting them, they will be more willing to accept changes, even if they are adversely affected. But if they believe that those changes have been imposed on them either by outsiders or by illegitimate governments who have not taken their concerns into account, then resentment is more likely to mount and to lead to socially destructive outcomes.'[2]

Orthodox champions of the cause of labour may not agree with such benign projection. Serious concerns have been expressed regarding the process engendered by globalization which may serve to reinforce global inequalities of wealth and quality of life, accelerate changes which lead to the degradation of the ecosystem and strengthen non-democratic forms of governance.[3] Alan Simpson, representing the Labour Party in British Parliament, does not mince words when he argues, 'globalization is little more than a front for corporate capitalism. It is about the transfer of decision-making powers from elected governments to global business, making the rights of corporations greater than those of citizens and redefining the welfare state in ways that makes corporate welfare indispensable and personal welfare unaffordable'. And further that it is a 'war against democracy, against accountability and against ecology. Most of all, it is a war against the poor.'[4]

The record of globalization creating an ambience of democracy and spreading it beyond the bounds of the so-called 'illegitimate' governments into the margins of society is hardly encouraging. Though the number of democratic states went up – from 44 in 1985 to 82 in 2002, enabling at least 57 per cent of the world's population to live in democracies, the regressions towards authoritarianism are not uncommon. How can one ignore the fact that as many as 3.6 million precious human lives were lost in civil wars or state-sponsored violence during the last decade?[5] Moreover, the much talked about benefits of globalization opening up the prospects of free flow of capital, technology and culture through a transnational policy network are more apparent than real, restricted as these are to a handful of countries.[6]

To mitigate the harshness of globalization, particularly from the point of view of the world's poor, Pranab Bardhan has referred to a policy option 'away from both state paternalism and harshness of market process' and relying 'more on local self-governing institutions and community involvement to improve the material conditions and autonomy of the poor.'[7] In this alternative scenario replacing 'the age-old state versus market debate', the state is not to withdraw to its minimalist role in classical liberalism (notwithstanding the media hype in favour of such neo-liberal theology). Instead, 'it is to play an activist role in local participatory development, in supra-local support for raising outside finance, in underwriting risks, in supplying training and extension services, investing in larger infrastructure and in coordinating some of the externalities across localities'. The state has to pay attention 'towards building local institutions and organization that are more sensitive to needs of the poor and to their opportunities'.[8] A democratic state may be coaxed, if not pressurized, into acting in the interest of its people at large. Indeed, governments are frequently sectarian in their actions and interventionist as they seek to promote or to protect the interest of the classes, or groups which can exercise influence.[9] The correctives against the operation of anti-poor market forces under globalization and anti-people political stances of the nation-state have to be sought, according to Nayyar, in situations 'where people are at the centre of economic development, not only as its beneficiaries, but also as the main actors'.

The Indian nation-state embarked on a comprehensive programme of democratic decentralization in 1993 through the enactment of the 73rd and 74th Amendments to the Constitution of India, giving due recognition to local self-governing institutions in both rural and urban areas. Panchayats and municipalities are now assigned specific jobs and allocated financial resources to administer villages and towns. Though the tradition of local governments was not new to this country, it is ironical that the Government of India became alive to the need for decentralized development only when it was called upon to abdicate its control over the economic life of the country by the votaries of globalization at home and abroad. One would not fail to notice that the changeover was more at the behest of the fund-bank regime than under prodding from a home-spun democratic regime. Be that as it may, for the poor and the marginalized, local governance harnessing people's initiative from below and utilizing local information regarding resources, market and even technical knowhow, was the only source of hope and succour amidst the vagaries of global force. While the nation-state capitulated to the dictates of the Fund and Bank, accepting all their conditionalities at a time when it had lost credibility at home, decentralization of developmental programmes was the only face-saving device for the powers-that-be. Hence, the stipulations of 1992–93.

Decentralization as an alternative policy measure, a 'corrective' was adopted by democratic governments at the sub-national level in West Bengal, Kerala and Karnataka, among others. In West Bengal, duly elected panchayat bodies had begun to function since 1978 under the Left Front regime. The planning process was made to follow a 'bottom-up' rather than a 'top-down' approach. By now, 16 per cent of total revenues of the state of West Bengal are marked as entitlements of the panchayats and municipalities to be distributed according to specific criteria amongst them for undertaking schemes of development in their respective regions. Seventeen items like education, health, public health engineering, irrigation, agriculture, etc. have been assigned to the local self-governing institutions in the state. Weaker segments of society, including the SCs and STs and women, have been assigned special roles in local-level development programmes. It is to be remembered that this move towards decentralization predated India's economic reforms and was not initiated as complementary to globalization.

II

There has been a vast array of literature on the functioning of the PRIs in West Bengal since 1978. Votaries and detractors alike have appreciated whatever achievements the Left Front regime has registered during the last three decades in the sphere of land reforms and empowerment of the poor and the marginalized segments of rural West Bengal through democratization of the PRIs, even long before the 73rd Constitutional Amendment Act came into effect. As the West Bengal Human Development Report, 2004 puts it, in the post-1977 era when the Left Front government came to occupy power, there was a major change both in the focus and the energy of land reforms. It was no more to be seen as a function of administrative meddling. The strategy of land reforms introduced by the Left Front government represented the outcome of the long period of struggle by the land-hungry peasants and social and political mobilization of the landless in the countryside. The protracted political struggles in rural West Bengal preceding 1977 provided the necessary social back-up to evolve a political consensus amongst large chunks of the middle and poor peasants, share croppers and agricultural labourers, bulk of them also representing backward communities like the Scheduled Castes and Tribes and minority community like the rural Muslims.[10]

Land reforms took shape mainly in the form of (a) redistribution of vested land and (b) securing of tenancy rights, which had already existed in law, through a programme of universal registration of tenants called 'operation barga'. The West Bengal Landholding Revenue Act (1979) and the Revenue Rules (1980), introduced by the Left Front government, provided for key changes in the share cropping system. These were in addition to two other measures of land reforms, namely, imposition of ceiling on large landholdings and reduction of *sub-infeudation* through the abolition of intermediaries between the cultivator and the landlord. The reforms thus initiated since 1977 were supported most effectively and consistently by the democratically-elected panchayats in tandem with local bureaucracy and with material inputs supplied through various administrative and financial agencies. According to one estimate, by 2002, 10.7 lakh acres of land were distributed amongst 26.66 lakh beneficiaries. The number of bargadars recorded around the same time was 15.04 lakh and the amount of land cultivated by them was 11.1 lakh acres; of the assignees of vested land (*pattadars*), the SCs and STs constituted 37 per cent and

19.31 per cent, respectively. For recorded bargadars, the corresponding figures were 30.51 and 11.03 per cent, respectively. Such access to economic resources in rural areas on the part of the poor and marginal farmers, the agricultural labourers and especially those belonging to the traditionally disadvantaged segments of society contributed significantly to the empowerment of the poor and the panchayats offered them an opportunity for holding on to and exercising such power. Post-1977 West Bengal with a decisive domination of the Left at the state, district and local levels of representative bodies came to be singled out as an example of pro-poor governance.[11]

Politics in rural West Bengal was controlled during the first two decades since Independence by the Indian National Congress through a widespread patron – client network with the landed gentry assuming the role of patrons who would deliver the goods to the rural underdogs in return for habitual loyalties to be encashed in ballot papers. The Left, occasional rumblings notwithstanding, would maintain a low profile in the village at least up to the time of the first split in the CPI in 1964. The process of what Arun Bose calls 'competitive mobilization' began thereafter as an offshoot of 'inter communist warfare', leading to a further split in Indian communism but also to increasing penetration into the villages as an alternative support base. Meanwhile, the Congress-sponsored 'green' revolution, by accentuating the gap between the rich and the poor in rural India, without mitigating the land hunger of the landless and the marginal farmers, created all the potentials for the 'green' revolution to turn 'red'. The Communists refused to miss the opportunity that had come their way and plunged whole hog into rural West Bengal, raking up the memories of the historic Tebhaga struggle and striving to build up an alternative power structure, opposed to the domination of landed, upper caste nobility, epitomizing rural leadership of the Congress. The process which thus set in and crystallized under the two short-lived United Front regimes during 1967–1970, picked up, after the five-year interregnum of Congress rule during 1972–1977. While retaining fidelity to its ideological moorings, the Left Front, and the CPI (M) in particular, has chastened its confrontationist stance for tactical reasons and concentrated more on programmes of rural regeneration through mass involvement effected through elected panchayats, taking care not to transgress what Atul Kohli calls 'the feasibility frontier'.[12]

Webster reported and evaluated the performance of two gram panchayats, situated in two different blocks in the district of Burdwan, during 1978–1990. He analysed the class-caste-gender composition of the gram panchayats in the three elections to the panchayats held in 1978, 1983 and 1988, respectively, evaluated their performances in respect of implementing various land reform measures and executing rural development schemes entrusted to them and finally assessed people's subjective perception of changes, if any, brought about in their objective conditions of life by the new politico-administrative activism unleashed at the behest of the Left Front regime in and around areas covered by his survey.[13] Endorsing the new perspective on rural development which calls for active participation of the beneficiaries in developmental planning from below, inverting the erstwhile relationship between the planners and the producers, and narrating the experiences of land reforms and rural development under previous dispensations, Webster offers insights into the quality and content of changes brought in. Putting the performance of successive panchayat regimes under scanner, he concludes that the tempo and zeal of the panchayat functionaries have begun to wane, resulting in a process of 'ossification' of existing social structures, by the end of the 1980s. This was evident from low participation of the illiterate, the low caste, and the women in panchayat meetings, leaving enough elbow room for the educated and articulate *babus* to think and act for them. An important observation made by the author is that the gender bias, rooted in the socio-cultural ethos of rural society, has continued to haunt and vitiate participatory democracy at the grassroots level despite intervention of the Marxists in Bengal.

Webster had written before the 73rd Amendment Act came into force but even after more than 15 years of reservation of seats for women in panchayat bodies, the scenario has not changed perceptibly with a few honourable exceptions, like the all-women gram panchayats in several districts of West Bengal and at least one all-women gram panchayat surviving more than two decades through open electoral competition for four consecutive terms at Kultikri in the district of West Midnapore.[14] Another interesting observation of Webster is the near rapprochement between local bureaucrats and ground-level politicians that has come about in course of gradual decentralization of power and devolution of resources from the centre and the state to the local panchayat organizations. It required strenuous efforts during the initial years to overcome reciprocal mental reservations of both and make rural development a cooperative venture. After a decade of induced honeymoon between the two, as observed by the author, the million dollar question is whether the meeting of minds did take place to the left of the administrators or to the right of the Leftist ground level politicians.

G.K. Lieten studied gram panchayats at work in a block in the district of Birbhum with his research queries focused on the changing interface between elements of 'continuity and change' in social-class configurations and political power structure in the village. In subsequent explorations undertaken by him, several other districts were covered and a full view of the performance of grassroots political organizations gradually emerged. In his early works, Lieten was both optimistic and euphoric about the Marxist experiments with rural development through a participatory framework. Lieten does not subscribe to the views of Ross Mallick and others that the Left has drifted, over the years, to a non-confrontationist posture, away from its erstwhile preoccupations with escalating agrarian class struggle. Rather, he finds the same 'govern and mobilize' strategy, formulated by the late Hare Krishna Konar, the chief architect of the agrarian programme of the CPI (M) in West Bengal, doing the rounds even at the present political conjuncture. Lieten underscores the fact that the Left is holding the office of the state government in West Bengal within the overall class structure of the Indian state and committing itself to the constitutional rules of the game. 'A more radical deconstruction of the property relations', according to Lieten, would 'have been synonymous with self-defeating brinkmanship'. What the policies and programmes of the Left could bring about instead was 'repeasantization' of a large chunk of the landless or landed poor people of rural West Bengal by way of reducing landlessness up to a certain point, effecting the changeover from a top-down to a bottom-up approach to rural development and reconstruction, increasing access of the poorest sections of society to the administration and last but not least, institutionalizing the 'partial disintegration of the traditional hierarchy' through elective panchayat machineries. On empowerment of the poor, Lieten's submission is that empowerment does not imply the appropriation of a larger slice of the cake by the rural underdogs, but refers to the extent of sensitization of the poor to the need to be vigilant that their rightful share is not illegitimately usurped by others with the backing of an almighty state. The objective gains, accruing to the poor, may be small in quantitative terms as it is bound to be, given the constraints of resources, but subjectively the poor gain immensely by raising the level of their consciousness and by uniting politically against those at the apex of the social-class hierarchy.[15]

Direct election to the panchayats along party lines keeps alive the process of competitive political mobilization of the rural masses and compels all contending political parties to catch up with one another in reaching down to the poorest of the poor. This 'catching up process', as rightly noted by Lieten, enables more and more SCs, STs, women and other disadvantaged segments of the rural population to move up in the political power structure no matter whether the sponsoring parties heartily desire it or not, particularly since the implementation of the 73rd Amendment to the Constitution of India, which has brought about a new social churning. This again has a considerable amount of destabilizing impact on prevailing class structure and in egalitarian social relations in the village. Viewed in this sense, the panchayats in West Bengal do not represent a mere change in the forms of patronage or tinkering with the delivery system of a welfare state. These are to function as an alternative structure of people's power bridging up the gap between state and civil society up to a certain level. Translated into reality, such innovation in the role of panchayats would facilitate participatory rural development, 'putting the last first', in Robert chambers' coinage, and making the 'people' the real actors, not just passive beneficiaries of 'development'.[16]

Critics have noted some snags in the realization of this objective. Over-politicization through regular and vigorous intervention of political parties viewing the PRIs as mere instruments to expand the control of party machineries and relegating in the process the genuine urges and aspirations of the common rural folk to the back-burner, have led to a situation where democracy is being replaced by centralism and spontaneous people's participation is given a go-by.[17] In a recent article on 'participation and development', Mohit Bhattacharjee has classified participation into (a) manipulative, (b) incremental and (c) developmental modes. Pointing to the ambivalence of the incremental mode of participation in which 'people are consulted in planning and implementation but not in the formulation of policy' and wherein recognition of the value of participation 'does not lead to any institutional change', Bhattacharjee argues that it is only in the third mode, i.e. developmental mode of participation that the people are no more treated as targets of development. They are the 'real actors', the 'agents' who are empowered through enhancement of their capability in a progressive manner. In his perception, 'involving the user group or setting of beneficiary committees, although useful, still falls far short of the developmental participative mode.

In the ideal participative mode of development, there is no power differential between the donor and the receiver, between the administrator, the representatives of the people and the people themselves who can freely come forward to air their choices and preferences. It provides the means for joint learning and action.'[18] Measured against such ideal parameters, gram panchayats in West Bengal are yet to evolve as institutions facilitating 'cooperative decision-making', taking gram sansads and gram unnayan samitis into full confidence. Two more issues have been identified by scholars requiring urgent and immediate attention in order that participatory rural development may be truly meaningful in West Bengal. First, processing and procedural reforms are necessary to free development from the clutches of government departments that invariably seek to put the departmental priorities above people's perceptions. Hierarchically arranged departmentalism makes local-level integration of functions all the more difficult. Secondly, resources, both financial and administrative, have to be transferred to the local level. At present, the panchayats get very little unattached funds. The funds which they can spend are almost without exception pre-allocated against identified projects. To really inspire the people to plan for their localities, unattached funds have to be made available to them. The appropriate unit for this is the gram panchayat. It is at this level that participative planning can be really effective. But the starting point has to be the gram sansad in West Bengal.[19]

III

Decentralization has a peculiar status in the discourses on globalization. Critiques of globalization look upon it as a safety device for the poor. Given the prospects of deindustrialization, unemployment and inflation, the survival of the poor depends on planned efforts towards sustainable development at the grassroots level. Panchayats in West Bengal, Gramin Bank in Bangladesh and local county township and village governments in China play a key role in building up survival and development strategies at the local level, neglected for long by the national or transnational policy-makers.

Now, interestingly enough, World Bank-sponsored 'theologians of the market place' also have turned out to be the staunch advocates of decentralization of economy and polity. Local governance involving public officials, NGOs, political and non-political actors provides a fluid and flexible setting that may be incorporated within the global economic network without much political cost. This has been the new line of thinking on the part of the neo-liberal political right to out-maneuver the radical or post-modernist critique of capitalist globalization.

The civil society, NGO-centric *mantra* in recent years has been advocating development through depoliticization of panchayats. Much curiosity is expressed by various funding agencies about the role played by local political leadership in making or unmaking of decisions at the grassroots level. The Left Front's strategy of recharging the old-fashioned village panchayats, the 'little republics', was basically aimed at realizing the diametrically opposite objective of democratization and empowerment of the marginal men and women through political intervention which would be the key, determining variable in harnessing rural development. Many non-Left political parties contested the elections to the panchayats no less seriously than the Left, captured power at all the three levels of the panchayat hierarchy and strove hard to prove themselves better performers in the field than their Leftist counterparts. Democratic ethos, therefore, struck deep roots in the villages of West Bengal, unleashing forces of competitive political mobilization.[20]

In placing rural development through Panchayati Raj Institutions in West Bengal in its contextual specificities, we feel constrained to reiterate the fact that the agenda of the Left, theoretically at least, was for democracy to precede, and not follow, development. Critics often point towards a negative correlation between development and democracy substantiating their argument with the examples of South-East Asian countries and contrasting the same with the experiences of India. Thus, South Korea with an authoritarian regime having no accountability to the common people is eradicating poverty and illiteracy in larger measures than India which, despite being committed to the well-being of the majority of her people whose support the political regime needs to be in power, performs much worse in combating poverty, illiteracy and ill-health.[21]

The West Bengal experiment under Leftist dispensation was marked by an attempt to reconcile democratic ethos with developmental urges, with a pro-poor political bias and a more responsive and less ambitious bureaucracy, with the Marxist parties playing a catalytic role with considerable amount of self-restraint. The experiment was not free from all hassles. The Left Front fought and won most of the panchayat seats in seven consecutive elections to the panchayats conducted between 1978 and 2011. But, it did not by any means enjoy a near monopoly of mass support in rural West Bengal. Even amongst a large chunk of the rural poor, a sense of alienation grew over the years, as the office of the panchayat had created a new babudom emitting upper-caste, *bhadralokian* ethos. Women were not given their legitimate share in the decision-making process even when they had the mandate to lead a gram panchayat or a panchayat samiti. With the tempo of land reforms slowing down from the late 1980s, poor and marginal farmers and agricultural labourers lost their erstwhile political militancy and the panchayats became just an instrument for disbursing doles and seeking return from its clients in the ballot box at the time of the next election. This change of perception on the part of the Left had its repercussions at the time of elections to the panchayats held in 2008. This was soon followed up by the Lok Sabha elections of 2009 in which the Left received a bad drubbing and a signal that its rosy days in West Bengal are numbered.

Post-2011, the theoretical debates and dialogues centring around participatory rural development will have to address two questions now under the changed scenario in West Bengal with a new political regime taking over. First, how can an effective strategy of decentralization of power and devolution of resources combat the neo-liberal market forces having a necessary proclivity towards recolonization of the worse half of the world? Second, how should democracy be made to work not merely as a tool or technique for administering and managing development but as an end in itself, treating the intended beneficiaries of development not as objects but as 'agencies' to actualize Amartya Sen's idea of 'Development as Freedom' and fulfill Amit Bhaduri's ideal of 'Development with Dignity'.[22] As elections to the panchayats held in 2013, an immanent contest for deepening of democracy at the grass-roots level is set in motion. With a rise in the tempo of political one-up man ship in more than 38,000 villages of West Bengal; a new chapter on participatory and pro-poor democracy might unfold itself further before the curious observers.

Notes

1. World Bank, *World Development Report 1999*, New Delhi: Oxford University Press, 1999.
2. J. Stiglitz, 'Participation and Development: Perspectives from the Comprehensive Development Paradigm', Special Lecture delivered in Seoul, South Korea, 26–27 February 1999.
3. A. Brah, M. Hickman and Mac an Ghaill (eds), *Global Futures: Migration, Environment and Globalization*, London: Macmillan Press, 1999, p. 4.
4. *Morning Star*, London.
5. S. Ganguly, *The Statesman*, 9 August 2002.
6. Deepak Nayyar, 'Globalization: What does it Mean?', in K.S. Jomo and S. Nagraj (eds), *Globalization versus Development*, New York: Palgrave, 2001.
7. Pranab Bardhan, 'Research on Poverty and Development', paper presented at the Annual World Bank Conference on Development Economics, World Bank, 1995.
8. Ibid.
9. Deepak Nayyar, 'Globalization: What does it Mean?', in K.S. Jomo and S. Nagraj (eds), *Globalization versus Development*, New York: Palgrave, 2001.
10. *West Bengal Human Development Report 2004*, Kolkata: Department of Planning, Government of West Bengal, 2004. Apurba Mukhopadhyay, 'The Left in West Bengal: Government and Movement (1967–1982) ', in Rakhahari Chatterjee (ed.), *Politics in West Bengal*, Kolkata: World Press, 1985; and 'Contextualizing Rural Development through PRIs in West Bengal', proceedings of the UGC Sponsored Seminar on Development and Participation, Belur: Ramakrishna Mission Vidya Mandira, Department of Political Science, 2007.
11. Ben Rogaly, B. Harriss-White and Sugata Bose (eds), *Sonar Bangla? Agricultural Growth and Agrarian Change in West Bengal and Bangladesh*, New Delhi: Sage, 1999. N. Mukherji, and D. Bandopadhyay, *New Horizons for West Bengal Panchayats*, Kolkata: Government of West Bengal, 1993. Also Anil Chakraborty, Apurba Mukhopadhyay and Debesh Roy, *Beneficiaries of Land Reform: The West Bengal Scenario*, Kolkata: Spandan, 2003. Also *West Bengal Human Development Report 2004*, Kolkata: Department of Planning, Government of West Bengal, 2004.
12. Apurba Kumar Mukhopadhyay, 'Changing Profile of Rural West Bengal', in A.K. Mallik, P.K. Pal and A.R. Ghosh (eds), *Education, Society and Environment*, Burdwan: University of Burdwan, Academic Staff College, 1996.

13. N. Webster, *Panchayati Raj and the Decentralization of Development Planning in West Bengal*, Kolkata: K.P. Bagchi & Co., 1992.
14. Prabhat Datta and Panchali Sen, *Women in Panchayats*, Kolkata: Dasgupta and Co., 2003. And Atonu Chatterjee and Apurba Mukhopadhyay, 'Empowerment of Women: Waiting for Godot?', in Harihar Bhattacharya and Abhijit Ghosh (eds), *Indian Political Thought and Movements*, Kolkata: K.P. Bagchi & Co., 2007. Also Alok Mukhopadhyay, Satyabrata Chakraborty and Apurba Mukhopadhyay (eds), *Gram Panchayats in West Bengal*, Vol. 1, New Delhi: Mittal Publications, 2012.
15. G.K. Lieten, *Continuity and Change in Rural West Bengal*, New Delhi: Sage, 1992. Also *Development, Devolution and Democracy: Village Discourse in West Bengal*, New Delhi: Sage, 1996.
16. Robert Chambers, *Rural Development: Putting the Last First*, Essex: Longman, 1983.
17. Moitree Bhattacharya, *Panchayati Raj in West Bengal: Democratic Decentralization or Democratic Centralism*, New Delhi: Manak, 2002.
18. Mohit Bhattacharya, 'Participation and Development', proceedings of the UGC Sponsored Seminar on Development and Participation, Belur: Ramakrishna Mission Vidya Mandira, Department of Political Science, 2007. Also Mohanty, Ranjita and Rajesh Tandon (eds). *Participatory Citizenship: Identity, Exclusion, Inclusion*, New Delhi: Sage, 2006.
19. Ibid.
20. Alok Kumar Mukhopadhyay, Satyabarta Chakraborty and Apurba Kumar Mukhopadhyay, 'Introduction', *Gram Panchayats in West Bengal*, 2012.
21. A. Varshney, 'Why Haven't Poor Democracies Eliminated Poverty', in Varshney (ed.), *India and the Politics of Developing Countries*, New Delhi: Sage, 2004.
22. Amartya Sen, *Development as Freedom*, New Delhi: Oxford University Press, 1999. Also Amit Bhaduri, *Development with Dignity*, New Delhi: National Book Trust, 2006.

CHAPTER 8

Capacity Building of Panchayati Raj Institutions

The West Bengal Experience

Debnarayan Modak

It is now a journey of nearly three decades and a half since the revival of Panchayati Raj Institutions in West Bengal in 1978. The state has been regarded as a role model for grassroots democracy in different parts of the country and beyond. When panchayat system was revived in West Bengal in 1978, it was actually a pioneering step. At that time, the institutions of local democracy were either on the decline or almost non-existent in many other Indian states. With the new experiments in Panchayati Raj Institutions (PRIs) in West Bengal and in a very few other states in late 1970s and 1980s, and also in a changed political climate, there emerged a new trend of revival of local institutions in general and PRIs in particular throughout the country. This new trend culminated in the initiatives taken by the then Prime Minister Rajiv Gandhi for adoption of 63rd and 64th Amendment Acts in order to give effect to the emerging ideas in his own way. Although the attempts failed for some obvious reasons, subsequently, the dream to give the PRIs and local institutions constitutional status came true in a sense in 1992 with the adoption of the Seventy Third and Seventy Fourth Amendment of the Constitution. It is well known that one of the basic objectives of the Amendments was to make the local governments 'self-governing institutions' by giving them certainty, continuity and strength in different ways.

Now, more than two decades have passed since the adoption of the Seventy Third and Seventy Fourth Amendment Acts and we have come across several experiments on revitalizing local institutions throughout the country. Over the years, the mandatory provisions of the Constitution have, by and large, been implemented by almost all the states through 'conforming legislations' and related administrative measures. Theoretically, local governments have been regarded as the 'third stratum' of government with reasonable substance and content in terms of powers and authority as well as creating adequate space for women and marginalized groups in the federal set-up of the country. Decentralized governance was also extended to the Fifth Scheduled areas of states through the provisions of the Panchayat (Extension to the Scheduled Areas) Act, 1996. Several initiatives of capacity building of those institutions have been taken at different levels over the years. As such, the time has ripened now to assess the progress of different states in making local institutions really 'self-governing' by way of fulfilling the task of enablement and empowerment of those through devolution of *3Fs* (Functions, Funds and Functionaries). So far, various studies have been taken up in respect of the working of PRIs in different states. Some comparative assessments have also been made in this regard. It should, however, be remembered that the advances made in different states are highly uneven as regards devolution of functions and empowerment of panchayats, so that they could evolve as 'institutions of self-governance' and also plan and implement programmes for economic development and social justice. Naturally, the extent of capacity building differs from state to state, leaving enough scope for making comparative assessments. The present article, while concentrating on the initiatives of capacity building of local institutions in West Bengal, will also try to capitalize on the fruits of such comparisons in order to better understand the very nature of the advances made in this state in this regard over the years. But, before going into the initiatives of capacity building in West Bengal, and making a comparative assessment, we have to deal with some of the basic concepts to ensure clarity of thoughts in this regard.

Capacity Building: Conceptual Understanding

Capacity may be defined as the totality of inputs needed by an actor to realize its purposes. Applied to the local bodies, this will ensure that such institutions are able to function effectively as institutions of self-governance. The very term 'capacity' is taken here in a somewhat broader sense. It does not confine itself in assessing the capacity of the panchayat functionaries only. It tries to capture the whole gamut of the panchayati raj as 'institutions of self-governance'. Capacity is regarded here as a multi-dimensional attribute. It includes awareness, knowledge, skill, self-confidence, actions, etc. Building these attributes has become an integral part in the functioning of any system of governance. Capacity of such institutions can also be seen through different but interrelated aspects: intellectual, institutional and material capacity. *Intellectual capacity* implies capacity to think, reflect and analyse reality independently and in pursuit of self-defined purposes of local governance. *Institutional capacity* implies procedures, systems, structures, staffing, decision-making, transparency and accountability, planning, implementation and monitoring. It also includes mechanisms for building linkages with others. *Material capacity* includes material resources, physical assets, funds, ability, systems and procedures to mobilize revenues; and access and control over physical and natural resources and infrastructure; systems and procedures required for adequate management of funds and such infrastructure.

Capacity building is a long-term process of strengthening of an actor based on systematic learning of new knowledge, skills and attitudes. Like all learning, the actor must see the value of and take responsibility for that learning. This cannot be imposed from outside, but has to be developed from within. This does not, however, mean that there is no need for external intervention. Actually, there are many. Preparation of the actor to identify its particular capacity needs and motivation to take responsibility for learning those is a major part of capacity building intervention in such a framework. In order to assess the task of capacity building at any given point of time, one must keep in mind the *specific indicators of capacity building*, which may be known as *Capacity Indicators*. Those include: (i) conceptual understanding; (ii) awareness of decentralization legislations; (iii) extent of awareness of the powers and responsibilities; (iv) initiative in transforming local bodies into 'institutions of self-governance'; (v) planning for development. As regards *the need for external interventions*, the following aspects may prove very important: (i) Stimulation for preparations; (ii) Provision for opportunities of systematic learning; (iii) Accessing and making available resources; (iv) Supporting on-going and sustained capacity enhancement over a long term. Viewed in this sense, judging the capacity of a local body may mean an evaluation of its purposes at a given period of its life cycle. It involves change over time. One of the consequences of the above is an acknowledgement of diversity and temporal dynamism in the requirement of capacity of such actor.[1]

Constitutional Local Governance in India

With the passing of the Seventy Third and Seventy Fourth constitutional Amendments with provisions of establishing panchayats and nagarpalikas as 'institutions of self-governance' in India, the structure of federal governance in India has changed substantially from a two-tier system to a three-tier one with the Union, state and local level governments. A necessary condition for the transformation of panchayats and nagarpalikas into 'institutions of self-governance' is devolution of powers, resources and functions for capacity building among the elected representatives. One of the very important features of the new arrangement is the provision for ensuring representation of the weaker sections, including women, in the process of governance. The basic features of the constitutional system of local governance in India after the Seventy Third and Seventy Fourth Amendments may be summarized as follows: (i) constitutional status to panchayats and nagarpalikas; (ii) panchayats and nagarpalikas as 'institutions of self-governance'; (iii) three-tier local bodies at village, block and district levels, earmarking specific functions for each tiers; (iv) stability and continuity to local institutions with a provision for holding of regular elections every five years; (v) ensuring representation for socially oppressed sections through reservation of seats in proportion of their population; (vi) reservation of at least one-third seats to ensure women's involvement in governance; vii) providing the framework of devolution of *3Fs*: funds, functions and functionaries.

In this connection, it may be noted that the democratic base of the country has been widened significantly with the virtual adoption of the concept of the 'Third Stratum of Governance' through the Amendments. We now have 793 representatives (543 in Lok Sabha and 250 in Rajya Sabha) at the Union level (first stratum); more than 5,000 members representing 28 state and two Union Territories (second stratum); and nearly three lakh elected representatives belonging to the different tiers of local governments in the districts and below (third stratum). If we try to gather some more numerical figures relating to the representative bodies at the grassroots levels, we may see that we now have 537 district panchayats with 11,825 elected representatives, among whom 41 per cent are women, 18 per cent Scheduled Castes and 11 per cent Scheduled Tribes; 6,097 intermediate panchayats with 1,10,070 elected members which include 43 per cent women, 22 per cent Scheduled Castes and 13 per cent Scheduled Tribes; 2,34,676 village panchayats with 20,73,715 elected representatives of whom 40 per cent are women, 16 per cent Scheduled Castes and 11 per cent belonged to the Scheduled Tribes. Apart from the existence of the three-tier local bodies at village, block and district levels, if we take into account the scope for participation of our people through village assembly identified as gram sabha at the rural level or through ward committees in the urban settings, we may come to realize the extent of the opportunities created by the constitutional amendments in widening the base of Indian democracy.[2]

Given the scope for wider participation of the people in the democratic process of the country, the achievements so far may not be overlooked while making an assessment of the impact of the constitutional change. The important aspects of the change may be identified as follow: (i) increased participation of hitherto excluded sections; (ii) women's involvement in public life; (iii) developing awareness of the need for strengthening grassroots level democracy; (iv) popularization of the concept of decentralization and participatory development; (v) recognition of local bodies as nurseries for future leaders; (vi) rise of voluntary sectors/civil society organizations for strengthening PRIs/local bodies and local democracy; (vii) increasing concern about corruption and use of public funds; (viii) introduction of innovative ideas in participation: social audit, people's plan, lokpal, social capital; and (ix) de-mystification of governance.

Conditions for Success of Local Government

However, one should remember that the positive factors as mentioned above may not yield the desired results if the necessary conditions for success of local level governments are not fulfilled. In this connection, it should be remembered that Gandhiji's dream of giving 'power to the people' presupposes inclusive growth, which can only be achieved through inclusive governance. The key to this is an effective, well-functioning system of panchayats. As such, the functioning of the third tier of government crucially depends on the devolution of resources, transfer of subjects, and the passing down of administrative control of the civil servants. After the constitutional Amendments, although the states have met their legal obligations by passing conforming legislations, the transformations of the local institutions as 'institutions of self-governance' from mere state agencies varied across states depending on the willingness to give up power of those who draw power from the existing structures. Another necessary condition for the success of the local governance is to engage with elected representatives. There is great need for capacity building – in accounts, budgeting, monitoring and so on. It is only when elected representatives have the full responsibility of not only deciding on what work to undertake, but also to raise the finances for it, by taxes or otherwise, in a hard budget constraint situation, that changes become possible. Unless larger powers and resources are devolved and elected representatives are trained, local government in the true sense of the term will be a dream. Hence, there is the need for measuring the extent of awareness of the powers and responsibilities vested in the elected members of the local bodies.[3]

Accordingly, the conditions for the success of local government include, among others: (i) devolution of resources, transfer of subjects, and the passing down of administrative control of the civil servants (3Fs: Functions, Funds and Functionaries); (ii) capacity building – in accounts, budgeting, monitoring; (iii) need for measuring the extent of awareness of the powers and responsibilities vested in the elected members of the local bodies. Studies, however, revealed that, contrary to what is desirable, many of the elected members of the local bodies perceived themselves as the agents of the state governments, and the local institutions as extended hands of the state governments. Although many researches were undertaken as regards the social background and many other aspects of our local level representatives, we need to emphasize more now on their level of awareness and understanding of the decentralization legislations; their efforts in transforming the local bodies into 'institutions of self-governance'. A study undertaken among the elected representatives of Madhya Pradesh, Kerala and Tamil Nadu reveals that in Madhya Pradesh and Tamil Nadu, elected ward members are poor in awareness about their powers and responsibilities, but in Kerala it is different. In Madhya Pradesh and Tamil Nadu, panchayats are perceived as agents of state governments, whereas in Kerala they are taken as local governments. In all three states, panchayat presidents understand the legislation better but planning for development is a far cry as little effort seems to have gone into capacity building and devolution of powers and resources.[4]

Panchayati Raj in West Bengal

Turning to West Bengal scenario, at the very outset, one may have a glance of the length and breadth of the panchayati raj system as it prevails in the state at present. In West Bengal, there are 17 zilla parishads and one mahakuma parishad (17 plus 1) with 720 elected members; 333 panchayat samitis having 8,564 members; and 3,354 gram panchayats with 51,142 members. West Bengal also has a separate system of local governance for Darjeeling district under GTA in Hill subdivisions and three-tier panchayat under Siliguri Mahakuma Parishad. The total number of elected members of the three-tier panchayat bodies, thus, is 6,0426. Among the 60,426 members, there are 3,354 gram panchayat pradhans, 3,354 gram panchayat upa pradhans, 333 sabhapatis of panchayat samitis, 333 sahakari sabhapatis of panchayat samitis, 18 sabhadhipatis of zilla parishads, 18 sahakari sabhadhipatis of zilla parishads. Thus, the total number of chairpersons and vice-chairpersons at the three tiers is (3,705 plus 3,705) 7,410. Also, there are 13,416 *upa samiti sanchalaks* at gram panchayat level, 2,997 *karmadhyakshas* at panchayat samiti levels and 162 *karmadhyakshas* at zilla parishad levels. Accordingly, the number of other office-bearers gives us a total figure of 16,575. There are also 31,018, 4901 and 522 general members, respectively, at this upa samiti (subcommittee)/*sthayee samiti* (standing committee) levels in different tiers. Thus, the general members of the *upa samitis* and *sthaycc samitis* taking together all the tiers are 36,441. In addition to these elected components, there are more than 30,000 personnel directly associated with the three-tier panchayat bodies, either as PRI employees or as official members of panchayat samiti/zilla parishad sthayee samities and gram panchayat upa-samitis (being representatives of line departments).[5]

Panchayat Experiments: Roads Traversed

Keeping in view the all-India perspectives, it may be said that panchayats being a state subject, the state governments have the primary role in empowering, enabling and making accountable panchayats. Government of India has also an important role, both direct and indirect, in the *devolution of 3Fs* (Finance, Functions and Functionaries) upon the panchayats because of its basic responsibilities to ensure governance in accordance with the constitutional provisions and also because of the increasingly large fiscal transfers it makes to the states in the functional domains of the panchayats. As stated earlier, the emergence of the panchayats as units of self-governance requires adoption of appropriate policies on the part of the state governments, to make legal and organizational changes as well as to put in place several other associated processes. It is to be remembered that the quality as well as the pace of change envisaged by the Amendments are left to the state government by allowing it to decide the functions to be devolved to those bodies, resources to be transferred and tasks in building capacities to meet the requirement. In case of West Bengal, it is claimed that the process of empowering the local bodies was being carried out incrementally all along though the same got a boost with the Seventy Third Amendment of the Constitution, which recognized the panchayats as the 'third stratum of government'. However, there is a debate as to whether the capacity building should precede more devolution or the otherwise. It is claimed that West Bengal was adopting a slow yet steady path of gradual devolution of functions and simultaneous building of capacities for the panchayats to emerge as units of self-governance.[6]

One major area of change brought about by successive amendments to the Panchayat Act for strengthening governance by the panchayats was related to improving participation of the people. It was realized that it was not enough to leave the entire initiative to the people's representatives, *who are only the representatives of the people and not their substitutes.* Therefore, there was need for further deepening and strengthening the process of decentralization in order to make the panchayats effective institutions for economic development and social justice. The Amendments envisaged that the panchayat bodies interact with the people continuously and there were adequate interactions among various tiers of the panchayats. In this connection, it may be mentioned that while the PRIs in West Bengal struck their roots into the soil and started influencing decisions of the line departments in respect of their activities, which was supervised through various *Sthayee Samitis* (Standing Committees) of the upper and middle tiers of the panchayats, there has been little formal devolution by most of the departments. The panchayats are approached whenever any department wanted participation of the people in implementation of any of their plan or maintaining their assets. Such involvement, though not ideal, helped the panchayat bodies in acquiring some institutional capacities to think of holistic development and to act accordingly, though in a very limited way, with their own initiatives.[7]

The panchayats have been empowered under the state Act as also under the *constitutional mandate* to prepare a development plan with regard to resources available and also to implement schemes for economic development and social justice (Section 19 [1]) The State Panchayat Act, however, needs further amendment for accentuating the role of the panchayat as a unit of self-government for achieving the goal of human development, including economic development and securing social justice for all. The process was also facilitated by emergence of other institutions like the State Finance Commission to judge independently and recommend transfer of resources to the panchayats to discharge responsibility as well as the Central Finance Commission making specific recommendations towards transfer of funds from the Union government. A vision document adopted by the Government of West Bengal in 2009 claimed that those are the factors that have contributed to make the functioning of the panchayats more responsive, decentralized, transparent and accountable.[8] The document, however, listed some important initiatives that were taken by the then state government to cope with the needs as mentioned above. Those include:

(i) Provisions of six *sthayee samitis* (Standing Committees) were there at the zilla parishad and panchayat samiti levels at the time of the inception of the *new panchayats*. Some new *sthayee samitis* were added and some new subjects were also added to some existing *sthayee samitis* in 1992. Some alterations in the nomenclatures were also made in 1984 and 1997. Five *upa-samitis* were also constituted at the gram panchayat level in 2003;

(ii) Provision for representation of opposition members in *sthayee samitis* has been made in 2003;

(iii) Block Sansad and Zilla Sansads have been constituted as accountability forums for panchayat samiti and zilla parishad in 2003;

(iv) *Gram unnayan samitis* (village development committees) at the gram panchayat levels constituted by gram sansads as executive wing of the gram sansad, which may be regarded as the extended arms of the gram panchayat;

(v) Major initiatives of the gram panchayat should be validated by the gram sansad and on certain issues initiatives should begin at the gram sansad level;

(vi) *District council* for panchayats constituted with the leader of the major opposition party in the zilla parishad as its chairman in 1994, and

(vii) A realization that it is easier to amend Act and to make changes in the legal process but it is difficult to effect those changes through building capacities at all levels.[9]

Evaluations of PRIs in West Bengal

In this connection, it may be mentioned that the experience of the panchayati raj system in West Bengal is somewhat different from that of the other states in India. Ghatak and Ghatak, in their attempt to evaluate the experiments on panchayati raj in the state way back in 2002, noted that the experience of West Bengal panchayat system stands in sharp contrast with that of other states, and together with land reforms, it has been credited for playing an important role in the impressive economic turnaround of the state since the mid-1980s. It is also said that West Bengal is the first and the only major state which has had timely panchayat elections on a party basis regularly every five years since 1978, a year after the Left Front government was elected to power in the state. It may be noted that the Left Front government in West Bengal in its whole tenure of 34 years has not postponed or rescheduled panchayat elections even when electoral compulsions dictated otherwise unlike other states, including those where the panchayat system has otherwise made significant progress, such as Kerala and Karnataka. Quoting different studies, they added that for anti-poverty and employment generation programmes that are funded by the federal government and therefore provide a basis for inter-state comparison, West Bengal stood out in terms of reaching target groups and being relatively free of corruption. The involvement of the villagers in construction and supervision has led to dramatic reduction of costs in public projects (i.e. minor irrigation services) compared to the previous arrangements. Observing some of the important limitations of the panchayat system in the state, the researchers noted that 'West Bengal lags behind several other states today in terms of devolution of power, finances and functions to the panchayat'. They, further, observed that 'the extent of people's participation in the planning process is significantly less compared to that of Kerala, where under the ambitious People's Plan campaign launched in 1996 villages were directly empowered to prepare detailed development plans that are then put to vote in popular village assemblies'. Ghataks substantiated their arguments with the findings of different researches undertaken in this connection.[10]

In this connection, it may be noted that insofar as the question of 'institutional innovations' is concerned, West Bengal may boast of newly-created institutions, as some of the bodies developed in the process may help us substantially to achieve the goals of decentralization if they work satisfactorily. But the problem lies with non-functioning and mal-functioning of some of the very important institutions created as such causing enough harm for 'self-governing' panchayats: 'Legislation is no substitute for action ... In West Bengal, legislation is creating tier after tier of non-functional panchayat bodies without resources, functions and functionaries. The creation of *Village Development Committees* under the West Bengal Panchayat (Amendment) Act, 2003 is a case in point. It is a grand exercise in shadow boxing'.[11]

However, the most debated issue relating to panchayat experiments in West Bengal is the consequences of its party-based operation. It is said that despite substantial decentralization of power through Panchayati Raj Institutions in West Bengal, *it is due to its party-based nature, it becomes an instruments of patronage at the village level.* As a consequence, violent battles have invariably taken place during elections, as these are seen as necessary by all political parties to capture or retain hold over these institutions. Buddhadeb Ghosh and Girish Kumar unequivocally stated that one of the 'disquieting feature is the tendency of the political parties to create a patron-client relationship between the political elites and the masses'. Moitree Bhattacharya went a step further and said: 'Real authority lies with the appropriate party unit.' Harihar Bhattacharya also echoed the same feeling. In this connection, besides the debate on 'patron-client' politics, the issue of the 'politics of linkages' has also gained much ground. The debate as to whether the involvement of political parties is at all necessary at the local level got much prominence in this regard.[12]

As regards the controversy over the acceptability of party-based panchayats, George Mathew wrote that although there is a view that the involvement of political parties in the panchayat elections is the root cause of violence, it is necessary for a number of reasons. Referring to the CPI (M) arguments, he held that the official recognition of parties in the panchayat elections 'would put an end to the age-old tradition of rural coteries reaping the benefits for narrow sectarian and caste interests'. He also held the view that that 'the direct involvement of political parties could make the local level leadership more disciplined and responsible'. To him, the 'most notable achievement of the CPI (M) government is that clientism and patronage, based on religion, caste, communal or feudal interests, have almost disappeared from West Bengal'. He regarded it as a 'higher level of social development'. He, however, said that 'if it leads to violent tensions and conflicts, then steps are needed to stem the rot'. He considered West Bengal as still the 'role model for Panchayati Raj'.[13]

A very important study on West Bengal panchayats identified the key changes that followed the introduction of local government and noted that the 'rural population now got access to governmental instruments at the village, even the booth, levels'. It explains as to how the 'local governance got largely demystified and turned into a sphere of intimate interaction, changing such complex issues of rights and entitlements, bureaucracy and laws, and corruption and malpractice from obscure and unreachable areas of 'high' politics to subjects of candid discussions and everyday scrutiny'. Analysing the implications for such changes and identifying the distinctiveness of the experiments that took place in West Bengal, the study referred the pertinent issues as it viewed that the *success* 'is not without its own problems'. It noted that the very nature of 'decentralization has been partial to the extent that the gram panchayat failed to take up the function of local planning in any significant way'. It, further, elaborated the implications for the party-based politics that has 'created the conditions for political exclusion' at length. The very nature of the 'top-down format of reform' has also been identified as one of the negative factors. What is more important in this connection is the identification of some specific issues relating to the weaknesses of the West Bengal panchayats. Those include: (i) serious paucity of skills and personnel in running day-to-day activities and the lack of adequate infrastructure being the most important obstacle for smooth functioning of such institutions; (ii) the lack of transparency is telling in many places, signifying a kind of bureaucratic feeling; (iii) the mediation of political parties with a double effect, viz., facilitating political linkages on the one hand and aggravating 'political exclusion' on the other; (iv) tasks relating to resource mobilization ignored and the local institutions are turned into 'spending units' and not a 'generating one'; (v) the working of the institutions like village development councils is far from satisfactory. Thus, the very nature of 'incomplete decentralization' was unveiled in the study.[14]

Undertaking an overall assessment of panchayats in India, and raising the basic question: 'What then are the panchayats?', scholars observed:

Constitutionally they are institutions of self-government. In reality, they are not ... There are mandatory provisions in the Constitution as regards direct election to all the three tiers, obligation to conduct election every five years, reservations of seats and the position of chairpersons in all the tiers for women and SC/ST communities, constitution of State Election Commission and State Finance Commission, etc. But in respect of devolution of functions, the Constitution left the matter to the discretion of the state legislatures, the Eleventh Schedule being only in the nature of an indicative list of functions that could be transferred to these bodies. The states have taken advantage of this and have chosen to keep the 'powers and authority' of panchayats unaltered.[15]

In this connection, one may refer to a *Citizens' Report* for a comprehensive review on *Panchayati Raj in West Bengal* which was prepared in 2010 by the *West Bengal Social Watch*, a forum of voluntary organizations, and formally released on 1 July 2011 at Kolkata Press Club. The report was drafted by Buddhadeb Ghosh. It evidently reveals the fact that West Bengal panchayats function under several limitations. Rather than giving autonomous space to these institutions of self-governance, the state government tries to control the panchayats in several ways. Popular expectations, however, are getting bigger. People at large are gradually coming up with demands for better services and asserting their rights to be consulted on matters that directly affect their lives. The report also laments that the present structure of local administration cannot accommodate these demands. It advocates reform of the panchayat system by conceding autonomy to panchayats and empowering them in terms of financial and administrative resources.[16]

The report further revealed that when the panchayat system was revived in 1978, it was a pioneering step. At that time, these institutions of local democracy were either on the path of decline or almost non-existent in many other Indian states. However, the policies followed subsequently did not make panchayats self-governing institutions. Absence of autonomous functional jurisdiction and fiscal autonomy are the possible reasons. Several functions have been assigned to the panchayats over the years, but they do not have the capability to work despite having funds. They are not in a position to think they are autonomous. It noted that one of the most disturbing feature of West Bengal's panchayat system has been the tendency of political parties to control the elected representatives. Comparing West Bengal panchayats with other Indian states, the report stated that the panchayats here are assigned excessive works theoretically, but practically they can do nothing without express order of the state government. It is contended that Kerala is far ahead of all other states. As regards capacity building of the PRIs through training of elected representatives, the report held the view that the huge task of capacity building initiatives requires strengthening of the training institutes and centres used for panchayat training in the state. The use of ICT is also very important in making the capacity building exercises attractive and effective. The capacity building initiatives should also involve NGOs and academic institutions of excellence. One of the very important features of the report is the incorporation of the major findings in the form of annexure of the report.[17]

Roadmap for Strengthening Decentralization

One of the important documents published by the Government of West Bengal in 2009 made a self-assessment of the initiatives undertaken and listed the major areas of changes made over the years to make the PRIs more effective and self-governing. While delineating the success stories, the document admitted that 'it is rather easier to amend Act and to make changes in the legal processes but it is much more difficult to give effect to those changes through building capacities at all levels'. Keeping in view the limitations of the government on this score, the document proposed a lot of changes in different areas, which include:

(i) Amending the West Bengal Panchayat Act and Rules framed under it to enable the panchayat bodies to function more effectively as units of local government;

(ii) defining the functional domain of the panchayat bodies more specifically to enable them to focus their activities in improving the quality of services delivered by them and respond to citizens' demand for diversifying the areas of service;

(iii) improving capacities of the panchayats, including providing additional manpower support to the panchayat bodies;

(iv) putting in place a structured system for preparing and implementing participatory plans at the village level and their integration with the plans prepared by the panchayat bodies;

(v) taking up in-depth studies of various management practices of the panchayat bodies for business process re-engineering;

(vi) taking various steps for improving the ethical and functional framework for good governance and better delivery of citizen services.[18]

The roadmap suggested that in order to strengthen democratic functioning of the panchayats and to ensure popular participation and capacity building at the grassroots level in West Bengal, more concerted efforts are required in the following areas: (i) participation at the village level; (ii) organizing the poor for their participation in panchayats; (iii) strengthening functioning of the *sthayee samitis* and *upa samitis*; (iv) defining the role of the members who are not office-bearers; (v) increasing participation of the political parties in opposition; (vi) vigilance and redressal of grievances – District Council and Lokayukta; (vii) improving accountability and transparency; (viii) other ethical steps for good governance; (ix) interface between panchayat and civil society.[19]

Regime Change and the Panchayats in West Bengal

It is evident from the above that the panchayat experiments in West Bengal since 1978, with all its positive and negative virtues, have taken place under the aegis of the successive Left Front governments. Recently, the state witnessed a major political transition resulting in the end of 34 years' Left Front rule and the installation of a new government under the leadership of Mamata Banerjee. Naturally, people all around, particularly those interested in democratic decentralization, are very keen to see what policies the new government is going to adopt in this regard. Although it is too early to comment anything at the present stage, the indications manifest so far may not be regarded as encouraging on this score. The new government is yet to make a clear statement of its 'development path'. It is reported in the media that the government has empowered executive officers more and more at the panchayat levels to implement development programmes. If these bureaucrats would have the power to sign and release funds on behalf of the panchayats, a power thus far vested in the office of the *elected panchayats,* one may imagine its implications for local democracy. However, if it were an interim measure in view of the uncertainty caused by delayed panchayat elections in 2013, a glaring exception since 1978 for whatever reasons, one may understand the logic behind it. But, in no case should the very idea of 'democracy at the upper levels and bureaucracy at the local level' be encouraged. Even the argument that if the panchayat members are relieved of their financial duties, they may have more time to concentrate on the development of their constituencies, may not sound convincing.

In this connection, one may refer to the observations made in an article published recently under the title 'Weakening Panchayats in West Bengal', wherein the author noted that the new state government it yet to make its 'development path' clear. In absence of such declaration, the author questions: 'Will the TMC-led coalition government (Congress was in the Ministry then) seek to undo the past? Will it build on the institutional changes that have so radically transformed the West Bengal countryside, or will it undermine – or reverse – land reform and the panchayat system, as part of its new rural development regime?' Analysing the available indications, the author has actually portrayed a picture which may not be regarded as very encouraging. Reporting a field survey undertaken in two villages in Burdwan district (Raina and Kanksa) in 2011, it is stated that there was 'disruption of work in panchayats' and 'subversion of panchayat's decision-making functions' under new regime.[20] After so many twists and terms, panchayat elections and new panchayat bodies have been constituted now and it is expected that there might be a clear-cut policy prescription in this regard from the present government.

In Lieu of a Conclusion

Panchayat system in West Bengal is at the crossroads and the challenges of capacity building have become very acute today. There is no denying the fact that the success of the initiatives of capacity building of local bodies presupposes the acceptance of these as really 'institutions of self-government' not simply in legal terms, but in day-to-day practices as well. The question of 'political will' particularly on the part of the ruling elites is very important in this connection. Over the years, although no substantial departure at the theoretical level has been discernible, yet a shift of emphasis to control these for political reasons rather than making these viable instruments of self-government has become very much evident. As a result, the role of the panchayats as autonomous bodies has been neglected and these are made to act as institutions remote-controlled by the state government and higher level politicians. Even the attempts at reverse direction making these centralized and bureaucratic as before are seen from time to time. Accordingly, the tasks of capacity building have been seriously neglected and the panchayat institutions have acquired a somewhat stereotyped nature.

In spite of the 'political deficits' as mentioned above, there is no denying the fact that the panchayat system in West Bengal has demonstrated enough evidence of its potential to achieve the desired goals of democratic decentralization and popular participation. The success stories of the West Bengal panchayat, which have given it the 'pioneering status' all over the country and even beyond, should not be undermined in this connection. The rising expectations of the rural people, particularly in the sphere of 'service delivery', are to be seen from this perspective. Again, the growing awareness of the rural people in respect of their 'right' to be consulted in matters that affect their lives should also not be missed in this connection. The increasing demands for transparency and accountability are also very important in this regard. Hence, the tasks of capacity building of the panchayat institutions are to be viewed as 'the need of the hour' not only to honour the 'rising expectations' of the people at large, but also for the cause of advancement of popular participation, which is the hallmark of democracy and social justice.

Here enters the questions of 'reforming' the panchayat system in West Bengal to develop them as really a 'third stratum of governance' within the broad parameter of the constitutional directives and to make local democracy meaningful in the state. Granting real autonomy and devolution of 3Fs viz., fund, functions and functionaries to the panchayat bodies are essential for the purpose. Now, it is time to remember that we no longer enjoy the pre-eminent position, when compared to some other states in India at least on some important counts. Adopting appropriate administrative and legislative measures and initiating training programmes at different levels are no doubt very important in this regard, but what is more important is the 'political will' on the part of the ruling elites that can encourage people's initiatives in managing their own affairs. It is to be remembered in this connection that the task of widening and deepening of democracy and decentralization cannot go in isolation of the political process and the goals in this regard can be achieved only through concerted political actions. Hence, there can be no 'apolitical' solution to a 'political problem'.

Notes

1. Rajesh Tandon, 'Capacity Building for Effective Local Self-Governance: The Indian Experience', in D. Sundar Ram (ed.), *Panchayati Raj Reforms*

in India: Power to the People at the Grassroots, New Delhi: Kanishka Publishers, 2007, pp. 111–121. Also, http://leftgovtwb.blogspot.in/2012/02/weakening-panchayats-in-west-bengal.html, visited on 13 February 2013.

2. George Mathew, 'Panchayati Raj in India: An Overview', in Mathew (ed.), *Status of Panchayati Raj in the States and Union Territories of India*, New Delhi: Institute of Social Sciences & Concept Publishing Company.
3. V. Vyasulu, 'Transformations in Governance since 1990s: Some Reflections', *Economic and Political Weekly*, 5 June 2004, pp. 2383–2384. Also, V. Vyasulu, *Panchayats, Democracy and Development*, Jaipur: Rawat Publications, 2003.
4. D. Narayana, 'Local Governance without Capacity Building: Ten Years of Panchayati Raj', *Economic and Political Weekly*, 25 June 2005.
5. Government of West Bengal, *Strategy and Action Plan for Capacity Building of Panchayats and Municipalities in 11 Districts of West Bengal under Backward Regions Grant Fund 2006–07*, Kolkata: Department of Panchayat & Rural Development, February 2007.
6. Government of West Bengal, *Roadmaps for the Panchayats in West Bengal: A Vision Document*, Kolkata: Department of Panchayat & Rural Development, March 2009, p. 10.
7. Ibid.
8. Ibid.
9. Ibid.
10. Maitreesh Ghatak and Maitreya Ghatak, 'Recent Reforms in the Panchayat System in West Bengal: Toward Greater Participatory Governance?', *Economic and Political Weekly*, 5 January 2002. Also, Vikas Rawal and Madhura Swaminathan, 'Changing Trajectories: Agricultural Growth in West Bengal, 1950 to 1996', *Economic and Political Weekly*, 3 October 1998; Mathew George, 'Panchayat Elections: Dismal Record', *Economic and Political Weekly*, 20 January 1998; H. Gazder and S. Sen Gupta, 'Agrarian Politics and Rural Development in West Bengal', in Jean Dreze and Amartya Sen (eds), *Indian Development: Select Regional Perspectives*, New Delhi: Oxford University Press, 1997; and Dilip Mukherjee, 'Information Systems and Public Policy in Developing Countries', *Background Paper, World Development Report 1998*, New Delhi: Oxford University Press, 1998.
11. Debabrata Bandopadhyay, 'The Caucus and the Masses: West Bengal Panchayat (Amendment) Act, 2003', *Economic and Political Weekly*, 15 November 2003.
12. Buddhadeb Ghosh and Girish Kumar, *State Politics and Panchayats in India*, New Delhi: Manohar, 2003; Moitree Bhattacharya, *Panchayati Raj*

in West Bengal: Democratic Decentralization or Democratic Centralism, New Delhi: Manak, 2002; Harihar Bhattacharya, *Micro Foundations of Bengal Communism*, New Delhi: Ajanta, 1998; and Partha Sarathi Banerjee, 'The Party and the Panchayats in West Bengal', *Economic and Political Weekly*, 14 June 2008.

13. George Mathew, 'West Bengal: Still a Role Model for Panchayati Raj', http://www.pucl.org/Topics/Law/2003/wb-panchayat-raj-htm, visited on 13 February 2013; Also see, George Mathew, 'Decentralization and Local Governance: How Clientelism and Accountability Work: A Case Study of West Bengal', in Satyajit Singh and Pradip K. Sharma (eds), *Decentralization: Institutions and Politics in Rural India*, New Delhi: Oxford University Press, 2007.
14. Dwaipayan Bhattacharyya, 'Writers' Building and the Reality of Decentralized Rural Power: Some Paradoxes and Reversals in West Bengal', in Nirja Gopal Jayal, Amit Prakash and Pradip Sharma (eds), *Local Governance in India: Decentralization and Beyond*, New Delhi: Oxford University Press, 2006.
15. D. Bandopadhyay, Shaila K. Ghosh and Buddhadeb Ghosh, 'Dependency versus Autonomy: Identity Crisis of India's Panchayats', in Manoranjan Mohanty, Richard Baum, Rong Ma and George Mathew (eds), *Grassroots Democracy in India and China: The Right to Participate*, New Delhi: Sage, 2007. For the same article, see also, *Economic and Political Weekly*, 20 September 2003.
16. West Bengal Social Watch (WBSW), *Citizen's Report on Panchayati Raj in West Bengal*, Kolkata: A West Bengal State Social Watch Report, 2010.
17. West Bengal Social Watch (WBSW), Annexures I-V include: (i) The main findings of the study undertaken by the West Bengal Chapter of the Transparency International, India, and the Institute of Social Sciences conducted in 2007 (T11-WB2009) ; (ii) Excerpts from an article by Amit Bhaduri, 'Why an Alternative Model of Development?', in Manoranjan Mohanty (ed.), *India: Social Development Report 2010*, New Delhi: Oxford University Press, 2010; (iii) Excerpts from Nirmal Mukherji and D. Bandopadhyay, *New Horizons for West Bengal Panchayats: A Report for the Government of West Bengal*, Kolkata: Government of West Bengal, 1993.
18. Government of West Bengal, *Roadmaps for the Panchayats in West Bengal*, op. cit., p. 10.
19. Ibid.
20. Aparajita Bakshi, 'Weakening Panchayats in West Bengal', *Review of Agrarian Studies*, Vol. 1, No. 2, July–December 2011.

CHAPTER 9

People's Participation in Development through the PRIs

A Thorn in the Foot

Soma Ghosh

In the twentieth century, the 'Administrative State' started acting as the accelerator for economic and social changes; it also took the responsibility for providing modern amenities of life, education, health, and transport along with the opportunity for employment. In the context of the gradual expansion of state activity, public administration had to act in a way to embrace daily life of the individual as well as the community. In every nation starting from the capitalist United States of America to former communist Soviet Union (presently Commonwealth of Independent States) or the developing countries of Asia, Africa and Latin America, the need to extend the areas of public administration was felt.

Development and Role of the State

Growth of industrialization and urbanization, shift from individualism to social welfarism, change in the world of ideas and practice, two world wars and the resulting international situation, rise of several international institutions such as the World Bank, the IMF, vast increase in population creating scarcity of food, shelter and other essentials of life, etc. led to the emergence of 'Great Society', which in turn accelerated the growth of 'Big Government' in almost all industrialized and advanced nations, as well as in many developing countries. The fundamental principles of the welfare state led to the expansion of state's functions in the realm of administration. But this did not affect the level of participation in the political process. Welfare activities became mostly the government's headache.

New Managerial State

The striking change in the perception and practice about the role of state administration came with the advent of Thatcherite ideology during 1980s.[1] Thatcherite ideology proposed the introduction of the practices of management, thus bringing into focus the need for marketization of the state's governing and administrative practices, the transformation of public service individuals into 'entrepreneurial subjects' and the adaptation of the machinery of state to the mission of 'entrepreneurial governance'. This concerted drive towards 'entrepreneurialism', fitted to the new 'free-market', consumer-focused conception of 'governance' had made the market and market criteria the *modus operandi* of 'governance' and institutional life. The international monetary institutions, like the World Bank and the IMF, advanced elite ideology of neo-liberal economics and this started affecting the governance of the state. The state, now being the enthusiastic adopter of 'Public Choice' approach to the public sector, had to shift the balance of incentives from input to output, and to proceed for the contracting out of services, the spread of internal markets and outright privatization, re-constituting citizens as consumers or clients in the 'open market' and 'open society', ushering the way for 'New Public Management', instead of administration. This shift in the paradigm required a type of civil servants ready to abandon the principles of 'political impartiality' and to act in a more 'agency-driven' style.

Entrepreneurial Governance

'Entrepreneurial governance' endeavours to promote competition between service providers, favours the shift from bureaucracy to 'community', focuses not on inputs but on outputs, redefines clients as consumers, decentralizes authority through 'participatory management', and prefers market mechanisms to administrative ones. It promotes the idea that 'to govern better the state is to govern less but more entrepreneurially'.[2] Osborne and Gaebler suggested that governments should: (1) steer, not row (it is not government's obligation to provide services, but to see that they're being provided); (2) empower communities to solve their own problems rather than simply deliver services; (3) encourage competition rather than monopolies; (4) be driven by missions, rather than rules; (5) be result-oriented by funding outcomes rather than inputs; (6) meet the needs of the customer, not the bureaucracy; (7) concentrate on earning money rather than spending it; (8) invest in preventing problems rather than curing crises; (9) decentralize authority; and (10) solve problems by influencing market forces rather than creating public programmes.

For many years the conventional growth-oriented, top-down strategy of development was not producing the desired result; at the same time, there had been consecutive failures in the field of administration. The researchers in their urge to decipher the complex field problems found that most of the people were occasional participants in the political process. The main reasons detected were illiteracy, deficiencies and other kinds of pauperization, creating severe apathy. Several management strategies were suggested and many of these were introduced to fit local situations. Throughout 1970s, several community development projects designed to promote rural development were taken up and participation was conceived as an intervention methodology. The concept of 'entrepreneurial governance' tried to focus on the utility of decentralized authority, though the question of empowering the local communities for their own development had remained unresolved.

Good Governance

In 1990s, the World Bank came out with the concept of 'good governance', keeping in view the necessity of the common people's participation in grassroots decision-making process, without which, it was realized, community development would be ineffective. According to the UN, good governance has eight characteristics.[3] Good governance is:

- Consensus Oriented
- Participatory
- Following the Rule of Law
- Effective and Efficient
- Accountable

- Transparent
- Responsive
- Equitable and Inclusive

Good governance does not occur by chance. It must be demanded by citizens and nourished explicitly and consciously by the nation-state. It is, therefore, necessary that the citizens are allowed to participate freely, openly and fully in the political process. Good governance is accordingly associated with an efficient, effective and democratic government, enabling citizens' participation, responsible and responsive political leadership, enlightened policy-making, a free press, independent judiciary and a civil service imbued with a professional ethos. Thus, a bottom-up approach to social change, an efficient people-oriented government which is accountable, being able to involve all stakeholders, focused on development, are the needs of the hour.

In the era of 'post-modern' public administration, the common people are considered an integral part. With the advent of the concept of 'entrepreneurial governance', more stress is laid on the emerging necessity of people's participation in local development issues as well as in wider fields of governance. In this context, working towards empowerment of common mass is now felt indispensable, so that common people may exercise greater influence over matters of their daily concern and the 'entrepreneurial governance', along with its market orientation, can become responsive to the development of the community according to local needs. With this vision and mission, citizen's charters were introduced both in Britain and India in the 1990s as a tool to promote responsiveness in public administration. Thus, people's participation in local development issues as well as in wider fields of governance had become a highly important agenda for discussion, specially in the context of 'entrepreneurial governance' and 'good governance'.

Development and Participation

'Participation is involvement by a local population and at times, additional stakeholders in the creation, content and conduct of a programme or policy designed to change their lives.'[4] To understand the essence of the people's participation in decision-making and implementation process, it is worthwhile to mention the notion upheld by the People's Participation Working Group (PPWG), which was established in 1999 to promote the implementation of the Government of

Vietnam's Grassroots Democracy Decree. The principles of grassroots democracy at the commune level are: *'people know, people discuss, people decide, and people supervise.'*[5] This decree entails the right of people to be informed about local development policies and budgets, to be consulted about economic development and other plans, to participate in decisions about community contributions to projects, and to monitor the activities of the elected representatives at the local level. According to PPWG, 'Participation is a process to include and empower stakeholders in decision-making that affects people's lives and their development,'[6] which matches very well with the needs of the Indian society also.

The objectives of the PPWG are to promote:

- an enabling environment and capacity building for enhancing people's participation and
- promote coordination of activities for efficient use of resources.

This being taken as the modus operandi, one can identify the major determinants of effective participation:

- to create conditions for people to fully participate in the development process and to have equal opportunities,
- to strengthen the capacity and create opportunities for all people,
- to ensure participation in the development process so that they can enjoy the fruits of development.

There are three main dimensions of participation:

1. Civil Society
2. Decentralization
3. Democracy

In the planning and programming stages and throughout the implementation of development projects, important information is provided by the participatory process, which ensures the congruence between objectives of development and community values. It can be taken for granted that if the local people are more involved in the planning and programming stages and throughout the implementation of development projects, any change brought by the administrators for development will be readily acceptable to the community. Further, it will reduce the project cost due to utilization of local human resources in a more effective way. Active participation helps rebuild community cohesion and instills a sense of dignity in the community. People's participation keeps the governance legitimate.

It has been long cherished in the Indian society that the Gandhian ideas of *gram swaraj* and panchayati raj system can become the most suitable vehicles for bringing in the required social and political change by including all the stakeholders in the process of decision-making and public policy formulation. Hence, it is a highly appropriate and legitimate demand to revitalize the Panchayati Raj Institutions, make them efficient and effective vehicles of social, economic and political transformation and accelerate the process of development and make it more people-oriented. As Gandhi said, 'Panchayat Raj represents true democracy realized. We would regard the humblest and the lowest Indian as being equally the ruler of India with the tallest in the land.'[7]

Problems and Probabilities

People's participation in political and administrative process is not without hurdles. There exist several barriers; most important of them is the sluggishness among the people, which leads to apathy. The degree of people's participation largely depends on the socio-political orientation of the administration of the nation concerned. Previously, in most of the Asian and African nations in their pre-colonial phases, the administrators were mainly interested in collecting revenue and maintaining law and order; and administrative system was not at all accountable to the common people. After Independence, these nations, particularly India, adopted several positive principles for rapid socio-economic progress and modernization. At this juncture, probably for the first time, stress was laid on mass participation. To implement the scheme, Panchayati Raj Institutions along with several other community development programmes were introduced in order to improve socio-cultural life in rural areas. But all these efforts failed to produce the desired result. Being an early starter in this journey, the Indian people were expected to be more assertive about their rights, to be critically aware of their life situations and to be able to perceive the options for their own development. Unfortunately, however, in Indian planned development perspective, operative in the world of free market economy, still the central bone of contention is 'people's participation'.

Participation and Indian Political System

To facilitate people's participation in the democratic process in India, the Panchayati Raj Institutions were introduced in independent India, which became more relevant with the introduction of 'entrepreneurial governance' and free market society, reminding us of the urgent need to ensure balance between the necessity of linking the causes of globalization with those of localization. Actually, the concept of 'people's participation' is to evolve as the 'end', enabling people to steer the process of local level development, not just as the 'means'. At this point, 'it is imperative to revive panchayat bodies in the era of globalization and liberalization ... Thus, the rural-urban divide can be minimized using PRIs as an effective catalyst for making villages assertive, self-reliant and competitive'.[8]

In principle, the Panchayati Raj Institutions (PRIs) can be the effective bodies for local-level planning and implementation; but in practice, several factors have acted as constraints for political participation, perhaps visible in other states also. Most important among these are some crucial social and economic factors, ranging from discrimination in social status and income, lack of education, discrimination in terms of occupation, race, place of residence and most importantly, sex. Moreover, most of the panchayat members do not necessarily seek to achieve social goals and hence may not be sensitive to the needs of the people. Further, diversion and misappropriation of resources hinder the development of the remote areas, thus making people apathetic towards participation in the institutionalized development process. Most of the members do not have the necessary orientation in planning and implementation of development programmes. Often they are found to be uninformed about the local problems, specially the needs of the minorities, therefore failing to prepare priority lists relating to development issues. Over-politicization very often damages the spirit of decentralized management and people's participation in the development process. Lack of coordination and often blurred functional link between the various tiers of the panchayats in terms of administrative and financial control, as well as overt and covert bureaucratic interference, have made people's participation in planning and implementation awfully ineffective.

The Seventy Third and the Seventy Fourth Amendments of the Indian Constitution have tried to address some of the problems for decentralized management and people's participation in the development process. West Bengal has worked well in this direction since the years when most of the states of India could not even design properly about how to operationalize the decentralization process and ensure participation. However, this PRI system is still not functioning with desired pace and magnitude even in West Bengal due to lack of active intervention of the people from all squares of life and also due to narrowly-routed political currents and crosscurrents. The elite control (mainly politically coloured elite groups) over the system has not permitted it to be genuinely participative. PRIs have failed to ensure empowerment of the poor and the marginalized; neither could it ensure social equity and gender equity. Minorities and marginalized people often find it difficult to participate in the social and political process, which is governed by the dominant groups. Women and Dalits are the greatest non-participating majority. Dalit women are the most oppressed group in this respect, who are denied their right to voice their grievances against discrimination, thus making the need to participate in the development process a useless phenomenon for them. Women are the largest non-participating majority in West Bengal too, very much reflecting the Indian scenario with variation in degree.

Participation and Visibility of Women

Development must imply not the exclusion but rather the inclusion of marginalized people, their efforts, experiences, dreams and hopes. Women everywhere are generally excluded from crucial economic and political activities, and their role stereotyping compels them to remain dependent on men. The extent of equality of women with men varies in different societies, ranging from near equal to utter subjugation. The women are still marginalized, though consisting of nearly half of the human resource potential. Forced and unjust limitation in terms of making economic contributions by women has been found to be one of the reasons for their low status in society. Some have argued that economic contribution by itself is not enough for women to be allowed equal participation in the decision-making process of family and community. Women continue to face severe obstacles emanating from the structures of social and economic dominance in local society. Through the Panchayati Raj Institutions, over a million women have actively entered political life in India. As per the Seventy Third and the Seventy Fourth Amendment Acts, all local elected bodies reserve one-third of their seats for women. Women, thus, can have lawful claim over at least 33 per cent reserved seats in gram panchayat and municipal bodies.

Social norms in India strongly suggest patriarchy and the patriarchal society is not ready to see women in the decision-making position. Reservation for women can be a very good mechanism creating equal opportunity for men and women; socialization process and cultural orientation have always generated a feeling of insecurity among women themselves, leading to lack of motivation, which can be addressed only if women become visible in political life. Due to female foeticide and infanticide and issues related to women's health and mortality and education, women in India are in a submerged position.

Population Total	*Males*	*Females*	*Ratio Male: Female*	*Child Sex Ratio (0–6 age group) Male: Female*
1,210,193,422	623,724,248	586,469,174	1,000: 940	1,000: 914
Literacy Total – 74.04%	82.14%	65.46%		

It is expected that women's visibility in the decision-making process will give equal status to women. Women are supposedly more resistant to corruption. Therefore, the Acts may prove to be vital factors in restraining the growth and expansion of corruption. The basic assumptions on which this reservation policy has laid its foundation are:

- Women have the rights and obligations to take part in the governance of the country.
- They possess a diversity of talents and life experiences to assume such responsibilities.
- They have the knowledge and capacity to become competent decision-makers and to pursue gender-friendly policies.

Women's contribution to nation-building must be channelized properly. Although the percentage of women in various levels of political activity has increased considerably, yet women are still under-represented in governance and decision-making positions. Women are not asking for grace and charity. Therefore, reservation for women is not a bounty but only an honest recognition of their contribution to social development. The long-term plan to extend this reservation in Parliament and state Assemblies has failed. Women's Reservation Bill or The Constitution (108th Amendment) Bill, which proposes 33 per cent of all seats in the Lower House of Parliament of India and state Assemblies to be reserved for women, is still pending; though the Upper house,

Rajya Sabha, passed it on 9 March 2010, It has failed to get the mandate in Lok Sabha.[9] Every political party for the last few years has been assuring its support to the Bill and then a farce or dirty political tricks are being played out by some so-called libertarian leaders; some others don't hesitate to jump into the well of the House and tear copies of the Bill. Then the House gets adjourned, the Bill is thrown into the dustbin, till it is revived in subsequent years and revolves in the same cycle.

The question is, whether reservation in panchayat bodies has brought about any change in the perception of the society? It is freely admitted by all parties that because of the inbuilt prejudice against women, male candidates enjoy an unfair advantage in elections. In the reserved seats, in most of the cases, women are represented only by name, not by their own capacities. It was expected that reservation for women would make an avenue for more women to enter politics, which in turn would help check the muddy politics that the menfolk have brought about; it would bring a new orientation to political life and also help in removing the criminal-politician nexus. But planting puppets in the democratic bodies can never ensure empowerment and can never bring a fresh air of thought in the political climate. It is not enough to talk about removing discrimination against women and establishing gender equality. New mechanisms for the social, political and economic advancement of women must be invented so as to generate social awareness on gender issues, without which participation of half of the society will always remain a myth. Women have been suppressed for ages and their rights forcibly denied and privileges taken away from them, but the solution does not lie in sending some women to democratic institutions on preconditions.

There has been an increase in representation of women in the panchayati raj system in the past 10 years, the Rajya Sabha was informed. The percentage of women representatives at gram panchayat level in 2010 was 38.4 as compared to 31.37 per cent in 2000. Then Rural Development Minister Vilasrao Deshmukh said that their representation in panchayat samiti level rose from a mere 20.71 per cent in 2000 to 37.19 per cent in 2010 while in the zilla parishad level, it stood at 35.8 per cent.[10] Some states, including Bihar, Kerala and Tripura, have already introduced 50 per cent reservation for women in their three-tier panchayat system. Can any such attempt bring about any change in practice?

Traditional patriarchal norms are still relegating women to secondary status within the household and workplaces, including panchayats, even when the panchayats are headed by the women leaders. Women are never decision-makers because of hierarchical family structure. They never experience handling of business and finance; They are not supported by their families in promoting economic activities in particular (mainly organized sector); but always only viewed as reproducers and home managers. No or low income and consequently, no or low investment capacity. Fear of failure and success, fear of neglect of family and children due to busy schedule, low education leading to low confidence-level, strong objection from the family and community, etc. have been the major de-motivating factors for women to participate in the political and development process.

The issue of poverty, particularly affecting women from economically and socially marginalized groups, and the broader issue of human rights violations affecting all groups of women raise questions on the working viability of the women panchayat members on the outcome of the reservation. There are certain other grave issues, like male resistance to women to exercise power, upper caste resistance to Dalit women occupying public positions, women's lack of knowledge about functioning of governmental institutions and their limited access to literacy, numeric and other functional skills, their early marriage and early motherhood and over and above, a strong 'son preference', which make it difficult for women to establish their own security and autonomy. Therefore, mere reservation can lead us nowhere, excepting some political gains for the local political leaders who eat the fruits without adding due and responsible effort for it. Kemal Dervis, UNDP Administrator, observed on 6 September 2005, 'As we move forward with the implementation of the MDGs (Millennium Development Goals), it is important that we are fully committed to investing in policies and programmes that empower women and promote gender equality.'

A few examples may also be cited where all-women gram panchayats were introduced and they performed well, but faced typical experiences. A study conducted in Maharashtra before and after the Seventy Third Amendment in 1992 presents a unique state of affairs in empowerment and reflects the social milieu and the attitude of male members of the family towards the issue of women's participation in social activities. It narrates how when a village woman once asked her husband if she could attend a training camp on panchayats, he retorted, 'And who will make the chapatis?'[11]

In an account on Nimbut village,[12] 'If I Can Run the House, Why Not a Panchayat?' has been cited, which unveils a unique example of an effective 'All-Women Panchayats in Maharashtra'. The author writes that when Nimbut elected 13 women to its panchayat in 1963 – the first known all-women panchayat in Maharashtra – panchayati raj was itself a relatively new concept. Most states had passed legislation to establish panchayats only in 1959, two years after the Balwantray Mehta Committee Report of 1957 had emphasized the need for 'democratic decentralization'. The author subsequently focuses on another enabling factor, i.e. family support. Padmavati Ramchandra Kare, sarpanch in Mauje Rui[13] (Indapur tehsil), backed by her supportive family, started forming her panel. Maratha women were not encouraged by their men, so Dhangar women joined her and supported her in standing at the election. The author also narrates the story of uplifting of Padmavati on the backdrop of family support; her husband, Ramchandra Kare used to make 'poli bhaji' (chapati and a vegetable dish), bathe the children, feed and drop them to school, when Padmavati had to go for days at a time to meet the mamlatdar at Indapur; people were always critical on the issue and he was identified as the sarpanch's husband. Finally, Ramchandra told her, 'Do what you like, so long as you mind the kids.' Following Mauje Rui's success, several other all-women panchayats were set up in that state. Among them was the one in Ralegaon Shindi in Ahmednagar district which had shown how women could effect social change in a village. In all local self-government bodies, 50 per cent of the seats were reserved for women. Several villages also had all-women gram panchayat.

West Bengal's first all-women gram panchayat in Kultikri performed well. Kultikri is an insignificant and backward village in the tribal-dominated Jhargram sub-division of West Midnapore. The emergence of Kultikri has added a new dimension to the democratic decentralization of power at the grassroots level in the state. Moreover, it has also strengthened, at least theoretically, the very purpose of the 73rd Amendment, that is, political empowerment of rural women. Till August 1994, 53 people were given IRDR loans. The DWCRA scheme, though introduced in 1990, did not make much headway. However, the present gram authorities have set up a basket manufacturing centre at Phulbani with 20 members. Orchards were set up on 28 acres of land. Kultikri has taken a leading role in the district's literacy campaign.

Previously, out of a population of 7.685, 1.854 were illiterate. In the 1992 literacy evaluation, 1,608 were brought to the evaluating centres, of which 1.010 passed the tests and were promoted to post-literacy centres. The gram panchayat has been able to bring electricity to the subsidiary health centre and is now trying to equip it with a new labour room. Tribals are being taught at the PLCs the harmful effects of using contaminated water and the necessity of having their children properly inoculated.[14] There are a hundred positive stories of women who, having powered their way into officialdom, are now ensuring that devolution of power works at the ground level.

There are failures too. Even if some determined and confident women have been able to fight against the obstructions of society or family to come up in power ladder, their biggest challenge remains on how to cope with the problem of some state governments' deliberate attempts of setting up alternative machinery to curtail their powers. This is not, however, an attempt to furnish an account of success or failures; rather, it is an attempt to explain that by default any such instance may be the source of inspiration; but these exceptional or artificially grounded examples never indicate the success of the movement for empowerment of women. If it would have been so, they could have made their way to the Legislative Assemblies or Parliament without waiting for the reservation Bill to be accommodated by the male pillars of the patriarchal society.

What really matters is a candidate's merit and self-assertion about their rights, not sex. Sexual discrimination against women stems from the notion that one's sex determines one's identity. The outlook is that a man is superior to a woman, not because of considerations of merit or thought, but by anatomical considerations. The enforcement of such belief-systems upon women is carried out by persuasion, blackmail, threat of physical violence and sometimes direct bodily or psychological injury. Women's Reservation Bill proposes to fight injustice, but actually it is feeding the prejudices of the patriarchal sections of society. Supporting such a Bill may mean that women are still to fall pray to the charity of the patriarchal society and polity, as politics is still men's business; men will decide what they will donate, to whom and how.

Capacity Building of Local-Level Women

Capacity building of local-level women leaders should be the primary objective of the state, so as to ensure participation of women in greater numbers and with assured quality. Despite formal legal restraints, official protocol and local political pressure, the bureaucrats (or 'Sala' officers, to use Riggsian terminology, in the developing countries) in managerial level in district administration may take steps to undertake and promote socio-economic and legal justice for women of all sections with a special emphasis on backward section of the women, to the aged, sick, helpless and destitute widows and distressed women. They may try to educate these women and to conduct vocational and professional training for the self-sufficiency of the poor women and assist them for self-employment or may recommend for their rescue and rehabilitation. They may also take steps to arrange homes for the destitute and the homeless aged women of the society. There is a need to enhance women's access in the production process, to enhance women's access to productive endowments, to provide them with suitable work conditions so as to increase productivity, both qualitative and quantitative, to expand women's access in the commodity and labour markets, to enhance their ability to bargain, to expand women's ability to gain control over their income, their bodies, motherhood, sex and their identities, so that they can come out of their isolation and use their collective strength, to build their capacity to enable them to have access to the domain of political power.

These can be done by helping to create

- a negotiating space for the physical presence of women, specially those from the most marginalized and oppressed sections, in capacity building efforts;
- ensuring legitimacy of capacity building efforts and ensuring women's active participation in capacity building and in the development programmes;
- creating awareness about women's control over their body, sexuality and property
- encouraging women's agencies and enhancing their ability to further their own identity;
- encouraging competition in the domain of rural micro, tiny, small and medium-scale enterprises, so that they can withstand global competition;
- encouraging decentralization leading to empowerment;
- evolving a process of gaining control over ideology and the resources which determine power;

- changing the nature and directions of systematic forces which marginalize women in a given context;
- enhancing confidence and knowledge; and
- enabling to gain different identity within families and ensuring more influence and recognition in the communities.

These can be done by organizing workshops, especially cross-sectoral workshops, to build conceptual clarity on gender issues on leadership, advocacy, negotiation and overcoming resistance. Apart from structured training programmes, all-field interactions are opportunities for learning.

Since the 1980s, local government institutions and self-help groups have opened spaces for their participation, whereby poor women can reflect on their situation, can identify problems and can fight against injustice. District administrative apparatus is expected to provide positive help by sharing their expertise, skill and by virtue of having a better access in the state and central governmental decision-making level. The newly-emerging managerial state wants every citizen to become a very good consumer having a good bargaining skill and having a control over his/her own destiny. It becomes convenient for the managerial state if every citizen becomes his/her own kind of 'manager', because in that case the state can become more market-oriented, shifting its eyes from social utility functions.

In its resolution (A/RES/50/225) of May 1996, the General Assembly of the United Nations recognized that

> there is a need for public administration systems to be sound, efficient, and well equipped with appropriate capacities and capabilities through promotion of the role and involvement of women in public administration, development of cross-sectoral gender sensitive and multidisciplinary capabilities, which supports all phases of the development process as well as the promotion of opportunities for all to participate in all spheres of the public sector.

Now, it seems to be the most effective way to promote women as micro entrepreneurs for which district administration may take initial measures for the

- promotion of savings and credit Self-Help Groups
- transformation of society by encouraging the attitude to work in collectives
- organizing Entrepreneurship Development Programmes (EDPs) for women

- channelizing bank schemes for micro-enterprises through SHGs.

If these processes and mechanisms are to be multiplied on a wider scale, these will have to be institutionalized. The multiplication process requires a major political commitment by the state to provide the necessary political space and a policy framework for a sensitive support mechanism. This will call for, among other things, simplification of ground rules that would facilitate participation of grassroots level organizations in the development process, bringing about flexibility and dynamism among the providers of public services, and orienting the local self-governing institutions to be sensitive to the needs of the poor and disadvantaged.

Sustenance of this process and eventual involvement of the women in it will be possible, if mechanisms for proper and timely *information exchange, conflict resolutions, joint actions, strategic planning* and *enhancement of public awareness* and *education* can be effectively introduced. The primary objective of such mechanisms should be to frame simple gender-friendly rules, laws, guidelines, etc. to guide women and in a wider sense the individuals and groups to act for self-development on the one hand and for local development on the other.

The Lithuanian Institute of Public Administration has been offering a programme entitled 'Equal Opportunities of Women and Men in Public Administration'. The Division for the Advancement of Women held an Expert Group Meeting on national machineries in collaboration with the Economic Commission for Latin America and the Caribbean (ECLAC) in September 1998. The major goal was to make the participants acquainted with the relevant measures and programmes on the part of the government and in particular with the activities of the inter-ministerial Commission of Equal Opportunities. Gender equality issues pertaining to the municipal level of governance are separately discussed in terms of the prospects of administration improvement. The main target groups of the courses include: heads of the departments of state institutions and their deputies, those in charge of developing and carrying out programmes of in-service training, and those involved in shaping personnel policies. On the governmental level, any such attempt will definitely take us a step ahead towards genuine participation by both men and women in the developmental and administrative process and thus will ensure effective involvement of the people in the development process.

Notes

1. Apparently simply a neutral social technology, New Managerialism is really the vehicle by means of which neo-liberal ideas actually inform institutional practices.
2. David Osborne and Ted Gaebler, *Reinventing Government: How the Entrepreneurial Spirit is Transforming the Public Sector*, New Delhi: Prentice Hall, 1992.
3. UNESCAP, *What is Good Governance?*, United Nations Economic and Social Commission for Asia and the Pacific, 2009.
4. Furqan Ahmad, 'People's Participation in Development Administration: Problems and Prospects', *Indian Journal of Public Administration*, Vol. LVIII, No. 4, October–December 2012, p. 698.
5. The Government Decree No. 29 of 1998 with later amendments promulgated through the Decree No. 79 of 2003.
6. VUFO – NGO Resource Centre Vietnam, *PPWG Overview*, www.ngocentre.org.vn/node/121.
7. M.K. Gandhi, *Village Swaraj*, Ahmedabad: Navajivan Trust, 1962, p. 71.
8. K. Usha, 'Role of Panchayat Bodies in Rural Development: How to Improve the Functioning of Panchayat Institutions', *Indian Journal of Public Administration*, Vol. LVIII, No. 4, October–December 2012, p. 717.
9. 'Rajya Sabha Passes Women's Reservation Bill', *The Times of India*, 9 March 2010, http://timesofindia.indiatimes.com/ india/Rajya-Sabha-votes-on-Womens-Reservation-Bill/articleshow/5663003.cms
   (Note: Now the Bill stands lapsed to be passed to dissolution of the 15th Lok Sabha in May 2014. — editor)
10. 'Elected Women, Panchayati Raj, Ten Years', New Delhi, 15 March 2011, http//zee news.india.com.
11. Bishakha Datta (ed.), *And Who Will Make the Chapatis?: A Study of All-Women Panchayats in Maharashtra*, Introduction, Kolkata: Stree, 1998, p. ix.
12. Meenakshi Shedde, 'If I Can Run the House, Why Not a Panchayat', in Bishakha Datta (ed.), *And Who Will Make the Chapatis?: A Study of All-Women Panchayats in Maharashtra*, Introduction, Kolkata: Stree, 1998, p. 1.
13. Meenakshi Shedde, 'Do What You Like, So Long as You Mind the Kids', in Bishakha Datta (ed.), *And Who Will Make the Chapatis?: A Study of All-Women Panchayats in Maharashtra*, Introduction, Kolkata: Stree, 1998, p. 6.
14. Asim Mukhopadhayay, 'Kultikri: West Bengal's Only All-Women Gram Panchayat', *Economic and Political Weekly*, Vol. XXX, No. 22, 3 June 1995, p. 1285.

References

Datta, Prabhat, *Anchalik Rajniti Unnayan O Bikendrikaran*, Kolkata: Mitram, 2009.

Datta, Prabhat, *Public Administration and the State*, New Delhi: Uppal Publishing House, 1989.

Ghosh, Soma, *Jana Prasashan: Tatto O Pryog*, Kolkata: Progressive Publishers, 2011.

Harper, M., *Empowerment through Enterprise: A Training Manual for Non-government Organisations*, New Delhi: Oxford and IBH Publishing, 1995.

Human Development Report 1993, New Delhi: Oxford University Press, 1993.

Kurukshetra: A Journal on Rural Development, Vol. 54, No. 1, November 2005.

Parker, A.R., *Another Point of View: A Manual on Gender Analysis Training for Grassroots Workers*, New York: UNIFEM, 1993.

Raj, M.C., *Participatory Training Methodology: A Process and Content for Empowerment*, Chennai: Dialogue Group, 1995.

Sanyal, B.M., *India, Decentralised Planning: Themes and Issues*, New Delhi: Concept Publishing Company, 2001.

Sarkar, Siuli, *District Politics and Administration*, New Delhi: Scholar, 2010.

Sarkar, Siuli, *Public Administration in India*, New Delhi: PHI Publishers, 2010.

Sen, Manab, *A Study of Self Help Groups in West Bengal*, Kolkata: Dasgupta, 2005.

UNDP Reports 2001, 2006.

World Development Report: Equity and Development 2006, New Delhi: Oxford University Press, 2006.

World Development Report: Making Services Work for Poor People, New Delhi: Oxford University Press, 2004.

Yojana: A Development Monthly, Vol. 49, June 2005.

III

Issues in Decentralization and Panchayati Raj

CHAPTER 10

The Panchayati Raj and the Bureaucracy

An Insider's Recollections from West Bengal

Alok Kumar Mukhopadhyay

To begin with, a caveat will, perhaps, be in order: what follows has no pretensions to an academic paper. All attempts to explain the phenomena discussed here will be bypassed as far as possible. They will be presented in the form of a narrative based on the experience of an executive in the middle-tier as he grew up in government service. This will be designed as nothing more than a record of events that led to a major shift in the functioning of the socio-political life of rural West Bengal in the larger background of the country with the task of collating them left for the scholars. Some observations cannot, however, be helped; but these are also a part of looking at the process purely from a personal point of view.

Prelude

The journey of panchayats from Article 40 (1) of the Constitution of India to the Seventy Third Amendment in 1992 stretches over a period of roughly forty-four years. The years intervening saw various experiments in Indian states, some taking strides ahead of others, some others maintaining *status quo*. It was also during this period that the forerunners lost their initial zeal with their early efforts ending in smoke. The demand for decentralization, however, continued and there was no dearth of debates among academics and politicians on the possible shape of panchayats. The change of guard at the national capital also made its own contribution.

It was in this background that West Bengal started its experiments in 1978 following a change of government in the preceding year. The first panchayat general elections were held on the basis of universal adult suffrage. The system that emerged was carried through successive elections at regular intervals, accommodating itself comfortably with the constitutional mandate.

The story of the insider begins towards the end of the sixties of the last century immediately after he joined district administration. A short-term posting to a development block revealed that there was a four-tier panchayat system in the state: the Zilla Parshad at the district level, an Anchalik Parishad coterminous with the block, and below it the Anchal Panchayats, subsequently renamed as Gram Panchayats, and Gram Panchayats at the sub-Anchal level. Regular elections were a far cry, not to speak of an election based on universal suffrage. Development expenditure for any tier of panchayats was infinitesimally small. Whatever development work could be taken up was entrusted to the block set-up, and not to the panchayats. The line of communication with the people ended with a village-level worker assigned to an Anchal Panchayat, and this official with the good offices of the Anchal Pradhan, the head of the Anchal Panchayat, used to be the link between the government on the one hand, and the people at that level on the other. The strength of the population in this case was around 10,000. Individual members other than the Pradhan had no existence for any practical purpose. Even the Adhyaksha, the head of a Gram Panchayat of those days, was hardly known to the people. A three-tier panchayati structure was brought on the statute book in 1973, but no steps were taken to implement the provisions in immediate future. It was, therefore, the bureaucracy alone which could touch upon the life of rural people in spite of its limitations.

Emerging Tensions

The general elections to the panchayats in 1978 based on the principle of universal adult suffrage and with minor modifications of the West Bengal Panchayat Act, 1973 brought a sea-change to the situation. The office-bearers of all the tiers together with other elected members now entered into the picture as an additional base of governance demanding their share from the bureaucracy. The system that emerged had the district magistrate and the block development officer as the executive officer of the zilla parishad and the panchayat samiti, respectively. Thus necessary official support was made readily available to the first two tiers from the existing set-up, while the pradhan, the head of the new gram panchayat, was given executive power. It was expected that the pradhan and his team would receive guidance from the block office.

The most important opportunity that was offered by the system concerned the line of communication. Now, an elected member of a gram panchayat represented on an average 250 families from around the place of his own residence, and this implied that he could reach any person within his constituency in course of a short time in a day. He knew most of the persons by name and face because of sheer proximity. This was in sharp contrast to the earlier days when a single village-level worker, an outsider in all sense, had to struggle hard with a population of about 10,000 with whom he had no personal stake. From the people's side, it meant that they could act through their own representative living in the same locality, instead of rushing to the block office at the first instance. It was with this added strength that the bureaucracy, the panchayats and the people faced the devastating flood of 1978 and carried through the uphill task of rescue, relief and restoration work in an exemplary manner.

The second benefit that the bureaucracy came to enjoy was to be relieved of the unpleasant job of selection of beneficiary, relocating to itself the role of an umpire in the event of any dispute. As an off-shoot, this also provided a space for public discussion of local priorities. But then, there was the other side of the dynamics. The euphoria generated by uninformed pronouncements on democracy at grassroots level among a group of persons suddenly brought into the decision-making process led to a confrontation with the official machinery

To start with, each block office was decorated with a signboard of the office of the panchayat samiti. This was both necessary and desirable. What was totally uncalled for was, in some cases, an insistence on removing the signboard of the block office. Again, in some cases, not everywhere, the control of the official jeep was taken over by the panchayat samiti. The block development officers here became scared, and this led to an unpleasant relationship between the sabhapati of the panchayat samiti and the block development officers concerned. These were aberrations rather than the practice; even then, these instances created some measure of distrust in the lower rung of bureaucracy, and made a large section of young officers considerably skeptical. The persons above did not intervene presumably because the sentiment at the field-level did not matter much. A natural solution to the jeep question was, however, reached when it was realized that availability of funds for running the vehicle depended upon the initiative of the block development officer. For the signboard problem, wherever it existed, an order from the state headquarters had to be issued clarifying that the office of the block development officer was as much a reality as the other office. By that time, however, that problem became a non-issue. The scenario at the district level was totally different. Political leadership at the zilla parishad was mature enough to appreciate the age-old glamour of the district magistrate, and the district magistrate in turn was quick to cash in on a new found opportunity in settling his scores in many areas with the mediation of the sabhadhipati, the head of the district panchayat.

Era of Mutual Cooperation

Funds for rural development started flowing in large amounts since the 1980s and the same went on increasing every year under different schemes from the Government of India. This led to a completely new atmosphere where the panchayats, and also the bureaucracy in the field, could now bring a good deal of relief to the people. Apart from expansion of much needed wage-employment and self-employment programmes under different nomenclatures, attention was also focused on infrastructure development with funds flowing through panchayats. Agriculture received a major break-through with loudly acclaimed land reforms initiative taken up by the panchayats with active involvement of the bureaucracy. In spite of some excesses here and there, this was a big achievement reaching its peak by the end of 1980s. This was also the period when a sense of friendship developed between the panchayats and the associated officers in the field. Panchayats came out of their moribund status of the pre-1978 days to a vibrant entity.

The first two terms of the panchayats passed off more or less in a happy mood. With most of the panchayats led by the same political combine as that governing the state, there was very little opposition to the emerging practice. The voice of the panchayats controlled by parties not in state power remained feeble. Whatever frictions surfaced came from within the parties in the ruling coalition. There were some complaints of partisan attitude, but this could be tackled at a higher level, and also with the help of new-found friends in the bureaucracy. Free flow of funds also provided enough elbow room for buying peace. The threat of audit became an additional force to serve as a check on the gram panchayats where necessary expertise in handling cash was not readily available. By the time the country entered into the new economic order, the talk of democratic decentralization became loud through a lot of reports, meetings, seminars and field visits. Hospitality with the help of contingent funds became fashionable. Bureaucracy at all levels and panchayats at the upper tiers turned out to be members of a well-off household. Financial austerity, which had been a characteristic of public life in rural governance, started developing a serious cleavage within the system. Integrity took a dwindling turn, particularly at the grassroots level.

In the early years of the 1990s, three important developments took place. The government at the national capital established with doubtful majority introduced economic reforms in 1991 by opening up the economy through a policy of large-scale privatization, selective deregulation and entry of foreign players into the domestic market, a large chunk of which remained so far reserved either for the public sector or the domestic capital. The second was the demolition of the Babri Masjid in 1992, shaking the basic social fabric of the country. The third was the 73rd Amendment to the Constitution of India conferring constitutional status on the panchayats. It is generally admitted that West Bengal with a Muslim population of about 23 per cent survived the shock of Babri Masjid demolition mainly because of the strong grip of panchayats in rural areas. Bureaucracy was least prepared to tackle the sudden threat which could go beyond control had it not been for the panchayats to rise to the occasion with their mass contact in daily life. The 73rd Amendment, which required many states to reframe their panchayat Acts, could be comfortably accommodated in the West Bengal Act thanks chiefly to the practice in the state by the panchayats. The challenge of economic reforms was, however, entirely a different cup of tea insofar as it was not on the agenda.

All the three events had profound implications on the functioning of panchayats. While the event of Babri Masjid indicated the solid base of the panchayats with their capacity to mitigate social tensions in collaboration with the bureaucracy, the other two proved how the structure stumbled when the official line was organized with a different orientation.

Dilemma and Retardation

The central message of economic reforms was downsizing the government and in a way expansion of activities of panchayats and their constitutionalization served as a readymade answer. The statute came out with high ideals of making panchayats into institutions of self-governance. Subsequently, funds followed fanfares. International funding agencies became exceptionally panchayat-friendly. It was given to understand that the responsibility for improving rural life had now passed from the hands of the government at the Centre and the states to the panchayats, which were carefully advertised as the third tier of government. So long as funds were available, no one found fault with the idea. It was a fact that a lot of good work was done throughout the state both before and after 1990 under the leadership of panchayats, and their achievement was on a much higher scale compared to the days of the community development programme as implemented by bureaucracy alone. The institution of beggary almost disappeared from the countryside. And, if some individuals starved somewhere, it was surely due to the failures of the local panchayat. But none of these could absolve the state of its own responsibility to provide rural people with basic requirements of a decent living. The ideal could have been, therefore, the combined efforts of thc bureaucracy and the panchayats to strive for enriching the quality of life of these people. In a strange coincidence, the days since mid-1990s saw government officials assume in practice a different role. While people's representatives were called upon to ensure economic development with social justice, associated officers at all levels rose to be the final arbiters with funds, functionaries and a series of guidelines remaining under bureaucratic control. The officers decided what to do and how to do it with the instrumentality of government orders in all conceivable details. By the turn of the century, panchayats learnt only to parrot what was passed on to them. Officials in their turn changed their vocabulary in a fashion chosen by the funding agencies. Thus, the 'beneficiary' of the old language became the 'stake-holders', an improvement through a programme was termed value addition, and so on.

As a result, panchyats lost all powers of imagination even for the limited space they were left with. Once a pradhan of a relatively well-off area was asked how he could say who were the persons starving in his gram panchayat, and he replied that he would convene a meeting for that purpose. On the other hand, the panchayats readily succumbed to the emerging culture of consumerism. Of course, there were notable exceptions, but undoubtedly they were few and far between. Panchayats now had good office buildings with modern fittings right up to the gram panchayat level. There was no dearth of money for hiring vehicles and also for meeting other contingent charges, and government servants of almost all categories had their share of the amenities. There was plenty of money for implementation of schemes under different names, all carefully designed with detailed guidelines. Even funds released as untied grants under dispensations of finance commissions were subjected to bureaucratic value judgment.

All this was done in the name of democratic decentralization, and panchayats had no hesitation to gulp it down. A time was soon reached when the prime concern of panchayats was to receive funds, spend them, submit utilization certificates and face audit, and all this strengthened the hands of bureaucracy. The more the leakages, the merrier, for that again called for further intervention. It was time to talk about good governance!

Search for Good Governance and Dependency on Bureaucracy

The literature developed on good governance for panchayats required them to be transparent before and accountable to the people, and this brought in an over-shadowing emphasis on people's participation through methodologies developed by the bureaucracy at the state level. The simplest form of transparency indicated by the government in early 1980s involved disclosure of information through putting up a notice on the walls of the gram panchayat office. This was forgotten in no time. The Pradhan of Budhakhali, a gram panchayat in Namkhana, now under South 24-Parganas, practised the method sincerely, although he came from Opposition politics, and he won the next panchayat elections to become the sabhapati of Namkhana panchayat samiti. The West Bengal Panchayat Act provided for a platform known as the gram sansad, which consisted of all electors of a gram panchayat constituency. The gram panchayat concerned has to convene two half-yearly meetings of this gram sansad and obtain approval of their annual plan, budget and the audit report from the electors. This provision continued together with the constitutional requirement of holding gram sabha meetings with electors of the entire gram panchayat. The West Bengal Act thus sought to go one step further to ensure accountability almost to the doorstep of the people. If taken seriously, the gram sansad meetings could be the panacea of people's participation, and it showed excellent results in cases where political faith with bureaucratic zeal accepted the message. Unfortunately, for most of the actors, this was reduced to a mere formality. The government decided, it seems, to rely more on its own machinery rather than working through political mobilization. In spite of high rhetoric, the idea could not be sold to the Opposition through practice, and those in power remained largely apathetic. The general impression that received wide publicity was that the panchayats were no longer working for the people and that their sole concern was grabbing power for individual benefits. In the new jargon, the interests of the poorest of the poor were sacrificed in the hands of a band of scheming leaders.

While these allegations were not entirely untrue, instances were galore to show that panchayats were also doing good work that earned accolades in all-India platforms. Reduction of poverty was admitted to be faster in West Bengal than in many other states, and it was certainly above all-India average. People from other states and also from abroad came to see how the total sanitation programme was in progress in the state by the combined efforts of the panchayats and the field-level officers. When a review team visited Nandigram-II, the first panchayat samiti to be fully sanitized in the country, the proud people told them how they had worked together under the leadership of panchayats forgetting their political differences in other spheres. Even in the initial years of implementation of the National Rural Employment Guarantee Scheme, the performance of some districts received wide attention. But here, too, bureaucracy soon took over. Nobody cared to appreciate the underlying philosophy of development with dignity. The significance of the switchover from release of funds through executive orders to legal sanction got lost in the morass of arithmetic with mandays and fund spent. The monitoring mechanism mandated by the Government of India and developed by the state bureaucracy went over the head of the panchayat functionaries, making them hopelessly dependent on government officials, most of whom were their own employees. Information technology, a late starter in the state, was vigorously imposed on the panchayats by the beginning of the new millennium without meaningful orientation of elected functionaries. Curiously enough, the accounting system was computerized in gram panchayats much before its adoption in the citadel of state power! The consequence was again a hopeless dependence on appointed officials. Members were merrily left with muster rolls!

During this time, the theme of good governance through transparency and accountability continued to be a refrain in all discourses on panchayats without citing a single example of its practice in mainstream administration. Since gram sansads and gram sabhas did not function properly, the government decided to create a further structure at the sansad level. By an amendment to the West Bengal Panchayat Act in 2003, provision of a gram unnayan samiti (village development committee) within each gram sansad was made apparently to make the sansads functional. Thus, more reliance was placed on legislative powers than on mobilization of public opinion for reforming the erring panchayats. Since this came on the eve of the ensuing panchayat general elections, the idea was received with serious skepticism. As a natural corollary, the burden of reaching people fell once again on bureaucracy over the head of the panchayats, although legal provisions appeared to be giving the gram sansads an executive arm. Thus, bureaucratization of panchayats became nearly complete by the time the insider's journey came to an end in 2006.

In course of time, the basic distinction between bureaucratic hierarchy and inter-tier linkage of panchayats was blurred. The constitutional desire to see the panchayats grow as institutions of self-governance was kept respectfully confined to the statute book; in practice, they were treated as an extension of the government in the state and at the Centre. Curiously, such a metamorphosis was accepted by the panchayat functionaries, their political overlords and also by a large section of the admirers of decentralization without a voice of protest. The lone exception was the arduous work of the first Finance Commission of West Bengal highlighting the concept of devolution in terms of entitlements.

Conclusion

When all has been said, it must be placed on record that the recollections are not as grim as it might look. People of all faiths involved in a watershed development project in Ousgram-II Panchayat Samiti declare with pride that they feel like worshipping in every household the image of the Block Development Officer who worked day and night to lead the team and completed the project. His counterpart in Falakata at a later date could mobilize hundreds of men and women from backward communities for engagement in schemes under the national rural employment guarantee programme at a short notice from the additional district magistrate concerned. The success story of Sian Muluk, a gram panchayat in the district of Birbhum where panchayat functionaries, public servants and members of a non-governmental organization put in concerted efforts right from the gram sansad for implementation of schemes under the Act still serves as a source of inspiration and also as a model for those who have faith in the philosophy of decentralization. Instances were also not rare when panchayat functionaries took upon themselves the responsibility of protecting officials from undue criticism. On top of everything, the zeal and commitment with which some women functionaries elected to reserved offices delivered the goods in spite of a whole host of odds deserve heart-felt acknowledgement. These are only a handful of many cases which inspire hope. If potentials of a powerful structure have not been nurtured with care and respect, one can only bow out with a sad face.

CHAPTER 11

Institutionalizing Decentralized Planning in India

A Doable Project or a Futile Fantasy

Buddhadeb Ghosh

From the 1950s onwards, attempts have been made from time to time to introduce planning at the sub-state level. In early 1990s, the constitutional mandate was received to introduce planning at the level of panchayats and municipalities and to set up District Planning Committees for preparation of district plans. Yet, the goal of institutionalizing decentralized planning remains largely unrealized. This essay seeks to make a quick review of this history in order to identify the impediments that stand in the way of institutionalizing sub-state level planning process in India.

Early Attempts

While drafting the first Five Year Plan way back in 1951, the Planning Commission stressed the need for activating the village panchayats to shoulder some development responsibilities and to integrate the programmes undertaken by the panchayats with the development plan of the state. This remained wishful thinking. For, firstly, at that period of time, rural local government system was in tatters and when the system was given a new lease of life after the Balawantray Mehta report (1957), the Planning Commission's interest in decentralized planning faded.

The Planning Commission again showed some interest in sub-state level planning from 1969 onwards. But panchayats did not have any role in the initiatives taken by it. In 1969, the Planning Commission issued *Guidelines for the Formation of District Plan*. It advocated treating district as a unit of planning and specified a procedure for preparing a district plan. The planning process was essentially a bureaucratic exercise in which the role of local self-government institutions, including that of zilla parishads, was confined to one of mere consultation.

The concept of block as the unit of planning was introduced in 1978 in the report of the Planning Commission's *Working Group on Block Level Planning* chaired by M.L. Dantwala. If the main architects of the 1969 guidelines on district planning were the bureaucrats, those of the 1978 model of block-level planning were the specialists. According to the report, the planning process has to be a continuous dialogue between the experts and the public, but it cannot begin with the public. Decision will ultimately be taken by the experts who would seek people's view to calibrate their decisions, as it were, with the feel of the ground situation as revealed from the dialogue between themselves and the public.

In 1984, another working group was set up under the chairmanship of C.H. Hanumanth Rao. This report shifted the focus back to district-level planning. It also made a review of the progress of district-level planning in different states following the guidelines of 1969. It was noted that district planning committees had been set up in various states under various names under the chairmanship of minister or the collector. District planning offices had also been set up in a number of states. But so far as planning was concerned, the district plan was 'purely an aggregation of departmental schemes' and 'very little planning in the real sense (took) place at the district level'. It is also necessary to point out that like its predecessors, the model developed for preparation of district plan was technical in nature in which experts' decisions were to be given importance, if necessary even by ignoring the advice given by the local government institutions. They had the right to be consulted, but no right to take decisions.

In mid-1980s, West Bengal and Karnataka had introduced for the first time decentralized planning with the involvement of panchayati raj system. While the involvement of PRIs was partial in West Bengal, it was complete in respect of Karnataka, where 20 per cent of plan funds were given in the untied form to the ZP. Both the states introduced two-level planning – block and district in West Bengal, Mandal (GP) and ZP in Karnataka. But in both the states, the system broke down in early 1990s.

Constitutional Amendments and Decentralized Planning

The stage for decentralized planning was opened once again after the Seventy Third and the Seventy Fourth Constitution Amendments, and more particularly in 1996 when the LDF government of Kerala launched a vigorous decentralization policy with People's Plan Campaign. For the first time in the country, Kerala showed that it was possible to give practical shape to the idea of planning from below under which each tier of panchayat and individual municipalities could prepare holistic area development plans in a systematic manner. There was a problem initially with regard to preparation of district plans by DPC as required under Article 243ZD. But, over time, they devised some methodology to prepare such plans.

Despite Kerala's attempts, no other state has so far taken serious steps to introduce decentralized planning. The West Bengal Panchayat Act made specific provisions in the Act for preparation of both Five-year perspective plans and annual plans. So far no serious attempt has been made to act upon these provisions. If it is admitted that planning at the panchayat and municipal level and then at the district level are constitutionally mandated tasks,[1] why no serious attempt has been made so far in most states to institutionalize the planning regime said to have been envisaged in the Constitution? The answer that is very often offered is expressed in that catch-all phrase: there is 'no political will'. But why is there no *political will*? I think 'political will' is generated both from the supply side and from the demand side.

The political leaders and the bureaucrats constitute the supply side and the common citizens, who are the targets of public policy, constitute the demand side. The expectation that the collective actions of the political leaders and the bureaucrats are guided solely by public spirit is unrealistic. Echoing Adam Smith, one may surmise that 'it is not from the benevolence' of the powerful political actors and the bureaucrats that one may expect good public policy, 'but from their regard to their own self-interest'.[2] So long as decentralization of governance is perceived as a system that is against the 'self-interest' of the political actors and the bureaucrats, 'political will' in favour of decentralization will not be generated and vice versa. Since most of the senior political actors and bureaucrats perceive decentralization as a threat to the survival of the system that has given them the power and authority they enjoy, it is unlikely that they would be much inclined to take pro-active steps for decentralization, unless there is demand-side pressure expressed through signals coming from below demanding more powers and authority for the local governments. There is no such demand at the local level and, hence, the power holders also do not perceive any threat coming from the voters. Why should they show the zeal to adopt a radical policy which is clearly against their self-interest? To the question why the Indian voters, especially the rural voters, are not raising this demand, no definitive answer can be given. Political sociologists may, however, examine the hypothesis that with time Indian voters may have become right-conscious, but they still lack the republican spirit to take active interest in taking matters of common concern to the 'sphere of public authority' and even lack the urge to get involved in associational activities for public cause.

The Escape Routes

While it is understandable that no pro-active steps for adopting and executing a radical public policy can be expected from the state's administrative apparatus, unless there is a 'political will', what is perplexing is the question as to how can a government of the day deny fulfilling a constitutional obligation? On reading the Constitution, it seems that the escape route for the ruling class has been provided by the Constitution itself. To drive home the point, it would be worthwhile to take a fresh look at the constitutional provisions on decentralized planning. It has been argued by many that the Seventy Third and the Seventy Fourth Constitution Amendments have introduced a multi-level planning regime to give practical shape to the concept of planning from below. This does not appear to be a correct interpretation of the Constitution.

Vagueness in Article 243G

First of all, let us have a look at Article 243G, which is said to be the main source of power of the three-tier panchayats, including the power and responsibility to prepare development plans for their respective areas. The provisions of this Article are contained in two parts.

In the first part, the Constitution empowers the state legislatures to enact legislation in order to endow the panchayats 'with such *powers and authority* as are necessary to enable them to function as institutions of self-government'. The Constitution does not elaborate this point further. But since it wants panchayats to have appropriate 'power and authority', to function as institution of self-government, it is obvious that the Constitution wants panchayats to function *autonomously* over certain matters. The Constitution stops at this point, leaving us to wonder in respect of which subject-matters the panchayats would exercise autonomy.

Thereafter, the provisions of Article 243G move on to two other aspects, namely, empowering legislatures to enact laws for devolution of *power and responsibility* to the panchayats in respect of (i) 'preparation of plans for economic development and social justice' and (ii) implementation of 'schemes' on certain subject-matters of development as illustrated in the 11th Schedule. Since in this part of Article 243G, specific schemes are proposed to be devolved to the panchayats for 'implementation', such schemes have to be either centrally-sponsored schemes or state-sponsored schemes. Hence, 'implementation' of schemes as mentioned in the last part of Article 243G is in the nature of an agency function.

Planning, however, stands on a different footing. 'Preparation of plans' at the panchayat level is not an agency function. It is an original function, because the state government does not discharge this function presently. Since it is not an agency function, the panchayats may exercise autonomy over preparation of plans. Even then, to prepare plans is not an inherent power of panchayats guaranteed by the Constitution. The Constitution has not given any mandate to prepare plans at the panchayat level. At the most it has expressed its intention to do so. It remains an optional function for devolution to the panchayats and the state government (or legislature) may or may not devolve this function to the panchayats. Even if it is devolved, there is no guarantee that it will get implemented either by the panchayat or by others.

So far as the nature of the plan is concerned, it is not a sectoral plan. The objective of planning being 'economic development and social justice', the panchayat plans cannot be narrow-spectrum sectoral plans. They have to be broad-spectrum area plans cutting across various sectors. Taken together, Article 243G conveys the following.

- The functional jurisdiction of panchayat will be determined entirely by the state government/legislature. The Constitution does not guarantee any inherent power of panchayat.
- The states may devolve power and responsibility to the PRIs to discharge functions and activities, which may be of two types –

one set of responsibilities which panchayats would discharge independently and another set which would be discharged as agents of state government.

- Whether the task of planning would be devolved to the panchayats is for the state legislature/government to decide. Once devolved, the panchayats may exercise autonomy in discharging this task. Like national plans and state plans, panchayat plans are also supposed to be multi-sectoral and holistic area plans.

As the above discussion shows, the constitutional scheme regarding devolution of functions and activities from the state to the PRIs, as expressed in Article 243G read with 11th Schedule, is not as straightforward as that of Article 246 read with 7th Schedule that allocates functions among the central and state governments. It has to be constructed, as we have done above. Interpretations of the same Article other than the one of our own are also available. But there is no controversy on two points. First, panchayats can derive their functional responsibility from the state government/state legislature only, not from the Constitution. Second, following from the first proposition, there is no harm if planning function is not devolved or if panchayats are loaded with only agency functions and no functions or activities are specifically allocated to them which they could discharge autonomously. Thus, even though it is clear that the Constitution intended that panchayats should have an autonomous jurisdiction or that panchayats should be given planning function, the state government could easily ignore this.

It is no wonder that in the absence of constitutional mandate and lack of 'political will' of most state regimes, panchayat level planning has remained a non-starter. There are also other problems with the idea of panchayat level planning. We shall come to this later. Before that, let us have a look at the important provision on planning, namely Article 243ZD.

Implications of Article 243ZD

Contrary to Article 243G, the provisions of Article 243ZD are more direct. They envisage constitution of district panning committees (DPC) with representatives elected from among the elected representatives of zilla parishad and the municipalities of the district plus some nominated members, not exceeding one-fourth of the total members. DPC is a body that is separate from the three-tier panchayat system. It has a two-fold task: one, to consolidate the plans prepared by the individual panchayats and municipalities and second, to prepare a 'development plan for the district as a whole', but such plan will be a 'draft' plan, which is to be forwarded to the state government. DPC's duty ends there. What fate awaits its plan is not a matter that needs to be considered by the DPC.

Probably because of the fact that constitution of DPC and preparation of draft development plan for a district are mandated by the Constitution, the Planning Commission also could not ignore them and directed state governments to implement the provisions of Article 243 ZD. That is why DPCs have been established in all the states and some kind of district plans get prepared by them. But like the plans which were being prepared in the early 1980s or 1970s, the plans of DPCs are also nothing but the aggregation of departmental schemes and panchayat and municipal schemes. This means that even after creation of a planning body at the district level which is armed with the constitutional mandate of preparing a district development plan, the situation remains exactly where Hanumantha Rao Committee on district planning found itself back in 1984.

Beyond Political Failure

In the field of decentralized planning also, it is business as usual. The plans for 'economic development and social justice' that were supposed to be prepared by all the tiers of panchayats and by all municipal bodies in terms of Articles 243G and 243W, respectively, do not get prepared. In almost all the states, DPCs have been formed and many among these bodies prepare district plans every year. But among the plan documents of the DPCs, there may be only a few which go beyond aggregation of schemes of different implementing agencies and integrate them in accordance with the strategies adopted for achieving certain development goals.

Why did the introduction of district and village or city level planning fail even after the Planning Commission felt its need more than six decades ago and the Constitution made provisions for such planning to take place about two decades ago? It is perfectly reasonable to lay the blame for the failure on the political actors and the bureaucracy. But at the same time, one must be aware of the fact that there are some conceptual and institutional problems attached with the whole concept of district and sub-district level planning. It is strange that these problems do not get adequate attention at all in the discourse on decentralized planning.

Conceptual and Institutional Problems

Under the Seventy Fourth Amendment Act, the District Planning Committee was entrusted to consolidate the plans prepared by the panchayats and the municipalities within the particular district and to prepare a *draft development plan* for the district as a whole. Simultaneously, the Constitution also visualizes the panchayats and the municipalities as institutions of self-government and to be responsible for economy development and social justice. Now, confusion may arise relating to the position of the draft development plan prepared by the DPC and the plans prepared by the panchayats and municipalities. The stipulations of Article 243Z may provide clues, but not the solution. Moreover, lack of autonomy and coordination at and between different levels may also create confusion.

Gram Panchayat Level Planning

Among the three tiers of panchayats, the gram panchayat level planning has received most attention in the discourse on decentralized planning. Yet, some of the inherent problems of gram panchayat planning remain unsolved. These are as follows.

- If the gram panchayat has to prepare a holistic plan cutting across all development sectors, how can it get inputs of various development sectors (like agriculture or irrigation or health or education) which are looked after in the districts by the field units of various line departments?
- What should be the institutional format for all the line departments to work with the gram panchayat in order that the latter may prepare a holistic development plan for its area?
- Even if such a format is created, will gram panchayat be the appropriate unit for drawing up a multi-sectoral area development plan?
- If gram panchayat is not considered to be the suitable unit for drawing up a holistic area development plan, then what should be the specific role of the gram panchayat in decentralized planning system? One option may be that gram panchayat makes through participatory process a development plan for optimum use of its own resources in order to achieve certain development goals identified by the DPC for the district as a whole. Could it not be considered along with other options to give an alternative role to the gram panchayat in the planning process?

- Is the plan to be prepared by gram panchayat meant for implementation by the gram panchayat? If not, who will implement it? How to ensure that plans get implemented through the budget mechanism of implementing agencies?
- Every gram panchayat has to make plans for various flagship programmes of Government of India. How to integrate such plans with the overall development plan of the gram panchayat?

Panchayat Samiti and ZP Level Planning

If gram panchayats are allowed to prepare multi-sectoral development plans, what kind of value addition is expected of the panchayat samiti (PS) plan, which could not be introduced in the gram panchayat level planning? In other words, what additional contributions have to be made in the panchayat samiti plan apart from consolidating the plans of gram panchayat? If this boils down to the incorporation of certain additional schemes without establishing necessary interconnections between them and the gram panchayat plans, then panchayat samiti planning process would be a useless exercise. One may then go from the gram panchayat plans to district plans. Some states like, for example, Kerala and Karnataka, presume that planning at the intermediate level may be dispensed with. Some states, on the other hand, may think otherwise. In West Bengal's 1985 model,[3] the first level planning unit was block and planning at the gram panchayat level was dispensed with. An institutional format in the shape of Block Planning Committee (BPC) was devised to prepare one multi-sectoral development plan for the block as a whole. It is necessary to consider whether that would be a better option.

If the intermediate level plan is made by BPC, then what will panchayat samiti do? One option may be that the PS makes a development plan for optimum use of its own resources in order to achieve certain agreed development goals. If there is a district plan to be prepared by the District Planning Committee (DPC), then what is the necessity for zilla parishad to go through an elaborate process of preparing a holistic plan for all the rural areas of the district? Instead, its plan may consist of a list of schemes and activities to supplement the efforts of gram panchayat and PS to achieve certain agreed development goals. One option may be that gram panchayat makes a development plan for optimum use of its own resources in order to achieve certain development goals identified through a participatory process.

District Development Plan

Some of the problems of preparation of district plan are embedded in the constitutional provisions (Article 243 ZD). The Constitution has not clarified the nature of the district plan, as a result of which there is confusion about its role and its features. For example, it is not clear whether the district plan is only a local sector plan in the sense that it presents in a consolidated form the plans of the rural and urban local bodies in the district prepared within the limits of the available financial and other resources. Or, whether in addition to the plans of the rural and urban local bodies, the district plan should also take care of the activities of the state government agencies within a district by including the plans for the activities being discharged by the line departments of the state government. The externalities of such functions and activities of the line departments may either remain confined within the boundary of a district or may spread beyond the confines of a district. If the district plan also covers the functions and the activities addressed by the state government's line departments, then which among the above two types of activities should be the concern of the district plan?

Another set of confusion relates to the role of the DPC as regards its own contribution in the planning process, apart from the task of consolidation. It has to be remembered that the DPC is not an implementing agency. It cannot implement any part of the district plan. In this context, DPC can earn its legitimacy in the eyes of the implementing agencies, if it can take care of some problems or issues concerning the development of the district, which cannot be addressed properly at the individual levels of any other agency. In that case, its task goes beyond the consolidation of the plans of the implementing agencies of the district, including those of the rural and urban local bodies. It will then have an important role to play in providing a framework and also in ensuring revision of the sub-district plans, so that the concerns not addressed in such plans are taken care of. The Constitution has identified 'matters of common interest between panchayats and municipalities' as one item that falls within the category of such problem or issue on which DPC has the right to intervene. Are there other problems/issues, which also should be addressed by the DPC in its district planning process?

According to the Constitution, the district plan prepared by the DPC is a draft plan. If plans of individual panchayats and municipal bodies are 'final' plans, why should DPC's district plan be a 'draft' plan? The logic is not understood. If district plan is a draft plan, then a system has to be developed under which these plans will be considered by the State Planning Board (SPB) on a routine basis and then approved with or without modification. Even if the plan is approved, the question as to who will implement the plan remains unresolved.

In the states where districts are large (as in West Bengal), consolidation of numerous local bodies' plan at the district level is not possible, unless a system of two-stage consolidation – first at the intermediate level and then at district level – is developed. This would necessitate preparation of an intermediate level plan before preparation of district plan.

Concluding Remarks

For the last 60 years, we have been talking of decentralized planning. For the last 20 years, our Constitution has been carrying provisions on the same subject. But we have so far failed to institutionalize workable and effective models of planning at the district or sub-district levels. It is all right to put the blame on the shoulder of the ruling class. But it is also necessary that the development practitioners and experts must address the various conceptual, institutional and operational problems associated with institutionalization of decentralized planning process.

Notes

1. Numerous writers on Panchayati Raj agree to this view, but they seem to have divergent views on the concept and the method of preparing district and local government level planning.
2. The phrase 'self-interest' is used in the sense of 'enlightened self-interest' and is different from 'selfishness'. Even though it has some resemblance with the model of 'rational decision-maker' of public choice theory, it does not convey the sense that motivation for action of the politicians or the bureaucrats is determined *solely* by the desire of maximization of power.
3. The planning methodology and organizational structure of decentralized planning introduced in this model may be traced in Anil Kumar Jana, *Administering District Plans in India: Issues, Constraints and Choices*, New Delhi: Concept Publishing Company, 2004.

CHAPTER 12

Whither Partyless and/or Non-Party Panchayats?

Contextualizing the Answers

Sakti Pada Pal

Panchayat Raj in India is as old as her age-long ancient village administrative system.[1] This system of panchayat moved Mahatma Gandhi very much and captured a major part of his thought as he was concerned with the freedom of the country from the yoke of British rule. He also envisaged to keep the fetish fortune of Indian villagers free from procrastination so as to establish their self-rule, *Swarajya*. The later politicians, be they Gandhians or non-Gandhians, preferred to choose this particular terminology – 'panchayat', to incorporate it in the future administrative structure of the country for putting credence to the idea of *swarajya*. But in the Constitution it was added not as a mandatory provision, but as a moral dictum in the form of Article 40 in the Directive Principles of the State Polity: 'State should take steps to organize village panchayats and endow them with such power and authority as may be necessary to enable them to function as units of self-government.'[2] Inclusion of panchayat as a directive appeared to be a compromise between the Gandhians and the Ambedkarites with Nehru maintaining a stoic silence during the course of debates in the Constituent Assembly.

Introduction of Panchayati Raj in India

The Directive Principles of State Policy had an encouraging effect on the state to stretch its arm by creating panchayats, non-mandatory in essence. Amidst the debate between modernization and the Gandhian vision as a reluctant partner, the provinces under the guidance of the Centre set to establish the panchayats. Besides this, a clear shifting of focus from government to governance, played a vital role in the scene. The Indian statesmen or politicians became enthusiastic about panchayat system in the late 1950s. The first Acts were passed on Panchayati Raj Institutions (PRI) in Uttar Pradesh and Bihar in 1947. Odisha had the distinction of being the first state in India to introduce Gram Panchayats in the year 1948.[3] The first Panchayat Raj Institution was introduced in Rajasthan on 2 October 1959 following the recommendations of the Balwantray Mehta Committee.[4]

The study team led by Balwantray Mehta realized that unless the village communities understood their own problems, realized own responsibilities, exercised real power through own representatives and kept constant vigil over local administration, development would not come true. To cope with this problem, the necessity of creating an agency was felt. Hence, the committee recommended a three-tier panchayat, elected directly at the village level and indirectly at the block and district levels. Politics was considered inimical for the success of this body and unanimity was taken for granted as 'consensus', barring the entry of political parties. But very soon the 'consensus' was belied. The conflictual groups took control of this situation and, belying all expectations, villages remained at the vortex of conflicts and politics.

Panchayati Raj Institutions became operative in West Bengal in 1957. These replaced *union boards* by giving importance to Article 40, based on Gandhian principles. It consisted of two stages – *Gram* and *Anchal*. This venture was complete with the replacement of *district boards*, when Zilla Parishad Act was passed in 1963 by creating Anchalik Parishad at the block and Zilla Parishad at the district level.[5] It was not a directly elected institution body, but had an indirect connection with the people. The institution was not formed through party-based election and was mainly dependent on the landed, educated or high-caste and middle-class people.[6] Naturally, the then panchayat system consisting of four tiers fell short of the idea of being a self-sustaining rural institution. It only served the purpose of some national leaders' wishes for feeling proud and being complacent with regards to the introduction and nurturing of grassroots democratic politics in the country-side. The panchayats became completely dependent on the dictates of the bureaucrats to propel a village-based development programme for the marginalized section of the country in the form of Community Development Programme (CDP) and National Extension Scheme (NES).[7]

However, panchayats lacked real enthusiasm and initiative which could emanate only from grassroots people. Participation was not much to be exemplary. Further, it lacked political zeal and activities in the involvement. Secondly, no political parties came forward to activate the panchayats to run the risk of success. Party-based panchayat was prohibited. People's political zeal and initiatives mainly grew out of their participation in the activities of political parties. Though the panchayats were partyless in form, in essence they became the carriers of vested interests of the upper caste and stratum of the commoners, leading to become the vestige of the then influential parties – mainly Indian National Congress (INC).[8] It extracted a question – whether panchayat could be partyless and/or a camouflaged one or a devoutly party-based participatory political institution in the true sense.

The Changed Scenario

Since the fourth general election in 1967, the one-party domination was shattered. The coalition types of government consisting of some regional political parties of same faith and beliefs and groups were formed at least for a short period. This change had a profound impact on invoking interest in decentralization and in formation of the lower layer of rural administrative system. It loosened the meaning of the concept of decentralization of power that so far depended on the wishes of a central government for efficiency and more efficacies for the fulfillment of development programmes. Rather, it brought forth the ideas of widening the scope of power on to the very bottom of the rural locality. It also revived in some parts of the country the classical Gandhian idea of village panchayats through the political forums, represented by different political parties. It sincerely reflected the items of the recommendations of the Balwantray Mehta Committee, 1957.[9]

Thus far, the present bottom-most step of administrative machinery in rural India consisted of three-tier panchayats. Later on, from 1994, it became a constitutional provision being mandatory for each and every state to adopt the three-tier panchayat system. However, the practice of panchayati raj transgressed the very meaning of ideal content in Article 40: 'State may establish panchayats, which are units of self-government'.[10] In actuality, the practice of panchayat forsook the 'may' question from its agenda and rather took over the baton to establish the system as a positive institution of grassroots democracy. It is to be remembered that panchayats in India did not faithfully reflect the Gandhian idea as such whether in form or in functions. In the changed circumstances, it was not also necessary. From 1957, according to the reading of the study of Balwantray Mehta Committee, it was professed that village people were not given importance in the formulation and implementation of development plans.[11] Certainly it was because of the interplay of various kinds of vested interests that a sound decentralization of power was not accomplished in the country, whether on behalf of the central government or the state government. As the village panchayat preserved the organic character and continuity of Indian society from ancient ages, those might become the ideal and fit institutions of self-government in India. The Gandhian reference to village panchayat could be cited as thus: 'the government of village will be conducted by the panchayats of five persons, annually elected by the adult villagers, male and female, possessing minimum prescribed qualifications ...'[12]

After 1942, Gandhi himself admitted that the future society of India 'is largely beyond my grasp' and four years later he did not need to feel in his 'picture'.[13] That is, the age would change and so also the concept. For ground reality the panchayat system would be enlivened, but not in the sense that Gandhiji emphasized. However, village *swaraj* would be the common link between the ideal society and the ground reality. Institutionalized participative approach was adopted. Panchayat had been acknowledged as the political institution of village administration, but non-political peasant and labour organizations, as visualized, were not present as the organizational bases of village *swaraj* and had not replaced the political parties.[14] The party-based panchayats were established in common. Asoka Mehta Committee, 1977 recommended the organization of party-based panchayats in the country.[15]

Panchayat raj was rejuvenated during the Janata rule, the first ever non-Congress central government in India formed in 1977. Some ardent followers of Gandhi like Jayprakash Narayan (JP) tied the knot of some hydra-headed multitudes of non-Congress parties and groups together led by some elderly Gandhian Congressmen who either left the INC or were ousted from the party. Morarji Desai, Jagjivan Ram, George Fernandes, a Gandhian socialist, and some others were at the helms of affairs. At this opportune time, the Asoka Mehta Committee was formed by the central government to oversee the affairs of panchayat raj, after they were established in a new way following Balwantray Mehta Committee recommendations. The Asoka Mehta Committee sought an effective panchayati raj with *district* as the unit of administration and planning. It modified the three-tier system by adding *Mondal Panchayat* as the base unit. It expected panchayat as an agency for local level planning as well as for political and administrative functions. West Bengal, Karnataka and Andhra Pradesh tried to revitalize the system through efforts at political levels. In West Bengal and Andhra, there were political motivations for the strengthening of local bodies. Karnataka attempted to make the district government as the third tier in Indian federal system. The Mehta Committee (1977) emphasized to establish the PRI as a political institution in place of its being a development agency only.[16] However, a big impetus in respect to the establishment of panchayats came from West Bengal, when it put the long pending Panchayat Act, 1973, into operation in 1978, with some modifications.[17] This endeavour had historical and revolutionary effects on matters of field administration and local government in the rural denoted area in West Bengal.

The newly established panchayats on the whole served and fulfilled three prominent purposes and objectives; first, (i) the fullest decentralization of power up to the grassroots level in the true sense of the term;[18] secondly, (ii) ensuring the establishment of participatory democracy with open and voluntary cooperation and participation of the people themselves in matters of their own development and evolution, and thirdly, (iii) making the panchayat not only an administrative tier of decentralization nor a participatory means to maintain democratic norms and procedures, but also an instrument to make the people and masses the beneficiaries in execution of their own plans and action for progress.[19]

The Traditional Legacies

A threadbare dissection of the panchayats reveals its long structural legacy. Not to speak of ancient council of five men (panchayat) that existed in the self-sustaining village communities – idyllic, ignorant and non-political in respect of their linkage with the centre of power, the institutional history of local self-government commencing from Lord Rippon's Resolution of 1882, then the Government of India Resolutions of 1915 and 1918 and subsequent village panchayat Acts in various states up to the Government of India Act 1935, had something to tell about the composition of the panchayats, having two tiers – the union boards and district boards.[20] Its functional parts were built on the basis of experience gained and the needs arising out of the situation the country had to face in dealing with the CDP and NES. These necessities were focused through the findings of different committees set up in a row – Balwantray Mehta Committee, 1957; Asoka Mehta Committee, 1977; Singhvi Committee, 1986, etc.[21] This whole course of action and interaction reorganized the structures of the PRIs in *two*, *three* or *four* tiers.

The spiritual and inspirational turn in panchayats came from the absorption of Gandhian ideals of *village swaraj*, developed by the later Gandhians or the disciples of Gandhi – Jay Prakash and Vinoba Bhave. It stood that villages would be free like communities, self-less like chained cooperative of neighbours, conscious socially and politically about their aptitude towards development and progress. Villages were considered as the infrastructural elements of the Indian states. As such, when these villages would become full of freedom, peace and tranquility with a conscious aptitude for political participation and zeal, the state would get a self-sustaining tier and the burden of the central government and the state governments regarding implementation of the CDP and NES as well as maintenance of the administrative structure from the upstairs, might be lighter or the weight fully off.

Last, not the least, a newly-imposed urge for the restructuration of the PRIs began germinating in its body polity, after it was realized that this institution was not only an agency of transforming the village society into a system of participatory democracy, but also a political institution to undo the wrong-doings so far committed and to compensate the damages by performing a positive political role to turn and twist the villages into a vibrant chamber of self-sustaining, self-ruling and self-protracting actions.

Panchayati Raj and Political Parties

Panchayati Raj came into existence in early 1960s in most of the states. The elections were held by secret ballots on the basis of adult franchise. But elections were very irregular and mostly dependent on the pretexts of the state government.[22] There were no party centres in every district to maintain regular contact with the villagers. Some political functionaries belonging to upper class or caste had the opportunity to keep contact with the village people and to know their problems. Though elections were held on non-party basis, in reality they were guided by some political people.[23] The panchayats were not uniform in organizations and varied from two tiers to four tiers, though there was mostly a three-tier system. In the lower stratum of the village panchayat, the mode of election was usually direct; in the upper tier or tiers, it was indirect, except in Karnataka.[24] In West Bengal, grassroots panchayats consisting of two tiers were established in 1957, but the upper tier consisting of *anchalik parishad* and *zilla parishad* were established by the Act of 1963 as stated earlier.[25] During this period, the political parties were less developed and lacked clarity in their policy. They were unable to canvass their own manifesto and had no infrastructure in the villages.[26] To cite an example of Rajasthan, where the first PRI came into force, the third panchayat election was held in 1978 after thirteen years of interval and then in 1988 after ten years of interval.[27] In West Bengal, United Front ministry (UDF) superseded the anchalik parishad and zilla parishad and kept the lower stratum in animation for a long time. After eleven years, the election to panchayats was held in 1978 in West Bengal after the Left came to power. The panchayat was formed on the basis of the Act of 1973, with a few modifications.[28]

Second generation panchayats began to emerge after the Asoka Mehta Committee submitted its report in 1978. Direct elections to the village-level panchayats were held and the block level and district level bodies were constituted from amongst the chairpersons of the lower level bodies except West Bengal, Karnataka and Madhya Pradesh, where direct elections to district level panchayats and mandal panchayats were followed.[29] Madhya Pradesh, Andhra Pradesh and West Bengal introduced participation of political parties in panchayat elections.[30] In West Bengal, political parties contested at all the levels of panchayats, including the gram panchayats.[31] In Bihar, village-level panchayats were not elected directly – four members were elected directly and other four were nominated by the mukhiya.[32]

West Bengal contributed much to the growth of a sound panchayat system and the experiment could be considered as the most successful one.[33] It established a system of party-based panchayats at all the three tiers on the basis of direct elections at a regular five-year interval. The CPI (M)-led Panchayat Raj Institutions created an institutionalized structure with sound practices of devolution of funds and functions to the panchayats. The parties played a significant role in mobilization of rural people for reconstruction of villages. The Communist Party of India (Marxist) shelved its characteristic function for rural mobilization to foment class struggle; rather, it accomplished the functions of rural development.[34]

After the Seventy Third Constitution Amendments Act came into force in 1994, the third generation panchayats began emanating in the states. The granite foundation of Panchayati Raj Institutions had gained a solid stature in its second generation from 1978 to 1992, concerning its institutionalization[35] (provision for election commission, availability of funds, maintenance of office and, administrative staff, etc.). Timely elections, continuous development activities, management of rural areas, its roles in mobilizing people for mopping up their own planning and development also contributed to its strength and performance. The involvement of political parties extensively for development and extension of grassroots democracy turned the panchayats into political vehicles for mobilization of the masses. People's willful and conscious participation, as originally visualized by Gandhi and other Gandhian personalities like Jaya Prakash, carried over and brought forward the legacy and spirit throughout its third generation from 1994 till date to build up a solid configuration.[36]

Gandhian Ideals Reiterated

The journey from 1978 to 1992 achieved a miraculous equation to open a complicated chapter and caught hold of a spectacular political phenomenon. In some states like West Bengal, Karnataka, Andhra Pradesh and Kerala at a later stage - three-tier/two-tier panchayat systems were introduced with a devoted emphasis on their party-based institutions.[37] In some states, parties got involved in the electoral practices at upper layer of panchayats - panchayat samiti and zilla parishad. The lower and bottom-most gram panchayat elections were supposed to be held on non-party basis.[38] Can this be called partyless democracy? We may recount and quote Prafulla Chandra Sen, a long experienced politician and former Chief Minister of West Bengal, preaching party-less democracy:

Further, there is hardly any possibility of participatory democracy or involvement of the people in administration. Conversely, village units with 1,000 population can elect the best possible scrupulously honest and capable persons by adult franchise and through successive electoral colleges the best available persons will be chosen for Block, Sub-division, District, State and Central levels. The elections will not be expensive – these will not be unreal – these will not represent parties, but the people, who alone count.[39]

He added, 'Party-less democracy may bring to an end the supremacy of the political parties. For, the latter by their very terms of reference, have to look to the interests of their own partymen first.'[40] Even Jayaprakash Narayan articulated, 'Panchayat Raj even in Rajasthan, where it began, is yet a far cry from this consummation ...'[41] He again stated,

In regard to the elections to village panchayats, it is my emphatic view that they should be held without contest. This view has been severely criticized in some quarters; in others, opinion seems to have veered round to it. For myself, the more I have thought over this question, the more I have discussed it with others and the more I have learnt of the workings of the village panchayats, the more convinced I have become that, if Panchayat Raj is to succeed, contests at election to village panchayats must be avoided.[42]

The Realities

In contrast to these views, the real politic went the opposite way. In 1980s, N.T. Rama Rao of Andhra Pradesh and R.K. Hegde of Karnataka organized panchayat elections on party basis.[43] Later, Congress also started contesting elections on party basis. It was also observed that in spite of election on party basis, caste had a prominent role to play in these states. In Maharashtra zilla parishad elections, parties like INC, BJP and Shiv Sena played a crucial roles.[44] In Uttar Pradesh, BJP and INC had lost considerably in the panchayat elections in 2000. Gujarat also demonstrated a party-based panchayat election. West Bengal's story was the most impressive one. CPI (M)-led Left Front government participated in the panchayat elections on party line in 1978.[45] It gave vent to political mobilization. It was a success story that could tell how a party-based panchayat might generate so much enthusiasm for the institutionalization of the system, which was very much alien to a party like CPI (M) and to its ideological position.[46] There was a belief that the local community interest could be toppled by party politics and interests and that party politics should not be allowed to spoil the community-type interests contained in the panchayats. But the direct and party-based elections broke the preached parochialism that the panchayats carried so far with it along with the idea of community. At the village level, the block of votes was very often mobilized by the vested interests and camouflaged by the Indian National Congress to establish panchayat raj. This party-based electoral politics of panchayat required a different form of organization. This organization obviously necessitated the introduction of parties into panchayat.[47] Voters were offered the chances of voting a party rather than for an individual. In place of traditional village leadership, an arena of new leadership came into being.

The introduction of party-led panchayats brought a halt to the traditional leadership and in its place a new pattern of political leadership emerged consisting of various parties. The ground reality did not warrant any uncontested partyless system, rather a party-based organization was evolving into the local setup with a self-sustaining, self-reliant and reliable infrastructure. It influenced the political condition of the people and bloomed into a round-whole village society, having similarity with gram swaraj of Gandhi. Parties did not curb or deter the spontaneous growth of political panchayats in the country. Party-based panchayats made over the necessities in the society as a form of living – growing and evolving ever a better place for direct man to man human relationship.[48] Beginning from three-tier simple organizations, the panchayats grew into a multifaceted complex whole with gram sabha, gram samsad, gram unnayan samiti blended with numerous self-help groups. Political parties, in spite of their acrimonious relationships, came into terms with many other parties to live in a community.

Party and the Committed Panchayats

Now there is the need for comprehending the views and role of the communist parties and other Left parties in organizing panchayats. How could these parties make up their ideological perceptions with a Gandhian institution like panchayat? Had it been a partyless formulation, this unbelievable blending might not be possible. A party-based organization might perform a spectacular commitment like this. The party literature and the views expressed by the leaders of the CPI (M) may provide clues in this regard. In spite of the skepticism of the party about panchayat system, it changed its attitude and participated in the panchayat elections, held in 1978.[49] The party in its directive for management of panchayats (*Panchayat Parichalana Prasange Nirdeshika*, 31 January 1994) stated, 'New panchayats start their journey. Almost 70 per cent of the members are newly elected for the first time. Amongst them, the number of party members is insignificant. For this reason the task of running the panchayats is a major challenge to the party' (translated).[50] Again it reiterated, 'we must have to involve each and everybody including those in the Opposition irrespective of party and creed to work in the panchayats.'[51] Further, there was a realization that participation in panchayats could strengthen the party's mass base in rural area. The party considered the panchayats as instruments for mobilizing more and more people towards the struggle for people's democracy.[52]

Party ideologue E.M.S. Namboodiripad, in his note of dissent to the Asoka Mehta Committee Report, 1978 stated, '... what is required is that while certain definite fields of administration like defence, foreign affairs, currency, communication, etc. should rest with the Centre, all the rest should be transferred to the states and from there, to the districts and lower levels of elected administrative bodies.[53] In the same breath, another prominent leader of the CPI (M), B.T. Ranadive remarked that panchayats' efficacy could be cited but from the point of view of a communist. And that increased power of the local bodies should be taken as 'instruments of democratic advance and struggle', but not as 'decentralization of political power in scientific terms'.[54]

During the panchayat elections of 1978, the main aims and objectives of the CPI (M) were to unleash the initiative of the rural masses and to inculcate in them a spirit of self-confidence, so that a mass movement could be gradually built up against the age-old exploitation. In this manner, the Left Front government, exceptional on various counts, avoided the fear of arbitrary imposition of Article 356.[55] Skepticism regarding bureaucracy and the development of political base in the rural areas through government activities were the order of the day. Through a Left coalition government, the party fulfilled its own intention of creating a mass base by mobilizing people as well as creating suitable political conditions for future advancement. On the other hand, it consolidated people's zeal to go to the bottom-most level of political development.[56] Panchayat system slowly but steadily moved towards mobilization of masses and setting a goal for people's participation. Finally, the panchayat indispensably became dependent on the parties in turn and they (the parties) institutionalized the system of grassroots democratic institutions.[57] It has been contextualized whether the party had done well, whether the party had made spectacular success in ensuring development and whether panchayat had captured the scenarios of village society and established a full-bloom participatory democracy.

Since the amendment to the Constitution in 1993, the activities of political parties have increased. It went so far as it could do for mass mobilization. Gandhiji insisted on keeping the villages and panchayats away from politics, but the interest of all the political parties including the CPI (M) was not any short of zeal, rather it performed ground work for the establishment of the institutionalized panchayats, having been elected at regular intervals under an election commission, having some interest in mass mobilization for development and having been equipped with enough funds and its mobilization.[58] The parties through their capacity building programme, job training activities and their programme for campaigning in favour of effective panchayat system did a good job to preach impeccably for a party-based panchayat. Gandhian idea of partyless 'gram swaraj' through panchayats had been relegated to the backburner although the idea percolated into reality through party-based panchayats.

Panchayat and party – being in course of time a relational coordinate – absorbs the very idea of partyless one in its essence, while brightening up the arrangement of building a solid network to establish grassroots democracy – a democracy of autonomous village republics. Parties would secure local institutional base for implementing their programme into action in both short and long term, they had the opportunities to politicize the whole developmental work and they initiated in the mind of the villagers to stand for themselves to secure result-oriented programmes for their own.[59] The Left particularly had done this properly to achieve the agrarian success in short term in West Bengal and to induce the village minds in the long term to rise to the occasion of each and every political solution at the time of crisis from their own. In West Bengal, as well as in some other states, the bureaucrats faced a changed political climate to call for decentralization of power and popular participation in decision-making. A change from a conflictual to cooperative relationship appeared and gradually a smooth working relationship emerged.[60] In West Bengal, the society was full of diverse social and political movements in which the poor and marginalized section remained at the front. These poor and marginalized people were involved in the process. The more they were involved, the panchayats were strengthened by a self-sustaining process, for inculcating zest and zeal in the villagers as actors.

A Note of Realization

It is now well accepted that an ideal Gandhian panchayat system is nowhere in the country. Some may try to enliven the utopian and communitarian village swaraj through the foundation of 'partyless' panchayats. It may be a matter of long practice and conjecture but one thing, however, is clear – 'partyless democracy cannot be ushered in for the asking. We have to work for it.'[61] Some states practised it by declaring the formation of rural grassroots institutions, going to polls without party symbols. Reality shows that those ventures turned dirty; because, the returned members of those panchayats bore the vestiges of some political power and high-born and/or influential caste or castes.[62] From 1977 onwards, following the recommendations of Asoka Mehta Committee, the panchayat election were mostly party-based. Party panchayat became the order of the day, though some Gandhians realized, 'In a country like India, at least, only the Gandhian system with gram *swaraj* as the goal will thrive and help us resolve our complex problems. That is what sixty years of my political career have made me believe. That is where my journey into politics has brought me today.'[63]

At this point some questions peeped into the focus as to where to seek the answers. The present-day panchayat system is an all-India phenomenon. Can this structural burdened with the task of catering to some thought to be constitutional, legal and moral functions, be borne by such types of units?[64] Are these units turned into self-sufficient autonomous ones, bereft of any guidance from their more sophisticated higher counterparts?[65] Any advancement with regard to the acquisition of village level self-sufficiency is being done by the new addendum to the existing panchayat Acts; as for example, vide 16 (a); 6 (c) of the West Bengal Panchayat Act, 1973, the gram unnayan samiti is constituted in each gram sansad area for the total development of poor, marginalized and backward people.[66] Are not these pampered attempts the outcome of party-based panchayats? These are completely alien to Gandhian ideal model. May not the question arise: whether the present state of affairs in the panchayat system of the country is capable of serving the original and fundamental task – the village autonomy with self-sufficiency, political consciousness and complacent freedom – all these with the help of party-based institution throughout India. Whether the party-based panchayats can do the needful was what concerned JP: 'The only remedy seems to be for the people to take their fate in their own hands and shape it according their will.'[67]

Exemplification: West Bengal and Kerala

Citing the examples of two states – West Bengal and Kerala – led by the Left Front government under the leadership of CPI (M) up to 2009, a case record in favour of party-based panchayats, whatever types of parties they may be, can be formulated.[68] With this formulation, the above inquisitive question would find satisfactory answers. In West Bengal, the CPI (M) was able to steer the gram panchayats in its own way. The party wanted to extend its control up to gram panchayat level. The step had ensured the coordination in the activities of the panchayats and enhanced the initiative and interest in the rural panchayat activities.[69] In the initial years, panchayats played the role of the catalyst of movement. The party gave leadership and the people were part of it. This type of popular participation enabled the panchayats to withstand the devastating natural calamities like floods in 1978. The people felt that they were part of the panchayat raj. In the later years, there was a phenomenal change. Panchayats turned into mere institutions. The people fell into 'we-they feeling' tussle. The CPI (M) was aware of it. It felt the need to increase intra-party democracy amidst the principle of democratic centralism.[70] A party, having faith in democratic centralism, if endeavoured to empower the people and encourage them to participate following the principle of democratic decentralization, can save Panchayati Raj Institutions from the decay and devil. It must be pronounced that panchayats should not be run on non-party basis.[71] Political will of West Bengal panchayat can well detect the lacunae of chaotic panchayat system in vogue in Bihar.

Now a turn to Kerala logically comes in. Kerala government's policy for decentralization was notably different. E.M.S. Namboodiripad's leadership, who in his dissenting note to Ashok Mehta Committee Report, 1978 crossed the limit of orthodox communist ideology, had given support to local democracy.[72] Democratic decentralism serves not a bit little the purpose of class struggle. It teaches the working class to rise against oppression. Democratic centralism is the principle of organizing party, but democratic decentralization is the principle of organizing people's own government. This will create a space from where common people may interact with democratic institutions.[73] Kerala government established such types of panchayats and was in the search of reorganizing and restructuring the same continuously, creating space for people's participation in their own government. The party-based panchayat in Kerala may well point out the lacunas of its counterparts of West Bengal.

Concluding Remarks

To conclude, according priority to the agenda for widening and deepening the grassroots democracy is the panacea of a party-based panchayats to get rid of its ills. The people of India have a commitment to the cause of making a future party-based panchayat into a success and should happily strive for the end of this journey.[74] The following observations made by Kuldeep Mathur in respect of status and *modus operandi* of panchayats in India are worth quoting: 'The constitutional mandate, notwithstanding its weakness, has made panchayats an important arm of Indian democracy. This is evident in the interest shown by political parties in the panchayat elections, including, paradoxically, even groups opposed to this state, as elections in Odisha or Kashmir have shown.'[75] Further, '... No doubt, there are conflicts and contestations, but these have only helped in shaking off long held mores and beliefs in society.'[76]

Notes

1. Jayantanuja Bandopadhyaya, *Social and Political Thought of Gandhi*, Howrah: Manuscript, 2000, p. 121. See also, R.P. Joshi and G.S. Narwani, *Panchayati Raj in India: Emerging Trends Across the States*, Jaipur: Rawat Publications, 2011, pp. 20–41.
2. *The Constitution of India*, New Delhi: Government of India Publications, 2005, p. 18.
3. Ramesh K. Arora and Meenakshi Hooja, *Panchayati Raj: Participation and Decentralization*, Jaipur: Rawat Publications, 2009, p. 254.
4. Joshi and Narwani, op. cit., p. 32.
5. Bhawani Prasad Chattopadhyay, *Panchayat Aain Ebang Gandhijir Panchayat (*in Bengali), Kolkata: Gandhi Memorial Committee, 1995, p. 9.
6. Ross Mallick, *Development Policy of a Communist Government: West Bengal since 1977*, Cambridge: Cambridge University Press, 1993, p. 125.

7. Joshi and Narwani, op. cit., pp. 29–30.
8. Buddhadev Ghosh and Girish Kumar, *State Politics and Panchayats in India*, New Delhi: Manohar, 2003, pp. 168–170.
9. Ibid., p. 169.
10. Mohit Bhattacharya and Prabhat Datta, *Governing Rural India*, New Delhi: Uppal Publishing House, 1990, pp. 110–115.
11. Joshi and Narwani, op. cit., pp. 30–31.
12. Bhawani Prasad Chattopadhyay (ed.), *Mahatma Gandhir Nirbachita Rachana (*in Bengali), Vol. V, Ahmedabad: Navajivan Publishing House, 2000, pp. 384–386. Also, *Harijan*, July 1942, cited in Jayantanuja Bandopadhyaya, *Social and Political Thought of Gandhi*, Howrah: Manuscript, 2000, p. 118.
13. Tendulkar and Mahatma, cited in Jayantanuja Bandopadhyaya, *Social and Political Thought of Gandhi*, Howrah: Manuscript, 2000, p. 119.
14. Bandopadhyaya, op. cit., p. 28.
15. Joshi and Narwani, op. cit., p. 36.
16. Ibid., p. 37.
17. Neil Webster, *Panchayati Raj and the Decentralization of Development Planning in West Bengal*, Kolkata: K.P. Bagchi & Co., 1992, p. 25.
18. Neil Webster, 'Panchayati Raj in West Bengal: Popular Participation for the People or the Party', in Kuldeep Mathur (ed.), *Development Policy and Administration*, New Delhi: Sage, 1996, pp. 231–233.
19. Ghosh and Kumar, op. cit., p. 187.
20. Bhattacharya and Datta, op. cit., pp. 13–42. See also, Joshi and Narwani, op. cit., pp. 20–41.
21. Joshi and Narwani, op. cit., pp. 30–41.
22. Ibid., p. 241.
23. Ibid.
24. Ibid., p. 242.
25. Chattopadhyay, op. cit., p. 9.
26. Joshi and Narwani, op. cit., p. 241.
27. Ibid.
28. Ghosh and Kumar, op. cit., pp. 172–176.
29. Joshi and Narwani, op. cit., p. 242.
30. Ibid.
31. Ghosh and Kumar, op. cit., p. 180.
32. Joshi and Narwani, op. cit., p. 243.
33. Ghosh and Kumar, op. cit., pp. 176–177.

34. Mallick, op. cit., pp. 134–136. See also, Webster, 'Panchayati Raj in West Bengal: Popular Participation for the People or the Party', op. cit., pp. 229–230. See also, Ghosh and Kumar, op. cit., pp. 180–181.
35. Joshi and Narwani, op. cit., pp. 243–246.
36. Ghosh and Kumar, op. cit., pp. 186–188. See also, Webster, 'Panchayati Raj in West Bengal: Popular Participation for the People or the Party', op. cit., pp. 229–230.
37. Joshi and Narwani, op. cit., pp. 244–245.
38. Ibid.
39. Prafulla Chandra Sen, *Partyless Democracy*, Kolkata: Gandhi Memorial Committee, 1981, p. 18.
40. Ibid., p. 13.
41. Jayaprakash Narayan, *Swaraj for the People*, Varanasi: Sarva Seva Sangh Prakashan, 1977, p. 14.
42. Ibid., p. 18.
43. Joshi and Narwani, op. cit., p. 246.
44. Ibid.
45. Ibid., p. 244. See also, Webster, 'Panchayati Raj in West Bengal: Popular Participation for the People or the Party', op. cit., pp. 230–232.
46. Webster, 'Panchayati Raj in West Bengal: Popular Participation for the People or the Party', op. cit., p. 231.
47. Ibid.
48. Bhattacharya and Datta, op. cit., pp. 174–175.
49. Moitree Bhattacharya, *Panchayati Raj in West Bengal*, New Delhi: Manak Publications, 2002, p. 163.
50. *Panchayat Parichalana Prasange Nirdehsika (*in Bengali), Kolkata: State Committee of the Communist Party of India (M), 1994, p. 3.
51. Ibid.
52. Ibid., Section 1, p. 3.
53. E.M.S. Namboodiripad, 'Note of Dissent to Asoka Mehta Committee Report, 1978', cited in Buddhadev Ghosh and Girish Kumar, *State Politics and Panchayats in India*, New Delhi: Manohar, p. 178.
54. B.T. Ranadive, *People's Democracy,* 17 July 1977, cited in Buddhadev Ghosh and Girish Kumar, *State Politics and Panchayats in India*, New Delhi: Manohar, p. 178.
55. Ghosh and Kumar, op. cit., p. 178.
56. Ibid., p. 179.
57. Ibid.
58. Ibid., pp. 164–165.

59. Webster, 'Panchayati Raj in West Bengal: Popular Participation for the People or the Party', op. cit., pp. 232–233.
60. Ibid., p. 235.
61. Sen, op. cit., p. 12.
62. Joshi and Narwani, op. cit., p. 242.
63. Sen, op. cit., p. 14.
64. Chattopadhyay, op. cit., pp. 21–22.
65. Ibid.
66. G.O. No. PN/0/1/IA/IA-1/2004, Kolkata: Government of West Bengal, Panchayat Department, 7 January 2004, p. 1.
67. Narayan, op. cit., p. 52.
68. Ghosh and Kumar, op. cit., pp. 186–187.
69. Ibid., p. 184.
70. Bhattacharya, op. cit., p. 187.
71. Ibid., pp. 187–189, citing *Party Chithi*, No. 6 of 1995 and No. 5 of 1996 of the CPI (M).
72. Ghosh and Kumar, op. cit., pp. 186–187.
73. Ibid.
74. Joshi and Narwani, op. cit., p. 276.
75. Kuldeep Mathur, *Panchayati Raj*, New Delhi: Oxford University Press, 2013, p. 59.
76. Ibid., p. 141.

CHAPTER 13

West Bengal Panchayat Elections 2013

Contemporary Debates

Chanchal Chakrabarti

The title of the paper itself clearly expresses that the author intended to deal with issues involving the controversies that cropped up between the Government of West Bengal and the State Election Commission. Fundamentally, there was one issue and the other issues emanated from the basic issue. The principal issue involved the question of status and authority of the State Election Commission (SEC) vis-à-vis the State Government in supervision, control and direction in all matters relating to elections to the three-tier panchayats in West Bengal. A very serious theoretical question arose. Where lies the supreme authority – in the State Government or the State Election Commission? The author endeavoured to open the discussion with a focus on the provisions of the Constitution of India. Does the Constitution of India allow the executive government to interfere and intervene in conducting elections to local self-government bodies?

There is no dispute in regard to the power and authority of the Central Election Commission (CEC) in conducting the elections to the Union and state legislatures, the office of the President and Vice-President of India. The authority of the CEC is established beyond doubt. The moot question was whether the State Election Commission enjoys the same power and authority as that of the CEC. The Government of West Bengal and particularly the Minister in charge of Panchayat Affairs on many occasions clearly expressed their views that the SEC does not enjoy the same powers and authority as that of the CEC. Actually, the whole controversy had originated from this sort of understanding of constitutional provisions, Acts and precedents.

Another very important aspect of the recent controversies was the role of the judiciary. The Calcutta High Court and then the Supreme Court had occupied a pivotal role in the resolution of the issues of conflict between the state government and the SEC. How far these efforts had been successful are discussed in the following pages.

The third important issue that surfaced was the role of the Union government and particularly the Ministry of Home Affairs in sending the central armed police forces to the state for conducting the panchayat elections in the state in a smooth, free, fair and peaceful manner.

The fourth and the last point the author wanted to examine was the outcome of the initial stage of the election. The process of submission and withdrawal was over. Therefore, an attempt could be made to assess the situation as to how far the process had been peaceful, free and fair.

I

To elaborate the first issue, let us begin with the debates held on the floor of the Constituent Assembly on 15 June 1949. Attempts should be made to read the minds of the members of the Constituent Assembly on this particular question of granting autonomy to the Election Commission vis-à-vis the Government. It may be stated firmly that if we follow the arguments placed in the Constituent Assembly, we would find that there was complete unanimity among the members regarding the status to be granted to the Election Commission to conduct the elections in India in future. Participating in the debates, B.R. Ambedkar had submitted in the Constituent Assembly:[1]

> The House will remember that in a very early stage in the proceedings of the Constituent Assembly, a committee was appointed to deal with what are called Fundamental Rights. That committee made a report that it should be recognized that independence of the elections and the avoidance of any interference by the executive in the elections to the legislature should be regarded as Fundamental Rights and provided for in the chapter dealing with Fundamental Rights.

It was evident from the submission of Ambedkar that the Fundamental Rights Committee formed by the Constituent Assembly considered to place the Articles relating to Election Commission in the chapter where other Fundamental Rights were enumerated. So much so, importance was accorded to the issues of composition, removal, powers and authority of the Election Commission. But when the recommendations of the Fundamental Rights Committee were placed in the Constituent Assembly, the House without diluting the fundamental nature of the provisions relating to the Election Commission proposed to place them suitably in some other parts of the Constitution. But on the question of autonomy of the commission, there was complete unanimity in the House, which was reflected in Ambedkar's speech delivered in the House on 15 June 1949:[2]

> When the matter came up before the House, it was the wish of the House that while there was no objection to regard this matter as of fundamental importance, it should be provided for in some other part of the Constitution and not in the chapter dealing with Fundamental Rights. But the House affirmed without any kind of dissent that in the interests of purity and freedom of elections to the legislative bodies, it was of the utmost importance that they should be freed. From any kind of interference from the executive of the day ... Therefore, so far as the fundamental question is concerned that the election machinery should be outside the control of the executive government, there has been no dispute.

The question might arise that the makers of the Constitution wanted to grant autonomy to the central election commission in regard to holding elections to Union and state legislatures, President and Vice-President of India. This kind of thinking or notion is the result of wrong interpretation or wrong understanding regarding the related arguments delivered in the Constituent Assembly by the learned members as well as the provisions of the Constitution. Before going to deal with the constitutional provision, it should be noted that the Constituent Assembly did not deliberate on the issues of holding elections to local self-government bodies. It was left to the states to enact appropriate legislation to organize panchayati raj system in chapter IV under the Directive Principles of State Policy (Article 40).

After four decades had passed since Independence, it was found that Panchayati Raj Institutions 'have not been able to acquire the status and dignity of viable and responsive people's bodies due to a number of reasons, including absence of regular elections, prolonged supersession, insufficient representations of weaker sections like Scheduled Castes, Scheduled Tribes and women, inadequate devolution of powers and lack of financial resources.'[3] In the light of this experience, it was considered that there was an imperative need to enshrine in the Constitution certain basic and essential features of Panchayati Raj Institutions to impart certainty, continuity and strength to them. Accordingly, the Seventy Third Amendment Act was passed to introduce the panchayati raj system uniformly throughout the country.

The Seventy Third Amendment Act is clear and specific on the powers, functions and authority of the State Election Commission. Article 243K (1) says – 'The superintendence, direction and control of the preparation of electoral rolls for, and the conduct of all elections to the Panchayats shall be vested in a State Election Commission consisting of a State Election Commissioner to be appointed by the Governor.'[4] After the Amendment, the State Election Commission had become a constitutional body which derives its powers and authority from the Constitution itself and does not depend on the mercy or whims of the state government. The Constitution under Article 243k (1) had unequivocally vested the power to supervise, direct and control the process of elections to the panchayats beginning from preparation of electoral rolls to the declaration of results and issuance of certificates to the victorious candidates. In a similar way, the Seventy Fourth Amendment Act had vested under Article 243ZA the power of superintendence, direction and control of the process of election to the municipalities of the state.[5]

The Constitution of India had not ignored the rights of the states as well relating to the elections to the panchayats within the state. The Seventy Third Amendment Act 1992 had allowed the legislatures of the states of India to make legislation 'with respect to all matters relating to, or in connection with, elections to the panchayats.'[6] Similarly, the Seventy Fourth Amendment Act had provided the state legislatures under Article 243ZA the power to 'make provisions with respect to, or in connection with, elections to the municipalities'.[7] It is to be noted here that the states enjoy these rights subject to the provisions of the Constitution, not independent of it. It implies that the states may make provisions with respect to all matters relating to or in connection with the elections to the panchayats and municipalities within the state, in consistence with the provisions of the Constitution. If any provision made by any state legislature is found as inconsistent, the provision made by state legislature shall be treated as void.

The Government of West Bengal had claimed that they exercised the power they were provided with under Section 42 of the West Bengal Panchayat Act, 2003 in deciding the dates of poll and distribution of districts. The Minister in charge of panchayat affairs had categorically said, when he unilaterally announced the dates and phases of panchayat election in April 2013, that the West Bengal Panchayat Act, 2003 had empowered the state government to declare the dates and phases of poll and the distribution of districts as well. Against this misconception of the state government and to make the constitutional position clear, four points need to be raised.

First, in support of the state government's action, they were referring to the constitutional provision which has empowered them to make laws relating to all matters with reference to, or in connection with elections to the panchayats. The state government had overlooked or ignored Article 243K (4), which clearly implies that state governments can certainly make legislation, but subject to the provisions of the Constitution.[8]

Secondly, constitutional provisions always prevail over the legislative provisions made by the legislatures, be it the Union or state, if any conflict arises between the two. This is so because the Constitution is the basic document and all other institutions are required to function within the limits framed by the Constitution. In case of doubt or confusions, Constitution is supreme.

Thirdly, although local self-government is mentioned in the Constitution under state list empowering state governments to enact legislations on any matter relating to local-self government, after the enactment of the Constitution Seventy Third and Seventy Four Amendment Acts, the status of the state government had changed. The provisions made by the state legislature with respect to any matter relating to, or in connection with the elections to the panchayats or municipalities in the state are subject to the constitutional provisions made in the Seventy Third and Seventy Fourth Amendment Acts. Thus, the Constitution has vested the powers of superintendence, direction and control of elections to the panchayats and municipalities in the state election commission. Therefore, the power conferred upon the state government under Section 42 of the West Bengal Panchayat Act, 2003 to declare the dates of poll should be viewed as merely nominal or formal which should be exercised by the state government in effective consultation with the state election commission.[9]

Fourthly, this cannot be regarded as infringement of states' rights over state subjects. The Constitution of India itself has vested power of amendment to the Constitution in Parliament and that too according to the provisions laid down in the Constitution under Article 368. Article 368 very categorically and elaborately mentions the procedure of amendment to the Constitution. In other words, Article 368 prescribes different procedures for different areas or parts of the Constitution is the case in point.

Article 368 stipulates that amendment to the Seventh Schedule (state list) of the Constitution requires consent of at least fifty per cent states along with approval of Parliament. It implies that the Constitution Seventy Third and Seventy Fourth Amendment Act 1992 are based on the consent of the states.[10]

Apart from these arguments, what is required is to comprehend the provisions of the West Bengal Panchayat Act, 2003 and see whether it has actually armed the state government to ignore the views of the SEC. In no way it had done this. Under Section 42 of the West Bengal Panchayat Act, 2003, the state government is empowered to declare the dates of poll for any election to the panchayats. But this power would have to be exercised in consultation with the SEC. And here 'consultation' means concurrence or consensus opinion with the SEC. This interpretation of 'consultation' may face questions from those who think that Section 42 of state Act of 2003 empowered the state government to declare dates of poll after consultation with the SEC, even if the Commission disagrees to the dates suggested by the state government.[11]

In response to this argument, two points may be raised: one, powers and authority of the SEC have to be judged in the light of powers and functions of the Central Election Commission. Under Article 324 of the Constitution of India, the Central Election Commission has been provided with supreme powers in all matters relating to elections to the Union and state legislatures and President and Vice-President of India.[12]

Two, an argument had been forwarded that the status and position of the State Election Commission is not the same as that of the Central Election Commission. The argument is untenable. In view of the orders pronounced by the Supreme Court of India, in the case of Kishan Singh Tomar versus City Municipality of Ahmedabad, Gujarat, it had become crystal clear that 'the same powers are vested in the State Election Commission as the Election Commission of India under Article 324.' Not only that, as per the Supreme Court's view expressed in the same case, 'the State Election Commissions are to function independent of the concerned state government' in the discharge of its duties.[13]

Taking into account all the arguments placed and discussed above at length and 'applying the golden rule of interpretation' by the Supreme Court, the powers and authority of the State Election Commission shall have to be judged. And if that was done, the supremacy of the SEC could be seen as clearly established vis-à-vis the state government. It had also been upheld by the Calcutta High Court Division Bench Comprising Chief Justice Arun Misra and Justice Joymalyo Bagchi in its Judgment on 13 June 2013.[14]

II

The conflicts and controversies that emerged between the Government of West Bengal and the State Election Commission are unprecedented, uncalled for and unwarranted. From the very beginning of the election process, the state government had shown an attitude which implied that the SEC was subordinate to the state government. This had been disproved by the foregoing discussion.

The dates and stages of poll became a major issue of conflict between the state government and the SEC. At the first instance, the dates and phases of poll were announced by the Minister in charge of panchayat affairs without consultation with the SEC. In the declaration, it was expressed that the government had wanted to hold the panchayat election in two phases – fourteen districts out of total seventeen in the first phase and the remaining three districts (Murshidabad, Malda, North Dinajpur) in the second phase. The SEC did not issue a notification following the government notification. The Commission had differed on both the issues. First, they were of the opinion that the panchayat elections should be held at least in three phases. Secondly, the distribution of districts was made with a heavy political overtone. In the press, electronic media and the political circles as well, the government's decision was subject to severe criticism on the ground that the government had deliberately segregated three districts in the second phase where Congress had a predominant position.

Under intense pressure, the government had to backtrack and redistributed the districts as twelve (first phase) and five in second phase. That also could not satisfy the SEC for obvious reasons. They stuck to their original position that elections should be held in three phases. At the same time, the SEC was raising the security issue. From the beginning, the SEC wanted the election to be held with the security posting of central forces and categorically demanded 800 companies of central forces, 300 from the date of nomination and the remaining 500 companies till the declaration of the results. On the other hand, the state government had been contradicting the SEC's demand for central forces, sometimes on the plea of availability, times on pretext of huge expenses. It was very surprising to note that the Governor did not intervene at this stage. He could have instructed his government to make available the security forces as required by the SEC. As a last resort, the SEC had to move the Calcutta High Court appealing to the court to give directions to the state government so that the government accepts the supremacy of the SEC in all matters relating to the panchayat elections.

Justice Biswanath Samaddar in his judgment on 10 May 2013 clearly upheld the supreme position of the SEC in matters relating to panchayat elections. The main points delivered in the judgment were as follows:

1. The panchayat election shall be held in three phases.
2. The SEC's authority to decide the dates of poll and make district-wise grouping was recognized. However, the SEC was directed to communicate the dates of poll and district-wise grouping to the state government immediately upon the receipt of exact details of availability of security personnel from the government.
3. As far as security personnel were concerned, the government was directed to arrange forces by bringing in central forces as well as forces from other states to the satisfaction of the Commission.
4. The state government was also directed to provide to the Election Commission the rest of the names of observers as well as the exact details of the security arrangements latest by 11 May 2013.

The state government was aggrieved at the High Court judgment and the panchayat minister was so visibly agitated that he challenged Justice Biswanath Samaddar to come forward and do the things within 24 hours. The state government moved the High Court for revision of the judgment passed by Justice Samaddar. A Division Bench comprising Chief Justice Arun Misra and Justice Joymalya Bagchi passed an order on 13 May 2013, the main points of which were as follow:

1. The panchayat election shall have to be held in three phases and the entire poll process is to be completed by 15 July 2013.
2. The dates for the election shall be notified by the government in consultation with the SEC.
3. The court classified the 58,000-odd booths into four categories: (i) Highly sensitive (ii) Sensitive (iii) Less sensitive (iv) Normal and set the principles of security posting in the following manner.

   Highly sensitive: Two armed policemen and two unarmed constables; Sensitive booth: two armed police men; Less sensitive: one armed policeman and one unarmed constable; Normal: one armed police personnel per premises.
4. The Division Bench did not accept the SEC's view that 800 companies of central armed forces were required to conduct the panchayat election in West Bengal in a free, fair and peaceful manner.

   The court directed that the state government may procure forces from other states or the Centre, if necessary.

The court also said that the order was passed with the 'consent' of both the parties – the SEC and the state government. The 'consent' word was seriously contested by SEC's senior counsel Samaraditya Pal and it was modified accordingly in a subsequent order on 13 June 2013 by the same Division Bench.[15]

This order of the Division Bench made the state government jubilant and more aggressive towards the role of the State Election Commission. The apparent reasons were two: one, the state government got the message that by the Division Bench's order the authority of the SEC had been curtailed. Two, the state government's dilly-dallying tactics regarding deployment of forces had been encouraged. Actually, the Division Bench had usurped the SEC's authority. It was the authority of the SEC to decide the quantum of security forces required to be deployed for holding elections to local self-government institutions. There was another important point the Division Bench had overlooked. Their order regarding the deployment of forces was actually meant for poll dates. There was no mention in regard to the deployment of forces for pre-poll period, namely the nomination paper submission stage. This had weakened the position of the SEC and the ruling party took full advantage of it. But the constitutional mandate was clear enough in this regard. It was the State Election Commission which was authorized to decide about the personnel required for holding the elections in a free, fair and peaceful manner. The Governor was under constitutional obligation to arrange the personnel as requisitioned by the State Election Commission.

In view of the Division Bench's order dated 14 May 2013, it seemed that the stalemate was over and the panchayat election could be held. Following the state government's declaration, the State Election Commission duly notified dates of poll in three phases on 2, 6 and 9 July 2013. Still the election commission was not satisfied with the government's decision to hold elections to the nine districts in the first phase on 2 July on the ground that availability of adequate security forces was not made clear by the state government. However, the SEC, on the basis of sensitivity-linked formula laid down by the High Court, wrote two letters dated 20 May and 10 June to the state government requesting them to let the SEC know in concrete terms in regard to the availability of the security forces, but received no positive answer or assurance from the Government.

Under such circumstances, the Commission again moved the High Court for deletion of the word 'consent' from the 15 May order as well as sought the court's views on the primacy of the SEC for holding elections to the local self-government bodies. The Commission further demanded the Division Bench's direction to the state government for arrangement of security forces. The Division Bench 'upheld the supremacy of the SEC in conducting the panchayat polls'. On deployment of forces, 'the Bench clarified that the Commission must get what it wants – not outside the deployment plan specified by the May 14 ruling – and it was up to the state government to arrange the personnel.'[16]

Even after this, the situation remained the same as it was before. The SEC sent another letter, but no result came out. Meanwhile, the central government had expressed its inability to provide central forces. Availability of forces from other states was near to zero possibility. It became almost clear that the election would have to be held only with the deployment of state forces. Even out of the state forces, the quantum of armed forces was not known to SEC. On the other hand, the government, particularly the Chief Minister and the panchayat minister, had been saying routinely that the election will be held in time. It implied that the state government had their own plan. They would treat the maximum booths as normal and thereby reduce the requirements of armed forces. The SEC was calculating the requirements on the basis of the sensitivity position of the booth areas as specified by the district administrative authorities and mentioned in the order of the court.

III

The state government and the SEC were locked in a stalemate situation over the deployment of security forces, which the Division Bench of the High Court could not even resolve. It was a clear direction of the Division Bench in its order of 14 May 2013 that it was binding upon the state government to arrange the forces as prescribed in the order itself. Where from the forces would come, it was up to the state government to decide and arrange. Chief Justice Arun Misra expressed the same spirit in his observation on 13 June 2013.[17]

Meanwhile, the state government communicated in public that out of the three states they had approached, only Punjab had verbally agreed to provide their forces, which even as on 27 June seemed to be uncertain due to lack of follow-up action by the state government. As far as central forces were concerned, the state government vehemently opposed the idea of deployment of central forces, as desired by the SEC since September 2012. At the last moment, under compulsion of the High Court order of 14 May, the state government wrote to the Union home ministry seeking 300 companies of central forces for the panchayat election in the state on 29 May. The Union home ministry expressed its inability to send security forces for the rural polls. In a subsequent development, after the initiative unleashed by the state Congress leadership, the Union home ministry signaled that the central forces would be made available. The Union Home Minister himself communicated to the press in Delhi on 11 June that he had already instructed the Union Home Secretary in this regard. The Chief Minister in Kolkata informed the press that she had personally talked to Union Home Minister, who assured her regarding the deployment of central forces. The Home Minister in his press briefing said that the state government was required to write a fresh letter seeking central security personnel.[18] But, surprisingly, Kolkata vernacular daily *Ananda Bazar Patrika* reported, referring to sources at Writers' Building, on 13 June 2013 that the Chief Minister had requested the Union Home Minister for central forces, but that is not for the panchayat election. Request was made for central forces to arrange additional security posting in the districts bordering Jharkhand and Odisha.[19]

The officers of the Union Home Ministry were surprised to know the claim made by their counterparts at Writers' Building at Kolkata. They claimed that the Chief Minister had sought central forces for panchayat poll. The state Congress president said, 'The Home Minister personally informed me that the Chief Minister had requested him for central forces to be deployed for the panchayat election.' Thus it further exposed the state government's unwillingness to hold the panchayat election with the central forces posted as guards. Even then the solution could have been found had the state taken an initiative to negotiate with the SEC and approached the court proposing to increase the number of phases by splitting nine districts scheduled to go for polls in the first phase into two or three legs as per availability of forces.

However, the state government simply did not do anything. They did not send a fresh application as suggested by the Union Home Minister, not discussed the issue open-mindedly with the SEC, nor approached the court for its direction. Ultimately, it was the SEC which submitted before the High Court on 24 June 2013 that it could not hold the election scheduled to begin on 2 July without adequate security forces. The hearing began on 24 June but remained inconclusive. The Division Bench directed the Centre's counsel to produce the Centre's views in writing on 25 June 2013.[20]

On 25 June morning, when the Division Bench met, the situation did not improve at all. In the afternoon, when the court hour was over, the situation remained almost the same. The only change was that the court suggested a five-phase election to which the Advocate General responded by pleading that a four-phase election was acceptable to the government. Then, the Calcutta High Court witnessed an unprecedented scene. Several calculators were brought in the court room and supplied to the counsels of both the parties to calculate the requirement of forces. Even at one stage it was seen that the Chief Justice was working with the calculator.[21] What the High Court was trying to do was not their business. The Division Bench was supposed to direct the SEC to let it know the requirement of forces and then direct the state government to arrange the forces to the satisfaction of the SEC. The Division Bench had virtually done the same in their order of 14 May 2013. Had the state government ensured the availability of forces as specified in 14 May order, the SEC would not have filed the petition expressing its inability to hold the election due to inadequate forces. Actually the Division Bench should have initiated *suo motu* contempt proceedings against the state government for its failure to comply with the court's order of 15 May.

'Holding of local polls is a state responsibility for which central forces are not used,' submitted Union home ministry counsel Mr S.S. Sarkar before the Division Bench of the Calcutta High Court. In this regard, two comments might be made. One, on earlier occasions, central forces were used for local polls in West Bengal. Two, although local self-government is a state subject, the Union government is under constitutional obligation to help the state government in the discharge of its constitutional responsibilities, if the central government is so requested by the state government concerned.[22] Similarly, if any state government is requested by the Centre to offer assistance in the discharge of constitutional responsibilities on any Union subject, the state government is expected to carry out the Centre's request.[23] This part of the Constitution of India reflects the principles of cooperative federalism. Thus, it was very difficult to understand the attitude of the central government. First, they rejected the state government's request, thereafter they agreed and again declined to provide central forces for the rural polls in West Bengal. The Maoist attack in Chhattisgarh and natural disaster in Uttarakhand may have influenced the Centre's decision. In that case, they could have requested the state to fix the poll dates as per their convenience to deploy central forces. That they had done, but under the Supreme Court's order on 28 June.

What happened in Calcutta High Court was surprising and unprecedented as well. It reflected the casual approach on the part of the state government and ineffective handling of the issues by the High Court on 24 and 25 June. On 26 June, just six days before the first phase of poll on 2 July, the Division Bench was still trying to find out a solution so that the poll could be held on 2 July. However, the State Election Commission had moved the Supreme Court praying for rescheduling the dates of poll, redistribution of districts and assurance of adequate security forces. So the battle between the state government and the SEC was shifted from Kolkata to Delhi.

The issues so long remained unresolved were settled by the Apex Court in just two days. The Supreme Court Division Bench comprising Justice A.K. Patnaik and Justice Ranjan Gogoi clearly showed that in the matter of elections to the local self-government bodies, the Constitution had vested supreme power in the State Election Commission. The Supreme Court had indicated from the beginning its firmness and determination to resolve the issues involved without delay. In fact, all issues were settled in just two days. The Supreme Court directed to hold the election in five phases according to new schedule (first phase on 11 July and last phase on 25 July). The court issued orders to both central and state governments to provide the security forces as specified in the order.[24] The Supreme Court of India deserved high praises for their promptness, prudence and efficiency in resolving the situation of impasse which had been continuing for three months. The Supreme Court Division Bench's commitment towards protection of democracy at the grassroots level was highly appreciable. In real terms, the Division Bench had vindicated the view of the State Election Commission and upheld the supremacy of the SEC in all poll-related matters of panchayats and municipalities.

IV

The Constitution had prescribed that every panchayat shall remain in office for five years from the date of its first meeting and no longer. Therefore, it is imperative that elections to the panchayats shall have to be held before the expiration of terms of the previous bodies. That was why the SEC had initiated the preparation well in advance in April 2012. The first letter they sent to the state government was in April 2012 and it was replied to by the government in August, 2012. The state government claimed that they wanted elections in the winter of 2012, but it were the Opposition parties and the SEC which did not want that the election was held. Was the allegation of the state government true? In fact, the election could not be held before 15 March 2013. At first the State Election Commission was required to complete the preparation of electoral rolls and then reservation of seats for SC/ST/OBC and women. The last date for completion of reservation being 15 March 2013, the election could not be held prior to that day. Polls to the panchayats could have been held any time between 15 March and 30 June 2013. Since at the earliest the term of some of the panchayats was scheduled to expire on 28 June 2013, there was enough time to hold the polls and ensure that no constitutional crisis was created. But that did not happen.

Now the question surfaced in different circles and media to shift the burden and incidence of unwanted delays and constitutional crisis. The issue involving religious sentiments in holding elections in the month of *Ramzan* was raised, and almost all political parties tried to exploit the minorities' sentiment. The state government from the very beginning had been attempting to decide the dates of poll and distribution of districts without effective consultation with the SEC. The government remained rigid on the non-deployment of central forces for the rural polls. Although they applied for central forces at the last moment on 29 May 2013, the central government declined. It actually strengthened the state government's original position. The state government initially insisted that the poll would be held on a single day, then agreed to hold it in two and later after the direction of the Calcutta High Court in three phases. As far as security forces were concerned, the state government's position remained unaltered. They intended to hold the election with the posting of state police personnel. But why was the state government so uncompromising on the use of central forces for the election? The reasons might be the experiences they had gathered from the byelection to the Howrah parliamentary constituency. Victory with a narrow margin and CPI (M) 's victory in two Assembly segments had made them think that the posting of central forces might lessen their chances of victory in a good number of panchayats. The Howrah parliamentary by poll clearly demonstrated the fact that deployment of central forces could make a huge difference.

The Supreme Court had rescheduled panchayat poll on the new dates in five phases with a rider that election be held on the basis of nominations that had already been submitted previously. During the period of submission of nomination papers, the SEC requisitioned for 300 companies of central forces. After realizing that they would not be getting central forces, they wanted 350 companies of state police personnel, which too they were not provided with. Thirty-two companies of state police force were ultimately posted to handle the security aspect during the nomination papers' submission. As a result, a large number of seats were won uncontested, of which 98 per cent went in favour of the ruling party. This fact had unmasked the government's design and provides the answer as to why the state government was insisting on holding panchayat election with the posting of state police personnel.

But was it the first time, that a huge number of seats had been won uncontested? Was it the first time that the government had arranged security forces to its advantage? No, it had precedence. The previous Left Front government and particularly the CPI (M) did the same thing. The panchayat election 2003 still remained ahead of the panchayat election 2013 in terms of the seats won uncontested. It was true that in 2013 election, 10.6 per cent of the total seats were declared uncontested. It was also true that in 2003 election, 11.6 per cent of total seats had been won unopposed by the ruling party. The most interesting fact was that in most of the areas where the CPI (M) had won uncontested in 2003, the TMC won without contest in 2013. In areas such as Arambag, Goghat, Khanskul, Pursura in Hooghly district; Kespur, Garbeta, Shalbani, Ghatal, Chandrakona in West Midnapur; Raina, Ketugram, Mangalkot in Burdwan district and many other areas, the CPI (M) had established their hegemony. They did not allow free and fair election to take place. In 2013 panchayat elections, TMC had been following in the footsteps of the CPI (M). They did not allow the Opposition candidates to submit their nomination papers. Even those who had been successful in submitting their papers were not allowed to campaign freely and fairly. Some people might say the right treatment was meted out to the CPI (M). Some even might say that the CPI (M) had been paid in their own currency. History was repeated, it was tit for tat. But the larger question remained unanswered. If this continues to happen, then what would become of grassroots level democracy?

Notes

1. *Debate in the Constituent Assembly*, Nirvachan Sadan: Election Commission of India, e-copy, p. 4.
2. Ibid.
3. The Constitution Seventy Third Amendment Act, 1992, Statement of Objects and Reasons, First Para (online material).
4. The Constitution Seventy Third Amendment Act, 1992, Article 243K (1).
5. The Constitution Seventy Fourth Amendment Act, 1992, Article 243ZA (1).
6. The Constitution Seventy Third Amendment Act, 1992, Article 243K (4). 'Subject to the provisions of this Constitution, the Legislature of a State may, by law, make provisions with respect to all matters relating to, or in connection with, elections to Panchayats.'
7. The Constitution Seventy Fourth Amendment Act, 1992, Article 243ZA (2).
8. The Constitution Seventy Third Amendment Act, 1992, Article 243K (4).
9. The West Bengal Panchayat Act, 2003, Government of West Bengal, Law Department, Section 42.
10. Article 368 (2) of the Constitution – 'An amendment of this Constitution may be initiated only by the introduction of a Bill for the purpose in either House of Parliament, and when the Bill is passed in each House by

a majority of the total membership of that House and by a majority of not less than two-thirds of the members of that House present and voting, it shall be presented to the President who shall give his assent to the Bill and thereupon the Constitution shall stand amended in accordance with the terms of the Bill:

Provided that if such amendment seeks to make any change in -

(a) article 54, article 55, article 73, article 162 or article 241, or

(b) chapter IV of Part V, chapter V of Part VI, chapter I of Part XI, or

(c) any of the Lists in the Seventh Schedule, or

(d) the representation of States in Parliament, or

(e) the provisions of this article,

the amendment shall also require to be ratified by the Legislatures of not less than one-half of the States by resolutions to that effect passed by those Legislatures before the Bill making provision for such amendment is presented to the President for assent ...'

11. The West Bengal Panchayat Act, 2003, Government of West Bengal, Law Department, Section 42.
12. Article 324 (1) of the Constitution -

    'The superintendence, direction and control of the preparation of the electoral rolls for, and the conduct of, all elections to Parliament and to the Legislature of every State and of elections to the offices of President and Vice-President held under this Constitution shall be vested in a Commission (referred to in this Constitution as the Election Commission).'
13. The Supreme Court's verdict on the case of Kishan Singh Tomar vs Municipal Corporation of the City of Ahmedabad on 19 October 2006, 'In fact, in the domain of elections to the Panchayats and the Municipal bodies under the Part IX and Part IX A for the conduct of the elections to these bodies, they enjoy the same status as the Election Commission of India. In terms of Article 243 (1) and Article 243ZA (1), the same powers are vested in the State Election Commission as the Election Commission of India under Article 324. The words in the former provisions are in *pari materia* with the latter provision.'
14. *Statesman*, Kolkata, 14 June 2013 ('A Division Bench of Calcutta High Court today upheld the supremacy of the State Election Commission in the holding of the Panchayat elections in the state as contained in Article 243 K of the Constitution of India.')
15. *Telegraph*, Kolkata, 14 June 2013 ('Calcutta High Court today removed the word 'consent' from a part of its earlier order and upheld the primacy of the State Election Commission in conducting the panchayat polls.')

16. *Telegraph*, Kolkata, 14 June 2013.
17. *Telegraph*, Kolkata, 14 June 2013 (Chief Justice Misra said, 'Whether it is from the Centre, other states or any other source, it will be up to the state to arrange for the forces.')
18. *Telegraph*, Kolkata, 12 June 2013 ('Yes, it [paramilitary forces] will be given,' – Shinde told reporters in New Delhi.)
19. *Anandabazar Patrika*, Kolkata, 13 June 2013.
20. *Telegraph*, Kolkata, 25 June 2013.
21. *Telegraph*, Kolkata, 26 June 2013.
22. Article 258A of the Constitution of India states, 'Notwithstanding anything in the Constitution, the Governor of a State may, with the consent of the Government of India, entrust either conditionally or unconditionally to that Government or to its officers functions in relation to any matter to which the exclusive power of the State extends.'
23. Article 258 (1) of the Constitution of India states, 'Notwithstanding anything in the Constitution, the President may, with the consent of the Government of a State, entrust either conditionally or unconditionally to that Government or to its officers functions in relation to any matter to which the executive power of the Union extends.'
24. *Telegraph*, Kolkata, 28 June 2013.

IV

Decentralizing Development: Including the Excluded

CHAPTER 14

Ethnopolitics and Self-governance in Darjeeling Hills

The Lepcha and the Panchayats

Tapan Kumar Das

This is a descriptive exposition of how the Lepcha, a marginalized and threatened ethnic community, participates in and intends to make use of the institution of Panchayati Raj for survival against domination of the diasporic Nepalese and the State.[1] Both the Nepali leaders and the State, often in collusion, try to use the panchayat as an instrument either for strengthening and expanding their hegemonic power or for control over the resources in Darjeeling hills. This process of control indirectly but effectively denies participation of the marginalized communities in the arena of power: political and economic. As the politics of the dominants and the struggle for survival of the Lepcha collide, the efficacy of the panchayat as a step to self-governance is questioned.

This study never tries to side with any pontificated theories or grand narratives. Rather, it is intended to lay open the multilayered tensions implicit in the political processes of the marginalized Lepcha that has put a shadow on the viability of this grassroots level institution of self-government. The primary source materials of this study come from the Government Register containing the results of the Gram Panchayat election 2000.[2] It is indeed a revealing election analysis because it exposes the nature of participation of the marginalized in the primary level of self-government. However, I am not using this space to focus on the benefits and success of the panchayat as an instrument of development. Secondly, It is proposed to reconsider the myth of representation through panchayat in a situation vitiated by ethnic hegemony of one over other marginal communities in Darjeeling hills. Not even constitutional provisions regarding reservation for the tribe ensure representation. Thirdly, in spite of having a glorified system of panchayats in West Bengal, it is doubtful whether making of a 'political panchayat' would be an appropriate step for the economically and numerically marginalized tribes living in different parts of West Bengal.

Demographic Profile

The Lepcha of Darjeeling hills are becoming the subject of media attention and government experiment of late for their struggle for survival in the face of hegemonic rule of the diaspora Nepalese.[3] Very recently, Bimal Gurung, the chief of the Gorkha Janamukti Morcha (GJM), threatened publicly that he would drive the Lepcha away from the Darjeeling hills if they would not kowtow before him.[4] Funny indeed: the diaspora wishes to drive the bhumiputras from the Mayel-lyang – the land of the Lepcha.[5] The Congress, BJP and the Left are keeping a strategic silence as they did in the past. Since their attainment of numerical majority, through continuous migration over decades, the dominant Nepalese diaspora community was trying to establish its hegemonic rule and redraw the mosaic of hitherto existing ethnic politics in the hills through denial of the separate identity to the native Lepchas and other ethnic groups. The ruling parties pamper the diaspora for political interests by dishonoring the spirit of the Constitution: building an egalitarian and strong state. I hope this sketch of ethnopolitics of Darjeeling hills is enough to set in motion my earlier premise that panchayat-tribe relation is to be looked at as multilayered tension-area. This is a skeletal analysis as very few of these layers can be considered in the anvil in this little space.

The majority of the Lepcha, a 'palae-mongoloid – brachycephalic' human group, are living in the subdivision of Kalimpong in West Bengal.[6] By religion, Lepchas are either Buddhists or Christians with indomitable inclination to their primitive animist faith; but their struggle for survival often faces hurdles due to religious rift. In spite of their Mongoloid lineage, they are conspicuously different from the Tibetans, Nepalese or the Bhutanese of the same stock. Their physical traits, history, language, and culture make them unique as an 'isolated tribe'.[7] As many as 32,377 Lepchas are living in West Bengal.[8]

Besides, small population status and high rate of dispersal has weakened the Lepcha to a great extent. Concentration of the Lepcha is comparatively higher in the subdivision of Kalimpong but penetration of the diasporic Nepalese in every corner of the subdivision again makes them numerically weak and scattered.[9] Besides, the geographical distribution of the panchayat constituencies often disregards the spatial concentration of the community. So, numerical weakness, scattered living and fragmentation induced by electoral laws stand in the way to full utilization of this occasion.

Majority of them are marginal cultivators owning 1–3 acres of land on an average. Profit from agricultural production depends on many things: on the one hand, amount of capital investment, weather and diseases and the market price, transportation and amount of debt one has to repay after final procurement of produce on the other. Hence, income is unsteady and seasonal, which cannot improve their standard of living. Roy shows that the Lepcha produce foodgrain mainly for the household consumption and cash crops and vegetables for marketing. However, production of foodgrain, like paddy, millet and maize, may not always be enough for the household and one has to buy the rest from the market either through cash or in exchange of any produce. In case of production of cash crops, the Lepcha are still undecided on investing capital and labour for profit. So, the Lepcha have to bear with the crises of subsistence economy.[10] Further, indebtedness among them is one of worsening nature as debt per borrower families in cash (₹ 1,442.60) and kind (55.5 kg) is highest in comparison to other major tribes of the region (like, the Rabha and Mech).[11] So, the Lepcha are the economically marginalized bhumiputras of Darjeeling hill areas. Could panchayat system be an effective instrument of participation and empowerment for the Lepcha under such circumstances?

The Lepcha and the Decentralizing Experiments

At the panchayat level, engagement of the Lepcha is more perceptible both in case of candidacy and electioneering. Since the inception of the system of panchayat in Darjeeling hills, the Lepcha have been participating in this system of self-governance. Due to unavailability of year-wise participation data, it is difficult to ascertain how much they can exploit this occasion for political advantage or benefit of the community. The doctoral dissertations of Sonam Wangdi Lepcha and Samit Ghosal will be helpful to understand the trend of Lepcha participation at the panchayat level. Although Sonam's observation was pretty optimistic, Ghosal noted a downward trend.[12] In his opinion, the panchayat cannot replace the authority of the traditional tribal council headed by the Mondal except in case of settlement of inter-ethnic disputes. This divide between the institution of Mondal (the village head) and the statutory institution of panchayat, is an obstruction to full use of the institution of panchayat. However, Ghosal's observation is more archaic in the sense that the institution of Mondal has to share power with the more powerful indigenous Lepcha Tribal Association (ILTA) of late.

We may now turn our attention to two very significant developments perceived in the hills during the decade of 1970s. The Lepcha of Darjeeling hills faced heavy assaults on their identity and existence in the 1970s. It is said that diasporic Nepalese threatened them not to reveal their Lepcha identity, the name and language, to the Census data collectors so that the Lepcha would be recorded as the Nepalese.[13] Under such veiled threats of ethnocide, the panchayat became meaningless to the Lepcha and it is an uphill task to use their reserved category status for self-rule. Indeed, during field tours in 1980s, I met very few old Lepcha panchayat pradhans and I did not find any Lepcha holding a position in the panchayat samiti or zilla parishad what Sonam has observed earlier.[14] Secondly, in late 1970s, the Left Front came to power and panchayats became the network of power of the Left, especially of the CPI (M), till the end of 1980s. However, the party rule never honoured the question of self-rule for the ethnic minority like the Lepcha.

Panchayati Raj Institutions in the hills have long worked under the Congress and Left rule. This was the first phase of panchayat politics in Darjeeling hills. The second phase began since 1980s. In 1988, the Gorkha National Liberation Front (GNLF) under the leadership of Subhas Ghising replaced rule of the CPI (M) and strangulated all political activities of the Opposition in the hills. As rule of the democracy was severely curtailed, the panchayat suffered extraordinary jolts.[15] A report of the Government of West Bengal on empowering the panchayat observes:

> Referring back to the earlier DGHC Act of 1988, one may recall that the ... Hill Council will be a substitute for the zilla parishad in the hill areas, the existing HADC and the District Planning and Coordinating Council. According to the provisions of DGHC Act, the Darjeeling hills have enjoyed the typical two-tier system of local governance; that too was opposed by Ghising and it ultimately ceased to exist from 2006. In Darjeeling district, local governance comprises Gram Panchayats and Darjeeling Gorkha Hill Council (DGHC) in the hill Sub-Divisions of Darjeeling, Kalimpong and Kurseong ...

It is crucial to note that while the entire country has been enjoying the benefits of the 73rd Constitution Amendment Act, particularly in terms of participation of the common masses in matters of grassroot level governance, the people of Darjeeling hills hardly had that scope. This was thanks to the Gorkhaland movement, which aimed at achieving self-rule, at the cost of rendering injustice to the common people and denied them the minimum opportunity to take part in the process of governance with whatever capacity they possess ... However, the single-tier system, which was in force since the last five years, now stands as a totally defunct body due to political reasons.[16]

So, the Darjeeling Gorkha Hill Council Act, 1988, a clear expression of the political understanding between the central and state leadership and clamouring Ghising, ignored the basic structure of self-governance and reduced it to Council dominated one-tier panchayat system. The civil societies in Darjeeling hills have not been in tune with Ghising's version of panchayat politics.[17]

In the third phase, the Gorkhaland Territorial Administration (GTA) Act, 2011, has been enacted repealing the Darjeeling Gorkha Hill Council Act of 1988. As per GTA agreement, the Department of Panchayats and Rural Development, including DRDA, has been transferred to the GTA. However, going back to the three-tire panchayat system requires new legislation or amendment. Interestingly, at the end of 2012, the GJM leaders like Bimal Gurung and Roshan Giri become conscious about the efficacy of the local government for the all-sided development of the hills. It should be recalled that when Ghising considered panchayat 'as a threat to the autonomous body', Gurung and Giri were his close aides. Political conscience often stands bereft of conscience in reality.[18] As this politicking in the hills shows, the system of panchayat has had to stride through a difficult terrain since 1980s but till 2005 the gram panchayat was the only institution through which participation of the local people could be ensured.

Voting Behaviour of the Lepcha and their Political Perception

Before giving a critical glance to the working of panchayat, a brief explication of the Lepcha voting behaviour in the state and national level elections would be helpful to provide contextual background of the problematic. Dearth of statistical data on community-wise voting pattern, which is vital for understanding the totality of Lepcha voting behaviour, is a great hurdle. In the colonial days, the Lepcha first tried to take advantage of election in 1937 with independent candidature and lost the election. It was the age of restricted franchise where rich and educated hill people could participate in the fray. The names of two or three Christian Lepcha leaders surfaced but under colonial administration and growing hegemony of the diasporic Nepalese. Truly, the Lepcha suffered from political infirmity and so their voting behaviour could not be a decisive instrument for survival. In the post-colonial period, immature leadership and helplessness of the Lepcha became evident when Mr Rongong, a Christian Lepcha candidate, withdrew his candidature in favour of his Nepalese rival in 1962. This certainly had a negative effect on the Lepcha voting behaviour. In 1977 Assembly election, a CPI (M) supported candidate, S.P. Lepcha, got a few thousand votes and lost. It was likely that only few of such votes were actually Lepcha votes because Left had no such base among the Lepcha due to its calculated indifference to the Lepcha. Instead, a tradition of independent candidacy and slight leaning towards Congress was prominent. In fact, the Lepcha voting behaviour is often vacillating between political party centric voting and independent candidacy. The panchayat election of 2000 was no exception.

Success of the Lepcha in securing seats in the state and national assembly in 1980s and 1990s (Goulan Lepcha in the Legislative Assembly of West Bengal and S.P. Lepcha in Parliament, respectively) created an impression of strong electoral favour of Lepcha masses to their candidates. Truly, the Lepcha Association of Kalimpong has carried out an ethno-centric campaign for Lepcha candidates with an expectation of welfare of the community.[19] Yet, in practice, the political parties in power rule the roost. For instance, the Gorkha National Liberation Front (GNLF), a predominantly Nepalese political party, had greater share in success of Gaulan Lepcha, once the MLA of Kalimpong area, as it enjoyed unequalled political power in Darjeeling hills. Gaulan Lepcha, a Christian fellow, made promises but did nothing; but he campaigned for the GNLF candidate among the Lepcha in council election.[20] On the other hand, the MP, S.P. Lepcha, was less reachable to its own ethnic community and was completely non-committal to the basic demands of the Lepcha community. In any case, both of them failed to translate dreams of good and honourable living for the Lepcha. As a result, the relation between the MLA and MP and the Lepcha community was no better than a strained relationship, which again negatively affected the voting behaviour of the community.[21] On the other side, till its heyday in Darjeeling hills, the GNLF with its violent ethnicpolitics undermines Lepcha support and fragments Lepcha community on party lines. This set of data concerns the gram panchayats of Kalimpong-I Development Block, one of the three Development Blocks of the Kalimpong sub-division.[22] To understand the role of other political parties, especially the 'working class' party like the CPI (M), among the Lepcha ethnic group in the sub-division of Kalimpong, a review of the result of the last gram panchayat election of 2000 is illuminating.

It is found that participation of the Lepcha at the panchayat level is more clearly perceived, which is more diffused at the assembly and parliamentary level. I have tried to comprehend the trend on the basis of the available data on the Kalimpong-I Development Block. There are 115 constituencies in the Development Block I, out of which 57 constituencies have no Lepcha candidates at all. This analysis concentrates on those other 58 constituencies where one or more than one Lepcha candidate was in the fray. In 115 constituencies, the number of candidates who stood for election was 353. Among them, only 71 that is about 20 per cent candidates belonged to the Lepcha community. The party affiliation of these Lepcha candidates is revealing indeed. Almost 54 per cent (excluding 12 forfeited Lepcha candidates) of the Lepcha have been registered as the GNLF candidates. Next to GNLF come the Independents, who accommodate about 35 per cent of the total Lepcha candidates. Although independent is not a politically independent group in true sense, it is difficult, in practice, to dispel the political leaning of the Independent candidates. To be fair enough, Independents might have been of any political parties and they certainly could not dare to expose their political colour for protecting their interests. There were six Lepcha candidates, only 8 per cent of the total Lepcha candidates, who contested with CPI(M) support. The CPRM, the breakaway faction of the CPI(M) in the Darjeeling hills, on the other hand, gave two (only 3%) candidates but with independent status.

This gram panchayat level election results show, among others, a close fight between two contenders – the Lepcha GNLF and the Lepcha Independent candidates. Out of that total votes cast (24,086), 8,660 (36%) votes were registered in favour of all 71 Lepcha candidates. However, the GNLF succeeded to garner 47 per cent votes and interestingly, where the GNLF succeeded in getting 32 seats out of total 38, the Independent candidates won only three seats out of 25. In spite of having 44 per cent of votes, the Independent candidates trailed behind. So, the percentages of votes polled in favour of independents and GNLF cannot give any lead to infer about the rate of success of the parties at the end. The reason is that while the GNLF appeared as a monolith, there was more than one candidate among which independent votes got divided. This has confirmed the win of the GNLF candidates. It is possible that there were a number of GNLF-supported candidates among the Independents, as candidates with support from CPI (M) or CPRM, for maintaining tactical upper hand over its opponents.

The CPI (M) and CPRM got only three and one seat, respectively. Among its 19 CPI (M) candidates in total, the CPIM fielded Lepcha candidates in six seats and won in three, including one uncontested. Although the result was better than the Independents, its minuscule existence among the Lepcha was exposed. So, in spite of dominance in the plains as a party of the workers, peasants and oppressed, the CPI (M) never made inroads within the downtrodden-agriculturist Lepcha community. Rather, the communists have always been sided with and pampered the dominant Nepalese since 1930s, including demand for a separate state of *Gorkhasthan* in 1947. Ironically, in spite of that, the CPI (M) and CPRM, the minors of minority, could not make any dent in the panchayat level politics in Kalimpong-I Development Block.

The religious affiliations of the Lepcha candidates apparently look irrelevant in such study (Table 3). However, this is certainly one of the inherent tension-areas that one way or other affects the *project survival* of the Lepcha through self-governance. Out of total (71) contesting Lepcha candidates, 55 per cent (39) were Buddhists and 45 per cent (32) of Christian religion. Among them, 21 and 17 were Buddhists and Christians, respectively. So, majority of Lepcha candidates, 38 candidates in actuality, fought in the Gram Panchayat election with GNLF tickets (See Table 4). Among the Independent contestants, 15 were Buddhists and 10 Christians. The religious denomination of the CPI (M) and CPRM candidates needed no special mention for its insignificant existence.

Table 1 *Basic Data of the Lepcha Candidates and their Political Affiliation*

Total no. of constituencies	115	
Total no. of constituencies with Lepcha candidates	68	
Total no. of constituencies without any Lepcha candidates	57	
Total no. of candidates in the election fray	353	
Total no. of Lepcha candidates:	71	(20.11% out of 353)
Total no. of Lepcha GNLF candidates:	38	(53.52% out of 71)
Total no. of Lepcha Independent candidates	25	(35.21% out of 71)
Total no. of Lepcha CPM candidates	06	(8.45% out of 71)
Total no. of Lepcha CPRM candidates	02	(2.81% out of 71)

Table 2 *Details of Election Results*

Total no. of votes cast in favour of all candidates	24,086	
Total no. of votes cast in favour of the Lepcha candidates of all parties	8,660	
Total no. of votes cast in favour of Lepcha GNLF candidates	4,094	(47.27% out of 8,660)
Total no. of votes cast in favour of Lepcha Independent candidates	3,838	(44.29% out of 8660))
Total no. of votes cast in favour of Lepcha CPM candidates	661	(7.63% out of 8660)
Total no. of votes cast in favour of Lepcha CPRM candidates	69	(0.79% out of 8,660)
Total no. of GNLF candidates won	148	
Total no. of Lepcha GNLF candidates won	32	(21.62% out of 148 Lepcha candidates)
Total no. of Independent candidates won	31	
Total no. of Lepcha Independent candidates won	03	(9.67% out of 31 Lepcha candidates)
Total no. of CPI (M) candidates won	05	
Total no. of Lepcha CPI (M) candidates won	03	
Total no. of Lepcha CPRM candidates won	01	
Total No. of forfeited Lepcha candidates	12	(14.81% out of 71 Lepcha candidates)

Table 3 *Religious Affiliation of the Lepcha Candidates*

Religions	*GNLF*	*Independents*	*CPIM*	*CPRM*	*Total*
Buddhists	21	15	01	02	39 (55%)
Christians	17	10	05	—	32 (45%)
Total	38	25	06	02	71 (100%)

The religious affiliations of the Lepcha candidates apparently look irrelevant in such studies (Table 3). However, this is certainly one of the inherent tension-areas that in one way or other affects the *project survival* of the Lepcha through self-governance. Out of total 71 contesting Lepcha candidates, 55 per cent (39) were Buddhists and 45 per cent (32) of Christian religion. Among them, 21 and 17 were Buddhists and Christians, respectively. So, majority of Lepcha candidates, 38 candidates in actuality, fought in the gram panchayat election with GNLF tickets (See Table 4). Among the Independent contestants, 15 were Buddhists and 10 Christians. The religious denomination of the CPI (M) and CPRM candidates needs no special mention for its insignificant existence.

Findings and Epilogue

The panchayat, it is believed and is often inculcated by the government agencies, is an exemplary institution of local self-government. It is an instrument of participation of the village masses in the arena of power where legislation and execution of policies affect their lives. The Constitution of India and its later-day amendments try to reassure self-governance of the women and the tribes in this system of governance. However, beyond principles, rules and amendments, the objectives of panchayat still remain unapproachable to the tribal community in practice. Or, it may be approachable for the fulfillment of interests of the dominant sections of the locality. It has as well been a venture of the tribal communities to make an optimum use of the institution under the flag of the dominant. Not only that, intra-community fissures may come out as some tribal leaders want to share the power with the non-tribal leaders at the cost of the community. Moreover, a close look at the patterns of function of any institution of urban and rural self-government reveals that it becomes a space for politics and corruption. Marginal ethnic community like the Lepcha is an alien and unwanted in this systemic aberration.

True to the fact, the advantage of panchayati raj is multifaceted but transforming the advantage into reality is a complicated process often intercepted by a number of dangerous intervening variables. This I call the present milieu of the self-governance which needs certain epistemological and ontological enquiry without delay to demystify the grand narratives on 'panchayati raj'. Besides, we must take into account multilayered tension areas: clash of endogenous elements and exogenous threats between people and politico-bureaucratic executives, within the system of self-governance. Again, absolutely crucial is the clash of ethnic interest that I try to delineate here: hegemonic rule of the diaspora towards the bhumiputra Lepchas undermines basic philosophy of self-governance. Therefore, the degree of advantage a community garners is primarily determined by the political, economic as well as numerical strength of the community concerned. In harnessing the advantages of the panchayats, they should have been provided with positive environment for a fight. None is ready for such commitment. Instead, we find:

(a) The Hill politics never shows any regard to the system of panchayat, especially since 1980s. The Panchayati Raj or such form of people's participation is intrinsically a part of the belief-system or culture. If participation is not sincerely valued, its execution for the benefit of the people would be seriously flawed. Hill politics of the diaspora Nepalese since its inception broadly stands in one point or other in the elite-autocracy continuum. The values of the panchayat system have never been accepted as a major thing. That is why GNLF chief Ghising takes the system of panchayats as infringement of power of the ruling caucus. Only the gram panchayat flickers for a short period. Relegation of three-tier system to nothingness is, therefore, normal to Ghising and his followers, including Bimal Gurung and Roshan Giri. During GJM reign, the elitist-autocratic character of the Nepalese leadership continues unhindered. The GJM leaders want a three-tier system of panchayats of late. Do they really have sincere interests in developing hill areas through this system? People like Bimal Gurung and Roshan Giri with a history of undemocratic obsession cannot make panchayat a success. In fact, democracy has gone into oblivion under GNLF and GJM rule. However, the GJM requires panchayat with same obsession to concentrate power in the hands of the new caucus. Indeed, panchayat will be a Foucauldian panoptic structure for surveillance over and strangulation of the Opposition as they have been taught through colonial and postcolonial politics of Darjeeling hills in particular and the state of West Bengal in general. So, instead of an instrument of development, the panchayat becomes an instrument of power certainly at the cost welfare of the hill people, irrespective of any ethnic community.

(b) Under such deformed system of panchayats, empowerment and development of the tribes will be an unaccomplished project. So, economically, the marginalized Lepcha are living in a system of subsistence economy and they are living in the villages without basic and proper amenities like, roads, markets, electricity, water and other supportive infrastructure.[23] Years after introduction of panchayati raj, no fundamental change is perceived till date. Experiences emanating from the field, that is village tours in Darjeeling hills, reveal that hill politics and its dominant actors as well as the State are indifferent to the proper execution of infrastructure development projects through panchayat or any other institutions. In the winter of 2012, I found, perhaps for the first time in more than two decades, that an important link road connecting remote villages with the nearest administrative centre in Kalimpong was under construction under 100-day work scheme. However, very few of such projects are undertaken and role of the panchayat in these development projects is yet to be ascertained. In fact, even the rule of the Nepalese-dominated GNLF and GJMM have paid little attention to the panchayats. It is now a redundant institution in Darjeeling hills. As big brothers are in the denial mode, the marginal Lepchas are hamstrung by such systemic obstacles. In spite of decades of operation of the panchayati raj, freedom from subsistence economy is still a fantasy for the Lepcha. For any kind of substantiation, government reports and Census reports are quite conspicuous.

(c) The Lepcha have a small population size and allegations of censoring their actual numbers by the dominant Nepalese really cannot be ruled out. In any case, numerical weakness cannot be appreciable to the politicians of all sorts, Left and right. In truth, none of the major political parties take care of their grievances till date, except the tactical steps taken by the present ruling party in West Bengal. Yet, the Lepcha have been forced to remain politically underrepresented in any rung of decision-making. The Lepcha candidates are found only in 50 per cent of gram panchayat constituencies. Setting aside its political colours, the Lepcha cannot file candidates in other 50 per cent constituencies of Block-I. The policy of seat reservation for the tribes fails to ensure representation of the Lepcha at the panchayat level.

(d) Community-centric bias often violates basic norms of the panchayati raj. The diasporic Nepalese leadership since the colonial days has been showing disregard to the bhumiputra Lepchas. In practice, the Nepalese leaders still try to deny the unique identity of the Lepcha. The leaders attempt to engulf them by categorizing the Lepcha as one of the castes within the caste hierarchy of the Nepalese. These attempts reach its climax when Bimal Gurung threatens to drive the Lepcha out from Darjeeling hills. The State, instead of protecting the minority, pampers the diasporic Nepalese as they are numerically the majority. So, the panchayats become a farce for a community suppressed by the dominant majority.

(e) Similarly, ideological tilt cannot bring fortune for the Lepcha community. It might be a fair assumptions that (a) Independent candidates stand for rejection of domination of the Nepalese-dominated GNLF and (b) the GNLF have also used a façade of Independent candidature to counter the ethnic protest against it. However, the party-wise breakup of those 71 Lepcha candidates is highly interesting not only for its political affiliation but also for its under-representation and fragmentation on the party lines. First, of the total number of candidates only about 20 per cent, that is less than a quarter of the total candidates, are the Lepcha candidates. It means that the Lepcha are politically under-represented in the area where density of the Lepcha population is highest than any hill subdivisions of Darjeeling district. Secondly, the Lepcha do not have political party of their own and they cannot take a united stand as they are divided into four political groups: the GNLF, Independent, CPI (M) and CPRM. So, this minority group is again divided broadly into GNLF (54%) and Independent contestants (36%). Thirdly, in spite of tradition of exploitation in the hands of the Nepalese, majority of the 71 Lepcha candidates that is, almost 54 per cent, fight on the GNLF tickets. In total, 55 per cent of the Lepcha contestants irrespective of party support have been elected. This is indeed an impressive victory provided the community could use it for the protection of community interests against the pressure of ethnic hegemony and party politics. Half of the Lepcha candidates lost and those who won have to remain under the domination of the Nepalese. So, development of the Lepcha can hardly be ensured through panchayati raj. It is indeed difficult to ascertain whether the Lepcha have succumbed to the pressure of the GNLF or it is a tactical move to realign with the GNLF for cause of the community. The dictatorial nature of the GNLF politics substantiates the former rather than the latter.

(f) Now, if we look at the success rate of the total number (71) of the Lepcha candidates, irrespective of party affiliation, with reference to the total number of candidates (353), the performance is abysmally poor. Whereas the GNLF has lost 13.51 per cent of the candidature only including one forfeited, 88 per cent of the Independent contestants got defeated in the election and among them 40 per cent forfeited their nomination fees. Greater is the failure if one looks at the fact that only three Independent candidates out of 25 (only 12%), succeeded in the panchayat elections even after getting 44 per cent of the total votes cast. So, for the GNLF, the opponents have either been dwarfed or fragmented. The field experience of the present researcher also reveals that the Lepcha in some cases fought against each other for lure of power or personal rivalry. So, this division of votes again exposes the internal feud and fragmentary nature of the Lepcha political representation. So alarming is the fact that an intra-community fight has been unleashed certainly at the cost of unity among its members. It is further observed that only 40 Lepcha candidates out of 71 won and 31 (including 12 forfeited) miserably defeated. So, a little less than half (44%) of the Lepcha candidates have been driven out of power. So, empowerment through self-governance remains a fantasy till date.

(g) Religious denominations also bring fragmentation and disunity within the Lepcha community. The majority of the Lepcha of Darjeeling hills, especially of Kalimpong, belong to the Buddhist religion and a great number of them lives in rural areas. They are the real protectors of Lepcha culture and language. And they are the most vocal and leading activists fighting for survival of the community. The converted Christian Lepcha, on the other hand, are indeed comparatively advanced in terms of education and economic standard. Till recently, there was a rift between these two sections of the Lepcha community. However, according to field experience, the Lepcha leaders, particularly the contesting candidates, of both religions never accept the diasporic Nepalese as just rulers of their land yet they fight with GNLF affiliation. They never have trust on the Nepalese leaders as past experiences have not been congenial to their survival. It is really difficult to resolve such contradictions but autocratic attitude, suppression, and if necessary expunging the opponents as policy of the diasporic Nepalese leaders cannot be an answer. In any case, the

Lepcha are divided either over the religious denominations or over the party lines that certainly enfeeble their attempts to turn panchayats into empowerment mechanism. So, the constitutionally recognized rules and institutions may not be the saviour of the Lepcha. Self-governance through panchayat is not an easy task as they are victims of various exogenous and endogenous threats. Such threats cannot easily be wiped out. Rather, these inimical conditions will continue under such socio-economic and political processes and the Lepcha have to suffer multilayered tension in the days to come. Political leaders of all colours can glorify the panchayati raj but it is they who create an impuissant State unable to save its crying citizens. Formation of 'political panchayat' is inefficacious for the Lepcha as they have no political party or strong political thrusters for protecting community causes. On the flip side, the Government of West Bengal has formed, with the consent of the Governor, a 'Mayel Lyang Lepcha Development Board' for the welfare of the Lepcha community of late.[24] It may ensure some sort of community participation in the process of empowerment of the Lepcha, but the aggressive GJM leadership would certainly impede the process. Unfortunately, the politics of the diasporic Nepalese leadership since its inception has been qualitatively so poor that they still cannot habituate themselves with the idea of a decentralized democracy and its basic institution: the panchayat.

Notes

1. Instead of the term *Gorkhas*, I have used the term *Nepalese* for its scientific authentication. For an interesting exposition of the term *Gorkhas,* please read Dipak De, *Prasanga Darjeeling, Gorkha Ke* (in Bengali), Allahabad: Anamika Prakashan, 2011. Among many books, *The Politics of Belonging in the Himalayas,* edited by Joanna Pfaff-Czarnecka and Gerard Toffin, New Delhi: Sage, 2011, is a good one with some in-depth articles.
2. Certified Handwritten Government Register Showing G.P.-wise Names of the Uncontested and Contesting Candidates, Panchayat Election–2000 (List of the Elected G.P. Members Result), Kalimpong-I Development Block Bearing Entry No. 1 to 58.
3. The present Chief Minister of West Bengal has proposed a Lepcha Development Council under the Department of Backward Class Welfare, Government of West Bengal.

4. *Eisamay* (Bengali Newspaper), A Times of India publication, 19 February 2013, p. 7.
5. It includes the whole of Sikkim, parts of Bhutan and eastern Nepal and areas of the plains up to Kishangunge of the present day. Darjeeling was a part of the state of Sikkim. Except imperial aggression of Nepal in the early days of 19th century, this region had never been a part of Nepal.
6. P.N. Bhattacharjee, 'Sero-Genetic Variations in the Lepcha of Darjeeling District with Special Reference to the Indian Mongoloids', *Bulletin of the Anthropological Survey of India*, No. 17, 1968, pp. 382–392; E.W.E. Macfarlane, 'Eastern Himalayan Blood Groups', *Man*, Vol. XXXVII, 1937, pp. 127–129; and H.H. Risley, 'The Tribes and Castes of Bengal', *Anthropometric Measurements*, Vols I & II, Calcutta, 1891.
7. G.B. Mainwaring, *A Grammar of the Lepcha Language*, New Delhi: Manjusri Publishing House, 1876 (1971 Reprint), pp. i-xxi.
8. Government of India, *Census Reports*, 2001.
9. Since last two centuries, migration of the Nepalese from Nepal has been continuing in and around the eastern Himalayan region. This migration heavily affected the Lepcha in all respects: political, economic, socio-cultural and what not. For an understanding of the nature of migration of Nepalese to India, please see Haraprasad Chattopadhyaya, *Migration between India and Nepal: A Socio-cultural Study*, Calcutta: Firma KLM Pvt. Ltd., 1996.

   Raju Bhattarai, 'Open Border, Closed Citizenships: Nepali Labor Migrants in Delhi', paper presented in the Seminar on International Migration, Multi-local Livelihood and Human Security: Perspectives from Europe, Asia and Africa, Institute of Social Studies, The Netherlands, 30 and 31 August 2007. Also, Dipak De, *Prasanga Darjeeling, Gorkha Ke* (in Bengali), Allahabad: Anamika Prakashan, 2011.
10. D.C. Roy, *Dynamics of Social Formation among the Lepcha*, New Delhi: Akansha Publication House, 2005.
11. S.K. Basu, *Indebtedness among the Tribals of West Bengal*, Calcutta: Cultural Research Institute, Monograph, 1974.
12. 'But their growing interest in politics can be seen in the result of Panchayat election of 1978. Several Lepcha candidates contested the Panchayat election and it is learnt that very few of them got defeated'. See Sonam Wangdi Lepcha, 'The Process of Detribalization of an Indian Tribe and Problem of its Modernization: A Sociological Study of the Lepcha of Darjeeling District', Unpublished Doctoral Dissertation, University of Bhagalpur, Bihar, 1979.

    'In the election of 1962, there were 10 Lepchas out of 15 members in the Pagang gram panchayat. But in the next election, which took place in

1978, the representation of the Lepcha community has come down to 7 from 15, though the Lepcha are numerically dominant group in this area. In the Nassay gram panchayat also the number of Lepcha members has become less in the last election ... This trend shows the decreasing interest shown by the Lepcha in the panchayat raj'. Samit Ghosal, The Lepchas of Darjeeling and Sikkim: A study in cultural ecology and social change, unpublished thesis, University of North Bengal, 1990, pp. 180–81.

13. Sonam Wangdi Lepcha, op. cit., p. 10.
14. Ibid.
15. Girish Kumar and Buddhadev Ghosh, *West Bengal Panchayat Elections 1993: A Study of Participation*, New Delhi: Institute of Social Sciences and Concept Publishing Company, 1996, pp. 101–102; and B.B. Kumar, *Small States Syndrome in India*, New Delhi: Concept Publishing Company, 1998, p. 95.
16. Strategy and Action Plan for Capacity Building of Panchayats and Municipalities in 11 Districts of West Bengal under Backward Regions Grant Fund 2006–07, Government of West Bengal, Kolkata: Panchayats & Rural Development Department, February 2007, p. 9. Also, Article 243M: The Constitution (Seventy Third Amendment) Act, 1992.
17. 'NGOs Unite for Hill Welfare', Darjeeling NGO Network, *The Telegraph*, 26 May 2004.

    'Contradiction in Darjeeling Hills: Panchayati Raj', Darjeeling Times.com, Sunday, 24 April 2011, 10: 02, written by Kalimpong news express, http: //Kalimpongonlinenews.blogspot.com, visited on 11 March 2013.
18. 'Push for 3-tier Rural System in GTA Area', *The Telegraph*, 23 November 2012, www.telegraphindia.com, visited on 12 March 2013. Also, '3-tier Panchayat in Hills Soon', Kalimpongonlinenews.blogspot.com, visited on 12 March 2013.
19. Conversation with L.S. Tamsang, 1999–2000.
20. *Field Survey*, 1998–1999 and interview with M.T. Lepcha, 1999. Further, according to C. Simick (1998), the former Secretary of the Lepcha Association, 'Our MLA, Gaulan Lepcha, is also indifferent. He never came to us; we have to go to his place if necessary'.
21. Before the election of S.P. Lepcha, one of the office-bearer of the Lepcha Association was asked whether they would vote for Lepcha, as he is a Lepcha. His first reaction was: 'Yes, but let's see, our association still does not convey any instruction to us in this regard. If it will instruct us, we the Lepcha must vote for him.' However, the next day, he observed:

'No, why should we do that, he is a CPM party cadre and he does only what his party instructs' (Interview with D.C. Roy, 1999).

22. Government of West Bengal, Certified Handwritten Government Register Showing G.P.-wise Names of the Uncontested and Contesting Candidates, Panchayat Election–2000, Kalimpong-I Development Block Entry No. 1 to 58.
23. Government of India, *Census Reports*, 1991 and 2001.
24. Government of West Bengal, *The Resolution No. 462-BCW/6S-73/2011*, Kolkata: Backward Classes Welfare Department, 12 February 2013, www.anagrasarkalyan.gov.in. Also see, D. Chakraborty, 'Role of Panchayat in Development Process of Hill Areas in the Eastern Himalayas: Environment and Economy', in R.L. Sarkar and M.P. Lama (eds), *The Plantation Workers in Eastern Himalaya*, Delhi: Atma Ram & Sons, 1986, pp. 532–538.

CHAPTER 15

Identity, Autonomy and Development through Decentralization

Journey from Darjeeling Gorkha Hill Council to Gorkhaland Territorial Administration

Jhumpa Mukherjee

With the formation of Gorkhaland Territorial Administration (GTA) in 2011, the people of the region have been filled with renewed optimism that the new arrangements would open up a plethora of opportunities with self-rule finally becoming a reality. The chapter tries to map the experiments of decentralization in the form of territorial autonomy and its effect on questions of development and identity in the hills of West Bengal.

Dynamics of Decentralization

Lexicographically, decentralization means both reversing the concentration of administration at a single centre and conferring powers of local government. 'It is concerned with the extent to which power and authority are dispersed throughout the geographical hierarchy of the state, and the institutions and processes through which such dispersal occurs'.[1] This is a generalized version of decentralization found in almost all the countries, whether unitary or federal. Much of the literature on decentralization focuses on the theoretical underpinnings of its different forms: political, administrative and fiscal. While political decentralization involves transfer of power; it occurs whenever political relations and responsibilities between new or existing levels of government are redefined with the effect of increasing the power of lower tier authorities; administrative decentralization occurs when the responsibilities are devolved to field agencies. Fiscal decentralization involves an attempt to transfer certain financial authority to local units, which have been granted autonomy in the sphere of raising taxes. In modern discourse, another connotation of decentralization has become popular, that is, privatization or market decentralization, which is the process of creating conditions in which goods and services are provided by market mechanisms primarily through the revealed preferences of individuals. However, it should be noted that in all these areas an element of democracy is operative. Yet, there is another peculiar form of decentralization, that is 'decentralization by default' – which occurred in Russia after the Soviet Union collapsed.[2] This was a highly politicized decentralization in the sense that in Russia, the state lost power to regional authorities that were generally not accountable either to the people or central government – a peculiar type in itself.

Advocates of decentralization argue, 'Decentralization will improve the efficient provision of services, the quality of governance, economic development and efforts to alleviate poverty.'[3] Again, decentralization is also advocated to improve the quality of democracy. Decentralization affirms the 'principle of subsidiarity', according to which decisions should be taken at the lowest possible level, and decision-makers should be accountable at that level.[4] Decentralization of power may enable the people of backward areas to take part in the decision-making process, make better utilization of local resources and ultimately make them a part of democratic governance. Rajni Kothari views decentralization 'as a clear counter to the processes of homogenization, globalization, modernization, liberalization and privatization ... a system such that people become the sources of decentralized governance, which should also mean a differentiated and pluralist structure of governance'.[5]

Decentralization and Cultural Identities

Such dynamics of power devolution get transformed in multicultural societies where decentralization may become a powerful tool of accommodation of demands of identities. It may be seen as an autonomous arrangement to protect identities. L.J. Sharpe observes:[6]

> ... it is possible to discern three distinct decentralist movements, each occurring at the three basic community levels of the nation state. At the most local level in urban areas, there is the wide variety of demands for some form of decentralization of power to the sub-community (Neighbourhood Council). At the next level in scale terms, there are the attempts in most western democracies to strengthen the capacity of the existing local government institutions so as to halt the upward drift of power and functions to higher levels of government. The last decentralist trend has been occurring at the regional level ... In some of the multicultural democracies, this movement has become a demand for the outright separation of regions where an ethnic minority predominates.

In India, decentralization is not a new administrative mechanism and has been operating since the investiture of the state in 1950, evolving in the process as a powerful medium of popular political participation at the local level. 'Decentralization in India has been a structural feature of Indian federation, and its implementation, when so resorted to, has helped to enhance state's legitimacy, and governance.'[7] The need for decentralized governance or *gram swaraj* was widely discussed in the Constituent Assembly. Granville Austin opined that 'the ideal of a revived village life with benevolent panchayats and decentralized government bringing democracy to the grassroots level appealed to Assembly members'.[8] This found expression in Article 40 of the Constitution of India that provides for the establishment of panchayats as units of local self-government. Accordingly, the Seventy Third and Seventy Fourth Constitution Amendment Acts, 1993 have provided for political decentralization through devolution of powers to the Panchayati Raj Institutions and urban local governments where a people-centred approach is followed to ensure the goals of democratic governance as stipulated in Part IV (Directive Principles of State Policy) of the Constitution of India. Since its formation, Panchayati Raj Institutions have been functioning regularly and democratically, evident from the regular holding of elections, reservation of seats for women, Scheduled Castes, Scheduled Tribes and so on. In this context, A.S. Narang observed:[9]

> The interests and aspirations of most people are concentrated in the localities in which they live and carry on their avocations of life. Normally, they would be content to compete at the level of the local self-governing bodies, making way for persons interested in larger issues of regional or national significance to opt for higher elective

forums. Decentralization of real power to these local institutions would thus help diffuse the threats of centrifugal forces, increase popular involvement all along the line, broaden the base of our democratic polity, promote administrative efficiency and improve the health and stability of inter-governmental relations.

It seems pertinent to mention here that the debates on decentralization focus upon its effectiveness in furthering grassroots democracy. However, PRIs as the third tier of the Indian federation are based exclusively on population and popular involvement; prime consideration being effectiveness of the local government to meet local demands. One finds that it has nothing to do with ethnic identity of the population. But in a complex multicultural society like India, identity issues do play a significant role. The people, that is the population, belongs to a distinct cultural marker – language, religion, tribe, etc. They have a deep sense of attachment to that primordial identity and protection and recognition of these identities are imperative for the integrity of the country. In India, and West Bengal in particular, the discourse on decentralization emphasized upon institutions and mechanisms mainly from public administration point of view, thus becoming highly theoretical and discursive. In the available literature and experiments on decentralization, identity issues are undermined; decentralization advocates better service delivery to people wherein magnitude of the population is of prime importance, thus underemphasizing the needs of diverse composition of the populations. Multiculturalism or multicultural needs of the ethnic populations are undermined in decentralization. Moreover, it has been found that though decentralization has become very popular in the agenda of governance, it is not inclusive; on the contrary, it has exclusionary potentialities. A case in point is the fact that the PRIs in Darjeeling do not conform to the specification of the Seventy Third Amendment Act in the sense that Darjeeling does not have a zilla parishad and panchayat samitis are absent in many blocks.

Decentralization should not, therefore, be seen merely as an administrative arrangement disconnected from ethnic, cultural, religious and linguistic issues. In India, creating social space for groups and communities as well as protecting them constitutionally and institutionally is envisaged as a prerequisite of multicultural accommodation and its political and institutional manifestations. In this context, Rajni Kothari argues that 'as far as the rationale of decentralization is concerned, there is need to see the evolution of decentralized processes in terms of a continuum. Merely setting up governing structures would in no way promise effective decentralization'.[10]

The ensuing discussion seeks to understand the functioning of GTA as a decentralized model of self rule to accommodate the identity concerns of the Gorkha within overall claims of autonomy and development. I will not delve deep into the Gorkhaland movement since the objective of the chapter is to understand the dynamics of decentralization in the hills of West Bengal and furthermore, to study the co-existence of PRIs and territorial councils and whether their interests overlap or contradict.

Governance in the Hills of Darjeeling

Historical evidence suggests that before 1835, Darjeeling was a part of the kingdom of Sikkim while Kalimpong and the adjoining territories a part of Bhutan. In 1835, Darjeeling was relinquished to the British East India Company by the King of Sikkim. Two further expeditions in 1850 and 1861 confirmed British possession of Darjeeling. In the year 1865, the Anglo-Bhutanese war led to the acquisition of Kalimpong and territories to the east of the Teesta river. Thus, Darjeeling was developed as a varied mix of Bhutanese, Nepalese, people from Sikkim and the plains. The district remained under the non-regulation scheme of administration till the passing of the Indian Council's Act of 1861. Later on, the Act of 1861 abolished distinction between regulated and non-regulated districts. Yet again, the Act of 1870 restored the pre-1861 status. In 1874, Darjeeling was declared as a Scheduled District and this continued until 1919 when its nomenclature was changed from 'Scheduled District'[11] to 'Backward Tract'. The Government of India Act of 1935 again changed its status to partially excluded area[12] within the province of Bengal. Thus, since its annexation, Darjeeling has been subjected to multiple experiments of autonomy but these did not portray a response to a specific identity concern.

The British Government had used Darjeeling as their *summer retreat* and had done nothing to ameliorate the plight of the ethnic community. They cultivated the seeds of 'difference', playing with the Gorkha sentiments of attachment to a geographical territory cascading into the demand for a separate state as early as 1907 when in a memorandum presented to the British Government, the Hill Men's Association demanded the formation of a separate administrative unit of their own comprising Darjeeling and the Duars portion of Jalpaiguri.

The grounds on which this demand was based on were: (a) geographical, (b) racial, (c) historical (d) religious, and (e) linguistic.[13] To pursue these demands in an organized and systematic manner, and to provide a political platform for their demands, the All India Gorkha League (AIGL) was established in 1923 under the leadership of Dambar Singh Gurung. Though the appeal of the Hill Men's Association for creating a separate administrative unit for Darjeeling was not immediately realized, their repeated demand for separation from Bengal sowed the seeds of a cleavage between the Nepalese of the hill subdivisions in Darjeeling and the inhabitants of Bengal in the plains.[14] The second type of demand for autonomy was formulated by the educated Nepalese middle class of Darjeeling, who submitted a separate memorandum to the British Government demanding the regional autonomy of Darjeeling within the province of Bengal. In lieu of their demand, under Section 92 of the Government of India Act, 1935, the district of Darjeeling was made a 'partially excluded area', although an 'independent administrative unit' as demanded by this Association was not granted.[15]

In the post-Independence period, the movement gathered momentum when the States Reorganization Commission failed to recognize the autonomy of the Gorkha. Disappointed, the Gorkhas asserted that 'post-Independence, Gorkha were the only community in the North-east left out during the reorganization of states even though they fulfilled the entire criterion'.[16] Both the colonial government and the independent state did not seriously dwell on the question of a Gorkha homeland.

The succeeding years witnessed movements for 'recognition of Nepali language' in the Eighth Schedule of the Indian Constitution as well as for the autonomous status of Darjeeling within the province of West Bengal.[17] Towards this end, the Government of West Bengal passed the Official Language Act in 1961 to give official language status to Nepali in the three hill subdivisions of Darjeeling. However, this was rejected by the then Central government, thus fuelling the fire for further discontentment among the Nepalis.

The Gorkha National Liberation Front (GNLF) was formed to pursue the long-cherished goal of a separate Gorkha homeland. The fundamental rationale behind this demand was the expulsion of Nepalese citizens from Meghalaya, the protest by the All Assam Students' Union (AASU) over illegal entry of Nepalese in Assam, protest by All Meghalaya Khasi Students' Union (AMKSU) for deportation of foreigners from Meghalaya, refusal of Sikkim and West Bengal government to accommodate them. Hence, the Nepalese of Darjeeling themselves took up the case of a separate homeland for themselves. Ghisingh-led GNLF emphasized that the name of Gorkhaland or the state of Gorkhaland is only one precious political asset and an authentic constitutional document for the whole Indian Gorkhas and also for the central government of India to prove the Indian national identity of the Indian Gorkhas: so as to give them permanent political and constitutional safeguard in India and further, no one can point out them as foreigners or immigrants in the soil of Indian territory.[18]

Nonetheless, the state government contradicted Ghisingh's views by endorsing the fact that 'West Bengal is as much a homeland for the Nepali-speaking population living here as it is for other communities. ... Nepalese, with their distinct language, looks, customs and habits are an integral part of the cultural heritage and landscape of the state of ours'.[19] Dissatisfied with the attitude of the state government, the GNLF revised its earlier position and started the second phase of agitation by demanding the status of separate statehood for Gorkhaland within the framework of the Constitution of India. To control the deteriorating law and order situation in the hills, the Chief Minister emphasized on a 'negotiated settlement', implying regional autonomy for safeguarding language and culture of the Gorkha. This settlement, however, was unacceptable to the GNLF. The GNLF led by Subhas Ghising strengthened their demand for the creation of a separate state of Gorkhaland and also demanded in addition, abrogation of the Indo-Nepal treaty and inclusion of Nepalese in the Eighth Schedule of the Constitution.

The years that followed during the Eighties witnessed violent agitation by the GNLF for the recognition of their claims. However, the movement was branded as anti-national by the Left Front government of West Bengal and the state government instead of encouraging the stand for a separate Gorkhaland contented that autonomous district councils may be created in order to protect the distinct culture of the Gorkhas. Ultimately, the loss of lives and property made the people crave for peace and the agitation came to an end with the signing of the agreement between GNLF and the government of West Bengal for the formation of an autonomous council. It was a tripartite agreement for the Darjeeling Gorkha Hill Council (DGHC) signed between Union Home Minister Buta Singh, West Bengal Chief Minister Jyoti Basu and GNLF president Subhas Ghising on 25 July 1988. The Council's mandate was to advance hill people socially, economically, educationally, culturally, by lending a measure of autonomy to the region.[20]

A tripartite Memorandum of Settlement (MoS) was also signed in New Delhi on 6 December 2005 between the Centre, West Bengal government and Gorkha National Liberation Front (GNLF) to initiate the process of according Sixth Schedule status to the GNLF-led Darjeeling Gorkha Hill Council. Under the Sixth Schedule, six tribes – the Bhutia, Lepchas, Sherpas, Yolmos and the newly included Tamangs and Limbus – will have greater representation in the proposed Gorkha Hill Council than the 70 per cent non-tribal population. The memorandum states: 'The objectives of this agreement are to replace the existing Darjeeling Gorkha Hill Council by an autonomous self-governing Council to be known as Gorkha Hill Council, Darjeeling, under the Sixth Schedule of the Constitution of India so as to fulfill economic, educational and linguistic aspirations and the preservation of land rights, socio-cultural and ethnic identity of the hill people and to speed up the infrastructure development in the hill areas.' This constitutional change will not only enhance its position, but give it more legislative and administrative power. But that remained only on paper.

All these declarations, albeit, failed to gratify the Gorkha. Malfunctioning of the Hill Council, lack of transparency coupled with undermining of democratic processes and Ghising's apathy towards securing a separate homeland for the Gorkha recrystallized the demand for Gorkhaland under the new leadership of Bimal Gurung-led Gorkha Jan Mukti Morcha (GJMM). Its first move was to turn down the inclusion of Hill Council under the Sixth Schedule. The Sixth Schedule according tribal status to the Gorkha was demeaning since the Gorkha were mainly caste Hindus and resented homogenization with the scheduled tribes. Since 2008, Gorkhaland movement gathered new momentum and Gurung adopted a non-violent form of protest by refusing to pay state taxes to the government due on electricity and phone bills, changing vehicle numbers from WB (West Bengal) to GL (signifying Gorkhaland). The new TMC-led state government kept its promise of an autonomous arrangement for the Gorkhas and the GTA was born.

The GTA: Roadmap to Recognition

A tripartite agreement between the central government, state government and Gorkha Janmukti Morcha was signed on 18 July 2011 for the establishment of a Gorkhaland Territorial Administration[21] with the objective of establishing an autonomous self-governing body to administer the region so that the socio-economic, infrastructural, educational, cultural and linguistic development is expedited and the ethnic identity of Gorkha established. From the beginning, the Act provided that the body should be established by direct election to root out anti-democratic forces unlike the DGHC (formed out of State Act) and the BTC (result of Sixth Schedule). An interesting observation is that the Act begins by a declaration (in which both state and Centre are parties) that the GJM is not dropping the demand for Gorkhaland whilst signing the GTA agreement, signalling the fact that GTA is only an interim arrangement and Gorkhaland demand may come up any day again.

The GTA Council or Sabha is composed of 50 members, 45 elected and five nominated by the Governor to give representation to members of SC, ST, women and minority communities. The Sabha shall be formed by direct election, thus generating popular confidence. The MPs, MLAs and chairpersons of Municipalities of the region shall be ex-officio members. There shall also be an Executive Body consisting of a Chief Executive, who will nominate 14 members out of the elected/nominated members as Executive Members. The Chief Executive shall nominate the deputy chief executive, but the Act is silent as to how the Chief Executive would be nominated. The GTA shall be provided with a Principal Secretary to be selected by the Chief Executive from the panel sent by the state government. The Act, however, is silent on the representation of the non-Gorkha communities.

The Act does not provide for legislative powers to the GTA but confers the power to frame rules/regulations under the state Acts to control, regulate and administer the 59 departments. The administrative, executive and financial powers in respect to the transferred subjects will be vested in such a manner to enable GTA to function in an autonomous manner. Some of the important subjects being, agriculture, education, irrigation, forest management, food and civil supplies, cottage and small-scale industries, land and land revenue, municipal corporation, panchayat and rural development, tourism, transport, welfare of minorities and SCs and STs, rural electrification – is a pointer to the fact that if GTA functions properly, it might really be autonomous and economically self-sufficient and bring about significant improvement in the lives of the hill people. Unlike the DGHC, the GTA is more powerful in terms of the subjects transferred to it and fund allocation by Centre and the state government.

GTA and Identity Concerns

Is the GTA an administrative body or is it concerned with recognizing the identity claims of the hill community? An interpretation of the objective of GTA reflects that it has been created to establish ethnic identity of the Gorkha through expediting socio-economic, infrastructural, educational and linguistic development of the region. This reflects that the identity concerns have been circumscribed within the larger issue of development. In fact, GTA aims to secure and promote Gorkha identity by addressing developmental issues. The entire GTA agreement focuses on the need for greater development to meet the identity claims. Thus, politics of development displaces the politics of identity in the hills, at least that is what the agreement portrays. Of the 50 members of the GTA Council, five are nominated by the Governor to give representation to members of SC, ST, women and minority communities. The Act is not clear about which minority communities is it addressing and the status of the Gorkha as SCs or STs because the Act itself speaks of referring the matter to the Backward Classes Welfare Department of the state government. There seems to be an ambiguity regarding representation of non-Gorkhas in the GTA.

GTA and Panchayati Raj Institutions

In India, decentralization is synonymous with institutions of local self-government and is a potential medium of popular participation and representation. No discussion on decentralization is complete without an analysis of the mode and functioning of PRIs. The Seventy Third Constitution Amendment Act, 1993 led to the establishment of three-tier Panchayati Raj Institutions in the country but Darjeeling was an exception since it had only gram panchayats and DGHC performed the role of zilla parishad. As per the DGHC Act 1988, the hill council will serve as a substitute for the zilla parishad in the hill areas and for the plain areas of the district, there shall be a Siliguri Mahakuma Parishad as a substitute for zilla parishad. In Darjeeling, district rural governance consists of only gram panchayats and DGHC and panchayat samitis are non-existent in the block areas. This has severely undermined the question of popular participation in grassroots institutions. After the signing of the GTA Act in 2011 and the transfer of department of panchayats and rural development including DRDA to GTA, till date nothing has been achieved. This requires amendment of the West Bengal Panchayat Act 1993 and creation of three-tier body in the hill areas. The

GJM leadership is apprehensive of the modalities of working of PRIs in the GTA area. The Agreement clearly states, 'A three-tier panchayat will be constituted by elections in the GTA region, subject to the provisions of Part IX of the Constitution of India. Notwithstanding anything contained in the West Bengal Panchayat Act 1973, the GTA shall exercise general powers of supervision over the Panchayats and the Municipalities.' Inclusion of PRIs within the GTA act is portrayed by the GJM as a significant achievement but it remains to be seen whether the ensuing panchayat elections this year in the state will really witness the functioning of two democratic institutions along parallel lines.

Conclusion

It is apprehended by some that the formation of GTA may open up other regional demands in the state, as already the Lepcha have started demanding an autonomous arrangement within the state. But the problem lies elsewhere. In West Bengal, development and local governance is envisaged as a part of decentralization without any focus on the identity concerns of the population. This creates a tendency for social exclusion and marginalization of ethnic identities. PRIs would never be able to meet the claims of Adivasis, Gorkhas, Lepchas or Bhutias of the state. The GTA may be envisaged as an experiment in West Bengal to guarantee politico-cultural representation to the people who have been denied political participation and self-governance since a long time.

Autonomous territorial arrangements offer mechanisms to protect identities as well as cater to developmental concerns. Again, identity questions can no longer be isolated from the development needs of the region. Hence, meaningful decentralization demands creation of institutional mechanisms to accommodate cultural identities and not just population-based local self-governing institutions. The notion of decentralization should move beyond traditional institutions to function effectively within a multicultural environment. Decentralization calls for democratic integration of cultural diversities.

Thus, autonomous decentralized multicultural institutions provide the institutional space within which the ethnic identities can make their own decisions and pursue their own values. In India, creating social space for groups and communities as well as protecting them constitutionally and institutionally is envisaged as a prerequisite of multicultural accommodation and its political and institutional manifestations. The significance of these decentralized units was well highlighted by Ronald Watts in that 'the desire for smaller self-governing political units has risen from the desire to make governments more responsive to the individual citizen and to give expression to primary group attachments – linguistic and cultural ties, religious connections, historical traditions and social practices – which provide the distinctive basis for a community's sense of identity and yearning for self-determination'.[22]

At present, it seems too early to comment on the efficacy of GTA but definitely the agreement for the formation of GTA reflects an appreciation of the political and cultural identities of the Gorkha and the recognition of the primary ties of the people. This integrationist model of decentralized governance definitely acts as a shock absorber in accommodating disaffected groups and identities within a democratic framework.

Notes

1. B.C. Smith, *Decentralization: The Territorial Dimension of the State*, London: George Allen and Unwin (Publishers) Ltd., 1985, p. 1.
2. *Local Rule: Decentralization and Human Rights*, Versoix, Switzerland: International Council on Human Rights Policy, 2002, p. 6.
3. Paul Smoke, 'Beyond Normative Models and Development Trends: Strategic Design and Implementation of Decentralization in Developing Countries', paper prepared for UNDP, November 2000, accessed at www.worldbank.org/wbicp/decentralization/library1/smoke.decentralization.pdf
4. *Local Rule: Decentralization and Human Rights*, op. cit., p. 9.
5. Rajni Kothari, 'Issues in Decentralized Governance', in A. Aziz and D.D. Arnold (eds), *Decentralized Governance in Asian Countries*, New Delhi: Sage, 1996, p. 40.
6. L.J. Sharpe (ed.), *Decentralist Trends in Western Democracies: A First Appraisal*, London: Sage, 1979, p. 21.
7. Harihar Bhattacharyya, *India as a Multicultural Federation: Asian Values, Democracy and Decentralization (in comparison with Swiss Federalism)*, Fribourg: Institute of Federalism, 2001, p. 135.
8. Granville Austin, *The Indian Constitution: Cornerstone of a Nation*, New Delhi: Oxford University Press, 1999, p. 31.
9. Cited in Harihar Bhattacharyya, *India as a Multicultural Federation: Asian Values, Democracy and Decentralization (in comparison with Swiss Federalism)*, Fribourg: Institute of Federalism, 2001, p. 152.

10. Ibid., p. 37.
11. The term 'Scheduled Districts' implied 'those remote or backward tracts or provinces of British India which had never been brought within or had from time to time been removed from the operation of the general Acts and Regulations and jurisdiction of ordinary courts or in which that operation was not complete, and officers were supposed to be guided by the spirit of indispensable laws or were actually guided by such laws as had somehow or other been considered to be in force'. See, C.L. Tuppar's 'Indian Political Practice', in Vijay Hansaria (ed.), *Sixth Schedule to the Constitution*, Delhi: Universal Law Publishing Co. Pvt. Ltd., 2005, p. 3.
12. Excluded areas implied those tracts exclusively inhabited by a compact tribal population and those areas where population comprised both tribals and non-tribals but the tribals were majority in number in denoted partially excluded areas.
13. Tanka B. Subba, *Ethnicity, State and Development: A Case Study of the Gorkhaland Movement in Darjeeling*, New Delhi: Har-Anand Publications, 1992, p. 78.
14. Atis Dasgupta, 'Ethnic Problems and Movements for Autonomy in Darjeeling', *Social Scientist*, Vol. 27, Nos 318–319, November–December 1999, p. 59.
15. Subba, op. cit., p. 80.
16. Priyadarshini Shrestha, 'Separation for Integration Status of Stateless Minorities in a Multicultural Democracy: A Case Study of the Indian Gorkhas', paper presented to the Summer University at the Institute of Federalism, University of Fribourg, 28 August–15 September 2006.
17. Dasgupta, op. cit., p. 61.
18. Press Release, 19 May 1983.
19. Cited in Snehamoy Chaklader, *Sub-Regional Movements in India: With Reference to Bodoland and Gorkhaland*, Kolkata: K.P. Bagchi & Company, 2004, p. 91.
20. *Statesman*, Tuesday, 26 April 2005.
21. Gorkhaland Territorial Administration, *Memorandum of Agreement*, Darjeeling, 18 July 2011.
22. R.L. Watts, 'Federalism Today: The Relevance Today of the Federal Idea', paper submitted at the International Conference on Federalism, Switzerland, 2002, www.forumfed.org/en/federalism/federalismtoday.php

CHAPTER 16

Mahatma Gandhi National Rural Employment Guarantee Scheme and Decentralized Development

Experiences from West Bengal

Dibyendu Sarkar

This paper is an attempt from the perspective of a practitioner at pointing out the strength and weaknesses, the opportunities and problems in implementation of the largest wage employment programme in the state of West Bengal. Mahatma Gandhi National Rural Employment Guarantee Act (MGNREGA), passed by Parliament in September 2005, is a path-breaking legislation in many ways. The Act provides legal sanction for the rural households' right to work, albeit in a limited way. In a complete break from the previously launched wage-employment programmes, MGNREGA is right-based and dignity of manual labour is recognized. A job-seeker has to be provided with employment within reasonable distance from the village and certain facilities have to be ensured at worksites. There is the provision for unemployment allowance when work cannot be provided within fifteen days from the date of application for work. All these features of the Act and the resultant Scheme (MGNREGS) are cataclysmic in nature and in a way revolutionized the entire gamut of rural development. However, implementation of the programme is not uniform across the country and while some of the states went far ahead of others in reaping the harvest, there are serious laggards. Section 1 of the paper charts out the course of wage employment programmes launched in India since Independence and the basics of the scheme. In Section 2, performance of the country as a whole in implementation of the scheme since inception has been analysed. Section 3 presents a comparison of ten states in implementation of the scheme in 2012–13. Section 4 presents the scenario of implementation in West Bengal based on performance of the districts, while section 5 deals with the lessons learnt from the experiences and the challenges faced in implementation.[1]

Evolution of Employment Programme in India

Since Independence and at the commencement of Five Year plans, the Government of India has been considering diverse ways of evolving a mechanism to improve the existing livelihood in rural areas. Accordingly, the first pilot project in the form of Rural Manpower Programme (RMP) offering wage employment on public works at minimum wages was initiated in 1960–61. The next intervention came after a decade when the Crash Scheme for Rural Employment (CSRE) was initiated, again on a pilot basis in 1971–72. Then followed the Pilot Intensive Rural Employment Programme (PIREP), Small Farmers Development Agency (SFDA), and Marginal Farmers and Agricultural Labour Scheme (MFAL) – all launched in the 1970s to benefit the poorest of the poor.

These experiments were translated into a full-fledged wage-employment programme in 1977 in the form of Food for Work programme. In the 1980s, this programme was further streamlined into the National Rural Employment Programme (NREP) and Rural Landless Employment Guarantee Programme (RLEGP). Later on, in 1993–94, NREP and RLEGP were merged into Jawahar Rozgar Yojana (JRY). A separate and more focused wage employment scheme named as Employment Assurance Scheme (EAS) was also introduced. Both the Employment Assurance Scheme and the Jawahar Rozgar Yojana subsequently merged into Jawahar Gram Samriddhi Yojana (JGSY) in 1999–2000 and was made a rural infrastructure programme. In 2001–02 again, JGSY was changed into Sampoorna Grameen Rozgar Yojana (SGRY) and National Food for Work (NFFWP), 2005. These wage employment programmes implemented by state governments with central assistance were self-targeting, and the objective was to provide and enhance livelihood security, especially for those dependent on casual manual labour. At the state level, the Government of Maharashtra formulated the Maharashtra Employment Guarantee Scheme and Maharashtra Employment Guarantee Act, 1977 to provide wage employment to those who demanded it.

The National Rural Employment Guarantee Act actually came into force on 2 February 2006 and was implemented in a phased manner. In phase one, the Act was implemented in 200 most backward districts of the country. Another 130 districts were added in 2007–08 and in the third phase, with effect from 1 April 2008, remaining 285 districts were brought under the Act. The acceleration was rapid and in fact even beyond the originally charted coverage plan. The Act itself in Section 1 (3) specifies the time-limit of five years for total coverage.

It shall come into force on such date as the Central Government may, by notification in the Official Gazette, appoint; and different dates or for different dates may be appointed for different states or for different areas in a State and any reference in any such provision to the commencement of this Act shall be constructed as a reference to the coming into force of that provision in such State or, as the case may be, in such area: Provided that this Act shall be applicable to the whole of the territory to which it extends within a period of five years from the date of enactment of this Act. However, the huge potential of the Act was identified at the very commencement of implementation and hence it took only a little over two years to bring the entire country within its ambit.

Difference between Previous Programmes and MGNREGS

Since Independence, all the wage employment programmes lacked in focus in so far as providing employment opportunities are concerned. While self-employment programmes like IRDP, SGSY focused on individual households, wage employment programmes were more community-oriented. In its emphasis on creation of durable community assets, the focus on providing employment opportunities to the rural households was somewhat lost. Moreover, there was no guarantee of work for the rural poor, no dearth of discrimination as there was no stipulation as to the right of the rural households in employment. Mahatma Gandhi NREGS, on the other hand, came with the primary objective of providing guaranteed employment to the rural households. Naturally, employment is provided to the rural households as their legally mandated right and not at the mercy of the local functionaries. The slogan is of work with dignity, work without discrimination. Another hallmark of the present scheme is the protection it offers to the workers. All payments are made through bank or post office accounts, an active grievance redressal mechanism is in place and public disclosure ensures accountability to the people.

The mandate of Mahatma Gandhi NREGA is to provide 100 days of guaranteed wage employment in a financial year to every rural household whose adult members volunteer to do unskilled manual work. Objectives of the Act and the Scheme (MGNREGS) introduced to implement the Act are the following:

- Ensuring social protection to the most vulnerable people living in rural India by providing guaranteed employment opportunities,
- Ensuring livelihood security to the rural poor through creation of durable assets, improved water security, soil conservation and higher land productivity,
- Strengthening drought proofing and flood management in rural India,
- Aiding in the empowerment of the marginalized communities, especially women, Scheduled Castes and Scheduled Tribes through the process of a rights-based legislation,
- Strengthening decentralized, participatory planning through convergence of various anti-poverty and livelihood initiatives,
- Deepening democracy at the grassroots by strengthening the Panchayati Raj Institutions,
- Effecting greater transparency and accountability in governance.

MGNREGS has become a powerful instrument for inclusive growth in rural India through its impact on social protection, livelihood security and democratic governance. The following are the salient features of the Scheme:

- The Act provides for registration of households and individuals for support under the scheme. Adult members of households interested to do unskilled manual work can register themselves by preferring applications to the Gram Panchayats.
- Once registered and positively within 15 days from the date of application, the gram panchayat, after conducting initial enquiry regarding residence of the household and age of the applicants, is to issue a Job card to the head of the household, which forms the basis for all future transactions with the household.

- A registered job cardholder is supposed to apply in writing either to the gram panchayat or to the programme officer (Block Development Officer) seeking employment. The application is supposed to indicate the period for which the household or the individuals in the household seek employment.
- Once the application is received, the gram panchayat is supposed to give a dated receipt and inform the applicant as to the work in which employment is assigned. Work has to be allocated within 15 days from the date of receipt of the application, failing which the state government is supposed to provide unemployment allowance for the delayed engagement.
- Minimum period for which employment is supposed to be sought and provided is 15 days as any engagement less than 15 days is deemed as non-viable in terms of impact on the household income. Moreover, this 15 days' engagement is supposed to be augmented by further periods of engagement within the over-all ceiling of 100 days for a household in a year.
- In case the gram panchayat or the programme officer fails to provide employment on demand, the household can seek unemployment allowance which the state government is supposed to provide for the days of unemployment despite written application seeking employment.
- Work is to be usually assigned within 5 kilometres from the residence of the job-seeker, failing which the job-seeker is entitled to an additional wage of 10 per cent of the daily wage as transportation charges and related expenditure.
- While assigning work, priority is to be given to women in the job-seeking household. A minimum of one-third of the person-days are to be generated with labour contribution of women only. The gram panchayats and the programme officers are encouraged to go beyond the stipulated minimum in engagement of women.
- MGNREGA being a rights-based programme, emphasis has been laid on providing certain facilities like drinking water, shade, first aid facilities and crèches for children at the worksite.
- Wages to be paid to workers are fixed by the Ministry of Rural Development on the basis of the agricultural consumer price index of the state and revised from time to time. Varied wages are fixed for different states and this is often more than the prevailing

minimum wages in agricultural activities. However, in some of the states, the situation is just reversed and agricultural minimum wages are higher than the NREGAs wage rate.

- Planning is at the core of MGNREGS and the process of planning is closely associated with the preparation of the labour budget, estimation as to the number of households seeking employment, number of days for such employment prospecting and associated financial estimation. Side by side with the process of preparation of labour budget, there goes the process of planning for work. Different works to be taken up during the year are identified a-priori through a participatory process at the gram sabha level. Works identified and prioritized at the gram sabha are processed by the gram panchayat and as part of a holistic plan sent to the intermediate panchayat (panchayat samiti) for further compilation. The panchayat samiti then approves the gram panchayat plans and as part of the panchayat samiti plan sends the same to the district. The zilla parishad at the district level finally approves the plans and the District Magistrate as district programme coordinator renders necessary support. The entire planning process is to be completed as per the schedule notified by the Ministry of Rural Development.
- In implementing the scheme, no contractor and machines replacing human labour can generally be engaged.
- Wages are to be paid to the wage seekers through accounts in financial institutions. All the wage-seeking households are supposed to have accounts in banks or post offices in which wages are to be credited within 15 days from the date of engagement, failing which the state governments are liable to pay compensation for delayed payment.
- Several transparency measures have been promoted in MGNREGS. Firstly, there is the provision of proactive disclosure. Technologically, the NREGAs portal of the Government of India is to be extensively used to provide information to the community on different aspects of the programme implementation. The portal is supported by a very detailed management information system (MIS) which brings most of the activities from identification of job-seekers to payment of wages in the public domain. Proactive disclosure in MGNREGS also includes wall writing at the gram panchayat offices, information boards at worksites, etc.

- Regular inspection of worksites by people from different tiers of the administration is another transparency measure. All inspection reports are to be acted upon and published on the website for wider dissemination.
- Social audit is the most innovative measure to bring about transparency in the scheme implementation. It is a mechanism in the hands of the local people to critically examine the works and identify the gaps in programme implementation, if any. A group of local youth is to be trained to conduct the exercise by way of
  - — collection of papers and documents;
  - — physical verification of work in the field;
  - — preparing the framework for the social audit;
  - — speaking with the community members; and
  - — placing the social audit report before the gathering of the community.

All India Progress in Implementation

In 2006–07, 2.1 crore households in only 200 districts were provided work and West Bengal reported highest figures followed by Madhya Pradesh, Uttar Pradesh, Andhra Pradesh and Bihar. In terms of person-days generation, however, West Bengal could not maintain its lead position. Total person-days generated in the country were exceptionally high at 90.5 crore. Total expenditure incurred in implementation of NREGAS in 2006–07 was ₹ 8,812.00 crore out of which 66.2 per cent was paid to the labours for wages earned during the year. Next year, additional 130 districts were brought under coverage and 143.59 crore person-days were generated by engaging 3.39 crore households. In 2008–09, rest of the rural districts (185) were brought under coverage, raising total number of districts to 615. There was also an increase in performance, 4.51 crore households were provided employment and 216.32 crore person-days could be generated. In terms of expenditure, it was ₹ 27,250.1 crore. No further increase in performance could be reported in 2009–10 when coverage of the programme in terms of person-days slumped slightly over the figures of the previous year; 257.15 crore person-days could be generated by engaging 5.49 crore households.

The downslide continued and in 2012–13 there was further reduction in person-days; 4.95 crore households were engaged and

226.48 crore person-days generated expenditure was high due to upward revision in wage-rate.

The following table gives a synopsis of physical performance in MGNREGS during April 2006–March 2013.

Table 1 *Physical Performance*

Years	*Cumulative Job cards issued (in crore)*	*Households employed (in crore)*	*Person-days generated (in crore)*	*Women percentage in person-days*	*No. of Schemes implemented*
2006–07 (200 districts)	3.78	2.1	90.05	40%	8.35 lakh
2007–08 (330 districts)	6.48	3.39	143.59	43%	17.88 lakh
2008–09 (all rural districts)	10.01	4.51	216.32	48%	27.75 lakh
2009–10 (all rural districts)	11.25 crore	5.26 crore	283.59 crore	48%	46.17 lakh
2010–11 (all rural districts)	11.98 crore	5.49 crore	257.15 crore	48%	50.99 lakh
2011–12 (all rural districts)	12.39 crore	5.04 crore	216.36 crore	48%	82.51 lakh
2012–13 (all rural districts)	12.72 crore	4.95 crore	226.56 crore	51%	101.45 lakh

Thus, since 2008–09, all the rural districts have been brought under the Scheme. In terms of person-days generated, highest performance could be registered in 2009–10. Thereafter, there was a relative decrease in terms of person-days, which is a cause of concern. There is also a major variation in terms of creation of job opportunities, which is the major plank of the scheme. A comparative evaluation of ten top ranking states on the basis of creation of person-days during 2012–13 financial year may be presented for analysis of performance.

These states are the top-ranking ones and share among themselves 80 per cent of person-days generated across the country. Looking at the achievement in distribution of job cards, these states issued 76 per cent of the cards whereas rest of country accounts for only 24 per cent as shown in the following table:

Table 2 *Number of Job Cards Issued*

State	Job card Issued
Tamil Nadu	88,55,944
Andhra Pradesh	1,22,28,014
Rajasthan	99,50,039
West Bengal	1,13,65,057
Uttar Pradesh	1,49,25,981
Madhya Pradesh	1,20,57,703
Chhattisgarh	44,05,667
Bihar	1,28,74,405
Maharashtra	70,42,522
Kerala	25,23,952
First 10 states combined	9,62,29,284
Rest of the country	3,09,39,227
All India total	12,71,68,511

Again, if we look into the performance in terms of creation of person-days and provision for household-employments, we find their respective positions. In addition to this, we may also get information pertaining to households provided employment by the states under comparison. The table also indicates percentage of the respective states in all-India scenario:

Table 3 *Creation of Person-days*

States	Person-days	Households Provided Employment	Share in all-India Households
Tamil Nadu	40,81,40,819	70,60,722	14%
Andhra Pradesh	31,80,73,754	57,86,101	12%
Rajasthan	22,03,03,090	42,17,157	09%
West Bengal	20,00,39,030	57,98,467	12%
Uttar Pradesh	14,03,52,329	49,31,708	10%
Madhya Pradesh	13,03,64,357	33,78,188	07%
Chhattisgarh	11,93,42,555	26,36,828	05%
Bihar	9,24,23,992	20,62,588	04%
Maharashtra	8,49,45,538	15,94,728	03%
Kerala	8,37,71,633	15,26,277	03%
First 10 states combined	1,79,77,57,097	3,89,92,764	79%
Rest of the country	46,78,84,409	1,04,91,853	21%
All India total	2,26,56,41,506	4,94,84,617	—

In the following table, respective positions of 10 states in terms of incurring expenditure during 2012–13 is given, which reveal certain interesting phenomena:

Table 4 *Expenditure Schedule*

States	*Total Expenditure Incurred*	*Share in all-India expenditure*
Tamil Nadu	4,12,056.39	10%
Andhra Pradesh	5,19,142.52	13%
Rajasthan	3,25,064.52	8%
West Bengal	3,83,421.08	10%
Uttar Pradesh	2,62,833.02	7%
Madhya Pradesh	2,86,062.98	7%
Chhattisgarh	2,22,065.53	6%
Bihar	1,89,086.5	5%
Maharashtra	2,17,808.15	6%
Kerala	1,41,637.05	4%
Combined 10 states	29,59,177.74	75%
Rest of the country	9,66,146.69	25%
All India total	39,25,324.43	—

From the table, it is revealed that in some states like Tamil Nadu, Rajasthan, Kerala, total expenditure vis-à-vis person-days generated is relatively low when compared to states like West Bengal, Andhra Pradesh. This was mainly because of the fact that states like Tamil Nadu and Kerala implemented extremely labour intensive schemes and cost of materials in those states was very low. This trend in implementing fully labour intensive works resulted in low expenditure despite high generation in person-days.

Analysis of the above tables presents certain interesting issues for consideration. First, despite having maximum number of job cards issued (1.49 crore), Uttar Pradesh fared low in terms of households engagement. Same also are the cases with Bihar and Madhya Pradesh where despite huge number of job cards, job-seekers engaged is substantially low. The base in terms of households as percentage of job cards is widest in Tamil Nadu (79.73%), followed by West Bengal (51.02%) and Andhra Pradesh (47.32%). Where the base is wider, it is extremely difficult to achieve higher per-household engagement despite substantially higher performance in terms of generation of total person-days. Ranking states in terms of average days of engagement per households provided thus is a misconstrued indicator in assessing over-all performance of the states. Secondly, despite generation of exceptionally higher person-days, expenditure incurred by Tamil Nadu is pretty low in the perspectives of the 10 states under comparison. Different reports available in this regard as well as the database in the Government of India portal suggests labour intensive nature of the programme in that state. More than 90 per cent of the expenditure was incurred there only for payment of wages to the job card holders for unskilled manual work. Emphasis on labour is certainly a healthy sign in implementation of the scheme. However, with minuscule expenditure in procurement of materials, serious issues regarding the quality of assets created have been raised. Andhra Pradesh somewhat maintains the balance between wage and materials. Even wage is much above the stipulated minimum of 60 per cent of the total expenditure in Andhra Pradesh. West Bengal is in a much better condition here as the wage-material ratio is more in line with the government stipulation. Here, we find two views in this respect. Those who are strongly in favour of the wage guarantee provision of the Act argue that the Tamil Nadu model is more akin to what's aimed by the provisions of the scheme. On the other hand, there are people who strongly advocate the secondary objective of the scheme, that of creation of durable assets which might help regeneration of the rural economy. The more durable assets created, the more the rural economy is capable of generating future employment opportunities, thereby gradually decreasing the dependence on MGNREGS wages for the rural households. Thirdly, in terms of works, Andhra Pradesh alone reported 46 per cent of total work implemented at the pan-India level. Such huge number of works implemented in a year is only possible when extremely smaller works are implemented where asset generation might be at risk. This needs further examination by policy-makers and experts.

Implementation and Performance in West Bengal

West Bengal may be taken as a case study in identifying the positive and negative forces in the process of implementation of the Mahatma Gandhi National Rural Employment Guarantee Scheme. In the previous sections, the analysis presented was mostly based on information culled from the Government of India portal (nrega.nic.in) which is supported by a management information system known as NREGASoft. As a secondary source of data, this is extremely rich and offers enormous information to the scholars, the monitoring personnel, the implementing agencies, and the citizens alike. Now, however, in addition to the secondary data available, I have drawn heavily from my own association with the programme at the state level. Being a direct stakeholder in the programme often makes one see the bright sides of the programme and has the propensity to be myopic to the shortcomings. But, I have tried to be as objective as possible in analysing the situation in West Bengal. Following table gives the basic figures pertaining to performance in 2012–13:

Table 5 *West Bengal District-wise Scenario*

S. No.	*Districts*	*Households issued job cards*	*Households provided employ-ment*	*Total person-days*	*Total expenditure incurred (in lakh)*	*Expenditure per GP (in lakh)*
1	South 24 Parganas	8,36,899	2,48,273	1,06,32,404	22,322.37	71.55
2	Bankura	5,86,063	3,53,066	1,36,98,987	22,987.73	120.99
3	Birbhum	6,60,015	4,52,300	1,92,73,296	33,503.03	200.62
4	Dakshin Dinajpur	3,05,764	98,781	27,26,656	6,889.5	105.99
5	Uttar Dinajpur	4,41,434	78,773	14,92,649	3,695.96	37.78
6	Jalpaiguri	6,54,496	4,14,169	1,07,50,506	20,628.46	141.29
7	Maldah	5,99,284	1,89,445	59,85,120	13,584.02	93.04
8	Paschim Medinipur	8,84,605	5,47,921	1,65,27,728	29,168.98	100.58
9	Murshidabad	10,44,249	4,21,143	1,11,86,802	23,226.63	91.44
10	Purulia	4,51,532	2,32,311	91,05,145	15,354.26	90.32
11	North 24 Parganas	7,49,593	3,56,599	1,60,01,387	30,978.98	154.89
12	Burdwan	10,28,158	7,56,617	2,36,50,949	46,451.67	167.7
13	Coochbehar	6,02,720	2,46,771	42,09,782	8,434.69	65.9
14	Hooghly	6,60,829	4,57,185	1,72,25,156	31,237.29	150.9
15	Nadia	7,15,573	2,74,765	1,07,62,083	15,131.51	80.92
16	Purba Medinipur	6,79,857	4,16,181	1,60,00,257	33,463.15	150.06
17	Siliguri MP	90,559	42228	8,43,426	1,834.81	83.4
18	DGHC/GTA	1,36,917	109840	66,53,549	16,951.66	151.35
19	Howrah	2,37,787	102099	33,13,148	7,465.33	47.55
District total		1,13,66,334	57,98,467	20,00,39,030	3,83,310.03	114.4

It is revealed from the above table that the state has a high number of rural households registered for job cards. In fact, nearly 70 per cent of the rural households in the state have obtained this document. While coming to the use of the job cards, West Bengal is one of the front-runners in the country. Despite such huge number of job cards having been issued, a little over 51 per cent of the job cards are used to obtain engagement opportunities. The table gives the district-wise picture. Nine districts are above the state average while there are 10 more district units where the average is lower than the state figures. Uttar Dinajpur with only around 18 per cent of the job cards in use is probably beset with the problem of governance. In terms of average person-days per household employed, despite such huge number of households provided, the state average could be raised to 34.5 which, however, is substantially below the national average. If we look at district-wise variations, there are nine districts which reported higher average than the state's over-all figures. Out of the remaining 10 district units, performance on this count was exceptionally low in the districts of Coochbehar and Uttar Dinajpur. In terms of coverage of households, both in absolute number and average days of employment per household, the hills of Darjeeling district falling within the jurisdiction of the Gorkhaland Territorial Administration (GTA) fared best in the state.

In terms of women's participation in labour, West Bengal was much below the national average. Even in the state average of 34 per cent of person-days generated with women labour, there was wide variation across the districts. Nine districts were above the state average whereas 10 district units fared worse than the state average. While Siliguri Mahakuma Parishad achieved special distinction on this count with 60 per cent women participation, Murshidabad fared extremely poor with only 17 per cent women in the workforce. In fact, half of the districts failed to achieve the minimum women participation as stipulated in the Act.

Table 6 *District-wise Share in Employment of Women*

District	*Total Person-days*	*Women Person-days*	*Per centage of Women Person-days*
Siliguri MP	8,43,426	5,06,316	60
Purba Medinipur	1,60,00,257	79,11,781	49
DGHC/GTA	66,53,549	29,34,387	44
Purulia	91,05,145	38,62,871	42
Jalpaiguri	1,07,50,506	44,18,427	41
Bankura	1,36,98,987	55,09,961	40
Uttar Dinajpur	14,92,649	5,33,712	36
Paschim Medinipur	1,65,27,728	59,69,696	36
Hooghly	1,72,25,156	62,50,826	36
North 24 Parganas	1,60,01,387	50,94,963	32
Maldah	59,85,120	17,99,061	30

Cont'd...

...Cont'd

Nadia	1,07,62,083	32,10,961	30
Dakshin Dinajpur	27,26,656	7,93,385	29
Burdwan	2,36,50,949	68,55,301	29
South 24 Parganas	1,06,32,404	28,24,444	27
Birbhum	1,92,73,296	52,16,423	27
Coochbehar	42,09,782	10,32,714	25
Howrah	33,13,148	7,74,476	23
Murshidabad	1,11,86,802	18,59,207	17
Total	20,00,39,030	6,73,58,912	34

The state government made efforts to rank the districts in terms of performance in implementation of the schemes in 2012–13. Deciding on the indicators for ranking is a very difficult exercise as there is no standardized template for such ranking. The ranking exercise undertaken by the West Bengal NREGA Cell has taken into consideration 10 indicators:

- Average person-days per household
- Participation of women in workforce
- Percentage of provided households completed 100 days
- Percentage of provided households engaged for less than 15 days (reverse ranking)
- Expenditure per Gram Panchayat
- Expenditure per rural household
- Income per provided household
- Percentage of Gram Panchayats in the district which could not maintain 60: 40 ratio in wage: material
- Work completion rate
- Percentage of households marked as BPL in the MIS against total BPL households in the district
- Percentage of worksite photographs uploaded
- Percentage of wage-seekers, photographs uploaded

The above indicators ranking respective positions have been selected from physical, financial and administrative performances. All the indicators were given equal ranking and from a simple average of the indicators the final ranking emerged. Following is the order of the districts in terms of the ranking exercise:

Rank	*Name of the district*	*Rank*	*Name of the district*	*Rank*	*Name of the district*
1	North 24 Parganas	2	Birbhum	3	Gorkhaland Territorial Administration (GTA)
3	Hooghly	5	Bankura	6	Purba Medinipur
7	Burdwan	8	Nadia	9	Purulia
10	South 24 Parganas	11	Paschim Medinipur	12	Malda
13	Howrah	14	Siliguri Mahakuma Parishad	15	Murshidabad
16	Jalpaiguri	17	Uttar Dinajpur	18	Dakshin Dinajpur
19	Coochbehar				

The position of the states (West Bengal) in terms of total person-days generated has seen considerable upward rise in 2012–13. During the previous three years, total person-days generated by the state was in the range of 15 crore. In 2012–13, it rose to 20 crore person-days, which was only fourth in the country in absolute number. There are other indicators where the state even achieved higher ranks. However, instead of discussing those achievements, it is necessary to examine the impact of the scheme on development and decentralization experiments in the states.

First, even with the limited number of days of engagement, the scheme has provided employment with dignity to the rural wage-seekers. It has largely dawned upon the wage-seekers that employment under the Act is their right and not dependant on the whims of the panchayats or the administrators. This amounts to creating psychological empowerment of the rural poor.

Secondly, though relatively low, 34 per cent participation of women in labour has made it possible for the women to earn wages equal to their male counterpart, which is barely the case in the unorganized agricultural sector. Earning wages equal to the male members in the family has certainly supported the process of empowerment of women. The Self-Help Group movement had given the women the power of collective bargaining. It made possible for the rural women to unite and lend their voices to various social issues. However, economic activities through SHG route take time to yield income. NREGS, on the other hand, has immediate potential for income generation. Wage earning is fast and this has helped rural women gain more prominence in the family. As has been pointed out in several studies on earning by the women, income earned by the women in the families has much more potential for gainful utilization in education of children, healthcare and other household activities.

Thirdly, in certain extremely poverty-stricken pockets where the villagers have little option of having been engaged in income earning activities and migration is the only option available to the poorest of the poor, MNREGS has raised the silver lining of earning in the village itself. Even when average engagement per household is low, in those pockets of Bankura, Purulia and Paschim Medinipur, people have got employment in the village, often at level much higher than the average and this has stemmed the outbound flow of labourers.

Fourthly, in the pre-MGNREGA era, gram sansad as the forum for people's participation in development was going haywire for inappropriate scope of implementation of the recommendations of the public assemblies. With MGNREGS inflow of fund multiplied by several times average expenditure on this scheme in a gram panchayat has increased. Such huge potential makes it possible to meet substantial part of the people's aspirations in terms of creation and development of local assets and thereby raise the level of people's participation in the gram sansads, both in terms of presence and participation.

Fifthly, as most of the works implemented belong to the sector of water conservation, minor irrigation and land development, it has been possible to create assets which in turn contribute to greater agricultural productivity. Vulnerability of the villagers due to changes in the climate has been reduced to some extent due to the positive environmental impact of the scheme.

Sixthly, works implemented in the individual beneficiary sector have made it possible for the rural households to access government fund for development of their own land. Excavation and re-excavation of farm ponds has made it possible for the small landowners to irrigate their own land and the land of their neighbours, especially in times of crisis. Smaller farm ponds in the western part of the state (in the districts of Purulia Bankura, Paschim Medinipur and Birbhum) have improved soil moisture by recharging the water table. These small *pond less* (locally known as 'hapa') have also been able to provide one or two critical irrigations to adjoining vegetable cultivations.

Seventhly, although implemented in an uneven scale in terms of depth of coverage, the process of social audit has improved transparency of the programme. Boards containing basic information on the works, including data on employment provided to wage-seekers at every worksite, has enhanced the scope of public scrutiny and reduced chances of pilferage.

Challenges in Implementation of the Scheme

Despite the positive impact and a host of other contributions of the programme in rural decentralization and development, there are quite a number of implementation challenges.

Delivery Mode Syndrome

The officials as well as the panchayat representatives have hardly been able to get out of the delivery mould. Despite repeated assertions, the scheme has largely remained a supply driven programme. Awareness about the scheme is near total in the rural areas: that job card is the essential document for receiving employment under the programme, that the programme intends to provide 100 days' employment to rural households, that equal wages are to be paid to the male and female wage-seekers, that all payments are made through bank and post office accounts of the wage-seekers – all these are well known in the villages. However, the demand driven nature of the programme has hardly reached the consciousness of the wage-seekers. People hardly know that only written application for employment is supposed to result in the allocation, that if an application is preferred asking for employment for a minimum period of 14 days at one go the gram panchayat is legally bound to provide employment, that in case employment cannot be provided within 15 days from the date of application the wage-seeker is entitled to unemployment allowance, that for delayed payment of wages the worker is entitled to compensation are the cardinal messages which have not reached the rural households. Existence of such shadow zones in awareness is not normal. Rather, it speaks of selective dissemination of information. For benefits to reach the poor in the villages, awareness on the demand aspect has to be improved through systematic communication-interventions. Implementation of the Act has already reached its eighth year. It is high time that the implementers make it mandatory to open work on the basis of written demand only. No demand, no work; every demand met to its fullest extent should be the slogan of the day.

People's Participation

In terms of participation of the rural people in planning, implementation and monitoring of implementation, there is a big gap. Although the scheme has made it possible to give shape to the aspirations of the people, often lack of proper facilitation has derailed the gram sansad meetings. Without paying any heed to the principles of holistic planning, works are planned in isolation and thereby hardly contribute to the development of the village as a unit. Rather, the gram sansads have prepared wish lists which have been compiled by the gram panchayats. Going by the name of annual action plan, the listed activities have been given shape and funding has been sought from the district. In 2012–13, however, an effort has been made to prepare the labour budget and the annual action plan through a more elaborate participatory process. Using the skilled facilitators of the SRD (Strengthening Decentralized Development) project, the initiative has resulted in some effective plans developed through participatory processes in which the villagers have contributed much more constructively.

Strengthening Decentralization

Although strengthening decentralization is one of the primary objectives of the scheme and active involvement of the three-tier panchayat system has been made mandatory in the Act and the guidelines, it has been the experience in the state that only the gram panchayats are actively involved in planning and implementation of the programme. Panchayats at the intermediate and the district level (panchayat samiti and zilla parishad) have hardly any role. Annual action plans generated at the gram panchayat level are to be compiled by the panchayat samiti and thereafter sent to the zilla parishad. Block development officer as programme officer is more involved in the enforcement part of the Act, whereas the developmental function under the programme is supposed to be looked after the panchayat samiti and its executive officer. At the district level, the district magistrate who is the district programme coordinator is supposed to provide support to the zilla parishad in scrutinizing the annual action plans and accord approval to the plans. In actual practice, the district magistrate himself approves the AAPs without referring the plans to the zilla parishad. Thus, the role of the district and the intermediate panchayat is much diluted. In order to ensure the capacity building of the Panchayati Raj Institutions, the practice has to be reversed.

Participation of Women

Participation of women is another area where there is enough scope of improvement. West Bengal's 34 per cent women labour is no match to the all-India average of 51.5 per cent. If we compare, we find that Kerala has the highest participation of women at 93 per cent. Tamil

Nadu too is substantially ahead of the average since the state has reported 74 per cent women participation. Rajasthan at 69 per cent too is substantially above the national average. Women participation in the scheme is very much possible if there is administrative will and political commitment. This is coming out very glaringly by the fact that even in West Bengal, Siliguri Mahakuma Parishad has been able to generate 60 per cent through labour of women job-seekers. At 49 per cent, Purba Medinipur occupies the second position. The more labour force has women representation, the better the implementation.

In the era of Integrated Rural Development Programme (IRDP) and in the earlier days of the Indira Awas Yojana (IAY), primacy to women in the households came as a major policy thrust. As a result, initially names of women from the families were added to the list of 'beneficiaries' from the same families. Such a kind of co-option opened the doors for the women in a vital asset in the family, the house to take shelter in, along with the asset used for productive purposes. With the passage of time, things became further institutionalized and the women emerged from mere additional names in the project to active stakeholders. When IRDP graduated into Self-Help Group based SGSY programme, there came a whole range of changes in micro-lending. Capacity building, self-reliance, group action and certainly women leadership – all became basic features of the programme. SGSY is now maturing further into National Rural Livelihood Mission where the entire SHG movement is growing and trying to achieve self-reliance in the true sense of the term in a mission mode. But the achievement in post-IRDP era was actually not a spontaneous change in the pattern of rural entrepreneurship. It cannot be said that one fine morning women came to overpower men in the matter of organizing themselves into groups and taking up group-based economic activities. It was a conscious policy decision of the state to organize Self-Help Groups with the poor women in the villages. The women folk came forward and supported the state initiative.

Women participation in the scheme is an issue which requires a conscious policy decision. It is a question of engendering MGNREGS and this can be done with some bold pro-women policy decisions only. There may not be a single intervention to set the things right. It may require a series of activities, directives from the highest echelons of power to the districts and the PIAs to consciously promote women participation and give priority to women in work participation in MGNREGS. It also requires religious exercises in the districts and down below to ensure that the directives issued by the State are put to practice and the entire machinery is geared up for giving due weightage to women power in NREGS. Some of the steps that can be taken for improving women participation in the programme may be the identified:

- Opening of separate accounts for all the job card holders. There are instances where women in the job card holding households are either part of a joint account or not even featuring in any account at all. This practice should be completely discontinued and all women in job card holding families must have their exclusive bank account. This single activity itself would probably ensure substantial progress in tapping the contribution of women who, although working in the field, are not being reflected in the musters.
- A team of officials at the block level should examine all the schemes identified in the labour budget and explore the possibility of developing all women workers groups in specific schemes.
- Involvement of women SHGs in planning, implementation and monitoring of activities should be appropriately explored.
- Women-specific IEC initiatives, including inter-personal communication, may be undertaken to make women in job card holding households aware of their rights and entitlements under the Act. In the sphere of IEC too, local SHGs and their clusters and federations may be utilized to the fullest extent.
- Selection of supervisors may be revisited and it should be ensured that not less than 50 per cent of the supervisors are women. In all cases where all women schemes are implemented, the supervisor must necessarily be selected from among women. The state-level instruction on giving priorities to the women SHGs in selecting supervisors should be followed in its true spirit and not as mechanical compliance.
- Special efforts should be taken to provide work to women closer to their home and of such nature that task can be performed with relatively lesser physical ability.
- The Operational Guideline, 2013 clearly indicates that women in special and difficult circumstances should be given priority for assignment of work. Widowed women, deserted women and destitute women are highly vulnerable and require special

attention. They should be identified and ensured that 100 days' work is provided for them. Pregnant women and lactating mothers (at least up to eight months before delivery and 10 months after delivery) should also be treated as a special category. Special works which require less effort and are close to their house should be identified and implemented for them.

Conclusion

It is a fact that tremendous progress has been achieved through implementation of the scheme in rural areas. The achievements cannot simply be measured in terms of generating employment or incurring budget expenditure. Apart from physical achievements, there are psychological achievements which are more vital in a developing society like ours. But there is still need for further interventions from both the government as well as from the non-state actors working in different fields of rural development. There is also the urgency in ensuring linkages between rural and urban programmes so as to create synergistic effect of development. The scheme has already expanded the basket of alternative works available to the villagers. Government of India has expanded the reach by adding a host of new schemes in the basket.

From a detailed analysis of the above facts and figures, however, it is established that there is no commendable progress in the state in taking up newer activities under the programme. The entire machinery is attuned to the traditional works like water conservation and water harvesting; excavation and re-excavation of ponds, canals, traditional water bodies; flood control; land development; social forestry; rural connectivity, etc. New works are hardly identified and prioritized. Hence, attention is required for diversification of works in order to keep generating person-days, creating durable assets and improve future livelihood opportunities.

Rural development is an integrated approach with multifarious dimensions and interacting implications. Hence, there is the urgency in pooling together the resources available for rural development under a single umbrella. Linkages in both planning and implementation of different programmes and schemes and also among functional agencies and departments are extremely poor. Convergence with the Nirmal Bharat Abhijaan (NBA) for construction of household sanitary latrines; convergence with the National Rural Livelihood Mission (NRLM) for greater involvement of the Self-Help Groups, convergence with the rural housing schemes like *Indira Awas Yojana* (IAY) or the state's own *Nija Griha Nija Bhumi* (Own House on Own Land) Programme; convergence with the *Pradhan Mantri Gram Sadak Yojana*; convergence with the Backward Region Grant Fund (BRGF) is possible and extremely required. All these schemes and programmes are implemented by the panchayats and rural development department which implements MGNREGS as well. There are schemes and programmes implemented by other departments where too convergence is required for better performance and sustainability. Integrated Watershed Management Programme (IWMP) is one of the most important programmes having possibility of convergence with this scheme.

Mahatma Gandhi NREGS is viewed as the most inclusive development intervention. Social inclusion is achieved through involvement of the entire rural community, including the marginalized, in the planning process and in public scrutiny through *Gram Sabha*; through creation of employment opportunities for the Scheduled Tribes and the Scheduled Castes; through making special provisions for the other-wise able individuals encouraging their participation in the programme. Last year, West Bengal reported 32.31 per cent Scheduled Caste person-days and 9.79 per cent Scheduled Tribe person-days. In otherwise able category, West Bengal is second to Andhra Pradesh only. However, here too the percentage is well below the legally stipulated 3 per cent. Financial inclusion is another priority, e-FMS, EBT should take care of financial inclusion. Implementation of the scheme in West Bengal has seen considerable churning in the recent past. However, that turn-around in terms of physical and financial performance has not yet been able to bring about systemic changes in programme implementation. Stronger policy intervention coupled with commitment to changes can bring about the desired pace and quality to the programme.

Note

1. Data and information used in this paper are taken from different reports and portals maintained by the Government of India and the Government of West Bengal.

CHAPTER 17

Delivering Guaranteed Employment

Experience of Half a Decade of Decentralized Development

Utpal Chakraborty

More than six years have elapsed since the largest demand driven employment programme of human history took birth in India and again it was guaranteed through the legislation of Parliament. Popularly known as *Eksho diner kaaj* (hundred days' work), initially National Rural Employment Guarantee Act (NREGA) and subsequently Mahatma Gandhi National Rural Employment Guarantee Act (MGNREGA), it has by this time designed as bottom-up, people-centric, self-selecting and right-based in its approach. It is also being accepted gradually and increasingly that the programme outline, subsequently Mahatma Gandhi National Rural Employment Guarantee Scheme (MGNREGS), has the potential to transform rural India at many levels, particularly its economic and social relations. Huge potential of the programme has already been evident, particularly in the enthusiastic response of the rural people, landless, wherever the marginal farmers and women workers in particular; wherever proper and adequate information about the programme has been disseminated. The programme has finally reversed the way the Indian state has traditionally dealt with the issues and envisages a radical change in the manner of interaction of the state, the local grassroots organizations and the local working classes in rural India.

Introduction

Since its initial launch in 200 districts in February 2006, the MGNREGS programme has spread countrywide and presently it operates in 596 of India's 625 districts. According to official sources, nearly 5.5 crore families were provided over 250 crore person-days of work under the programme in 2010–11. Over the last six years, the scheme has generated more than 1,100 crore person-days of work at a total expenditure of over ₹ 150,000 crore. The share of SC/ST families in the work provided under the programme has been 55 per cent and 45 per cent of workers are women. Average wages of workers have gone up by 54 per cent over the last five years. Moreover, nearly 10 crore bank and post office accounts of poorest of the poor have been opened by this time and around 80 per cent of wage payments are made through this route. The Act clearly states: 'An Act to provide for the enhancement of livelihood security of the household in rural areas of the country by providing at least one hundred days of guaranteed wage employment in every financial year to every household whose adult member volunteers to do unskilled manual work and for matters connected therewith or incidental thereto.'

Basic Objectives and Guidelines of the Scheme

The draft operational guideline submitted by Mihir Shah Committee[1] in February 2012 highlights the following goals of the programme as:

(i) Social protection for the most vulnerable people living in rural India.

(ii) Livelihood security for the poor through creation of durable assets, improved water security, soil conservation and high land productivity.

(iii) Drought proofing and flood management in rural India.

(iv) Empowerment of the socially disadvantaged, especially women, Scheduled Castes and Scheduled Tribes, through the process of a right based legislation.

(v) Strengthening decentralized, participatory planning through convergence of various anti-poverty and livelihood initiatives.

(vi) Deepening democracy at the grassroots by strengthening Panchayati Raj Institutions.

(vii) Effecting greater transparency and accountability in governance.

It is often said that the birth of MGNREGS is a paradigm shift in rural development programmes launched after Independence. It is different from any other employment programme in human history, particularly on the following points as are identified by the Committee:

(i) It provides a legal guarantee of wage employment.

(ii) It is a demand driven programme where provision of work is triggered by the demand and for work by wage-seekers.

(iii) There are legal provisions for allowances and compensation both in cases of failure to provide work on demand and delays in payment of work under taken.

(iv) The MGNREGS overcomes problems of targeting through its self-targeting mechanism of beneficiary selection.

(v) The Act incentivises states to provide employment as 100 per cent of unskilled labour cost and 75 per cent of the material cost of the programme is borne by the Centre.

(vi) Unlike earlier wage employment programmes that were allocation based, MGNREGS is demand driven and resource transfer from Centre to States is based on the demand for employment in each state. This provides an additional incentive for states to leverage the Act to meet the employment needs of the poor.

(vii) There is further a concomitant disincentive for failing to provide work on time, as the states then bear the cost of unemployment allowance.

(viii) Gram panchayats at the bottom level are to implement at least 50 per cent of the works and such order of devolution of financial resources is unprecedented.

(ix) Plans and decisions regarding the nature and choice of works to be undertaken, the order in which each work is to be triggered, site selection, etc. are all to be made in open assemblies of gram sabha and ratified by the gram panchayats. Works that are inserted at intermediate panchayat and district panchayat level have to be approved and assigned by the gram sabha before administrative approval can be given. The gram sabha may accept, amend or reject them.

(x) The decision of the gram sabha cannot be overturned by higher authorities, except to the extent of ensuring conformity with the provisions of the Act and its operational guidelines.

(xi) The bottom up, people-centred, demand driven architecture also means that a great share of the responsibility for the success of the MGNREGS lies with the wage-seekers, gram sabhas and gram panchayats.

(xii) MGNREGS marks a break from the relief programmes of the past towards an integrated natural resource management and livelihoods generation perspective.

(xiii) Social audit is a new feature that is an integral part of this programme. Potentially this creates unprecedented accountability of performance, especially towards immediate stakeholders.

(xiv) An annual report on the outcomes of MGNREGS is presented annually by the central government to Parliament and to state legislatures by the state governments, facilitating oversight by the elected representatives.

Performance Appraisal

Official sources reveal that under the scheme, an amount of ₹ 1,10,700 crore (66% of the total expenditure) was spent during the last six years (up to the financial year 2011–2012) as worker wages out of the total budget outlay of ₹ 1,72,500 crore. In 2011–12 alone, ₹ 24,600 crore of the total expenditure was incurred on wages and nearly 5 crore households (close to 25% of all rural households in the country) were provided with more than 209 crore person-days of work. Again, during these years, 337 crore (28%), 280 crore (23%) and 561 crore (47%) person-days were created for SCs, STs and women, respectively. A year-wise detailed picture of this achievement can be traced from Table 1.

Table 1 *An Overview of Performance (April 2006–March 2012)*

	2006–07 (200 districts)	*2007–08 (330 districts)*	*2008–09 (All rural districts)*	*2009–10 (All rural districts)*	*2010–11 (All rural districts)*	*2011–12 (All rural districts)*	*Total 2006–07 – 2011–12*
Households provided employment (in crore)	2.1	3.4	4.5	5.3	5.5	5	—
Person-days (In crore) (per cent of total person-days)							
Total:	90.5	143.59	216.3	283.6	257.2	209.3	1200
SCs	23 (25%)	39.4 (27%)	63.4 (29%)	86.5 (30%)	78.8 (31%)	46.2 (22%)	337 (28%)
STs	33 (36%)	42 (29%)	55 (25%)	58.7 (21%)	53.6 (21%)	37.7 (18%)	280 (23%)

Cont'd...

...Cont'd

Women	36 (40%)	61 (43%)	103.6 (48%)	136.4 (48%)	122.7 (48%)	101.1 (48%)	561 (47%)
Average person-days per employed household	43 days	42 days	48 days	54 days	47 days	42 days	**
Financial Details							
Budget outlay (in ₹ Crore)	11,300	12,000	30,000	39,100	40,100	40,000	1,72,500
Expenditure (in ₹ Crore)	8,824	15,857	27,250	37,905	39,377	37,303	1,66,516
Expenditure on unskilled wages (in ₹ Crore)	5,842	10,739	18,200	25,579	25,686	24,660	1,10,706
(% of total expenditure)	(66%)	(68%)	(67%)	(67%)	(65%)	(66%)	(66%)
Works (In lakh)							
Works taken up	8.4	17.9	27.8	46.2	51	73.6	146
Works completed	3.9	8.2	12.1	22.6	25.9	14.3	87

** Data cannot be averaged as households from one year to another are not distinct.
Source: Ministry of Rural Development, Government of India

Several studies have been conducted both by the government and private institutions by this time. There are distinct ways in which the scheme is likely to curb rural poverty, the most direct and obvious being the creation of work and income opportunities for the poor in the rural areas.[2] In surveying 1,500 households in three states, a study[3] observed that the share of the scheme in increasing income of the poor was highest in Andhra Pradesh (about 17 per cent). In Rajasthan, this share was 10 per cent and in Maharashtra it was 7 per cent.

There is also preliminary evidence that income from participating in the scheme is being used by rural households for starting their own ventures. An interesting research analysing revealed that around 17 per cent (out of 96 job card holders surveyed) of rural households spent their income to run, expand or start a new business.[4] Studies further reveal that a greater portion of income from 48 per cent to 66 per cent for men and women respectively spent their income on strengthening their own economic position.[5] As a result of this, urban migration from rural areas has considerably declined over the years.

Another important aspect of the scheme is to ensure that women have equitable and easy access to work, decent working condition, equal payment of wages and representation in decision-making bodies. During the period from 2006–07 to 2011–12, around ₹ 53,000 crore have been spent on wages for women and around 47 per cent of total person-days have been utilized by women. At the national level, the participation of women in the scheme has surpassed the statutory minimum requirement of 33 per cent; in 2011–12 alone, women person-days of employment came to around 50 per cent. However, the large inter-state variation in women participation has remained an issue for further study. In 2011–12, Kerala had the highest female participation (93 per cent) while Tamil Nadu and Rajasthan followed with 74 per cent and 69 per cent, respectively. Nine other states, including West Bengal, remained below the requirement of 33 per cent. A detailed picture on the percentage of women participation in the scheme as workforce can also be traced from the following tables.

Table 2 *State-wise Percentage of Women Person-days from 2006–07 to 2011–12*

State	*Women person-days (percentage of total person -days) 2006–07*	*Women person-days (percentage of total person-days) 2007–08*	*Women person-days (percentage of total person-days) 2008–09*	*Women person-days (percentage of total person-days) 2009–10*	*Women person-days (percentage of total person-days) 2010–11*	*Women person-days (percentage of total person-days) 2011–12*
Andhra Pradesh	55	58	58	58	57	58
Assam	32	31	27	28	27	25
Bihar	17	28	30	30	28	29
Chhattisgarh	39	42	47	49	49	45
Gujarat	50	47	43	48	44	45
Haryana	31	34	31	35	36	36
Himachal Pradesh	12	30	39	46	48	60
Jammu and Kashmir	4	1	6	7	7	18
Jharkhand	39	27	29	34	33	31
Karnataka	51	50	50	37	46	46
Kerala	66	71	85	88	90	93
Madhya Pradesh	43	42	43	44	44	43
Maharashtra	37	40	46	40	46	46
Odisha	36	36	38	36	39	39

Cont'd...

...Cont'd

Punjab	38	16	25	26	34	43
Rajasthan	67	69	67	67	68	69
Tamil Nadu	81	82	80	83	83	74
Uttar Pradesh	17	15	18	22	21	17
Uttarakhand	30	43	37	40	40	45
West Bengal	18	17	27	33	34	32
All India	40	43	48	48	48	47

Source: Ministry of Rural Development, Government of India

Findings of countrywide study suggest that the increased access to paid work has had a positive impact on enhancing women's socio-economic status and general well-being. 82 per cent of the widows in a sample regarded the scheme as a very important source of income and 69 per cent stated that MGNREGS helped them to avoid hunger. Studies further reveal that post-MGNREGS, women have gained greater control to spend their income on repaying small debts, paying for their children's schooling and bearing medical expenses, etc.[6]

One of the key objectives of this programme is the creation of sustainable assets that strengthen the livelihood resource-base in rural areas. Since inception, around 146 lakh works have been taken up. Of these, almost 51 per cent of works are related to water bodies (water conservation, flood control, irrigation, drought proofing, renovation of traditional water bodies and micro-irrigation) and over 19 per cent works are related to rural connectivity. All these works have the potential of providing benefits for the rural communities by improving irrigation facilities, enhancing land productivity and connecting remote villages to input and output markets. A detailed picture of resource generation can be seen from the following table:

Table 3 *Works Undertaken Between 2006–07 and 2011–12*

S. No.	*Type of works*	*Number of works completed from 2006–07 to 2011–12 (in lakh)*	*Ongoing works (in lakh)*	*Per cent of works taken up from 2006–07 to 2011–12*
1.	Water conservation and water harvesting (e.g. farm ponds, percolation tanks, etc.)	19.5	36.4	25
2.	Flood control and protection (e.g. check dams, culverts etc.)	3.9	5.9	4

Cont'd...

...Cont'd

3. Drought proofing (e.g. afforestation/tree plantation, agro-forestry, etc.)	5.2	13.0	9
4. Irrigation canals (Macro-and micro- irrigation works, etc.)	5.7	9.5	7
5. Renovation of traditional water bodies (e.g. desilting of tanks etc.)	6.6	9.8	7
Total Water Conservation and Water-related Works (sum of (i) to (v) above)	**40.9**	**74.7**	**51**
6. Works of lands of SC/ST/BPL/SMF and IAY and Land Reform Beneficiaries	13.0	19.9	14
7. Land development (e.g. contour bunds, field bunds, etc.)	13.9	18.8	13
8. Rural connectivity (e.g. village roads, etc.)	16.0	28.3	19
9. Others (e.g. Bharat Nirman Kendras)	2.8	4.6	3
Total Works	**86.6**	**146.3**	**100**

Source: Ministry of Rural Development, Government of India

Constraints in Implementation

In several states, steps have been initiated for converging the scheme with other schemes and other government departments such as are dealing with agriculture and horticulture. A significant part of financial allocation under the scheme (12 per cent in 2011–12 and 20 per cent in 2010–11) is found to be spent on works on private land. The works done on private land and holdings are found more sustainable due to definite ownership rights. Despite so many achievements as outlined above, the journey of this programme has not been a smooth sailing all the way. A radical departure from the age-old culture of supply-driven approach to this new culture of demand-driven, right-based, decentralized decision-making model has by this time encountered diverse problems. Besides independent evaluations, annual reports and audit reports of the Comptroller and Auditor General of India have identified different bottle-necks in implementation and delivery mechanism of the programme, which include lack of proper awareness about the basic objectives of the programme followed by improper planning, lack of transparency, delayed payment, non-availability of proper information at the worksite, etc. There is no denying the fact that awareness about the provisions of the Act is vital in strengthening the demand for work is an important element in the scheme. A study conducted by the National Sample Survey Organization in Andhra Pradesh, Rajasthan and Madhya Pradesh in one of its Rounds in 2010–11 indicated that awareness level among the potential beneficiaries about the provisions of the Act such as demand for work, claiming the unemployment allowance and grievance redressal mechanism, etc. were poor.[7]

On the other hand, performance audit report prepared by the CAG[8] has identified that planning and prioritization of the works by the gram sabha, which ensures proper address of the development needs of each locality through active participation of the villagers, is still below the desired level. The constraints they have pointed out are that gram sabhas are not held frequently, there is low participation at the meetings of the gram sabha for making prioritization of works. Again, work selection is very open, not done according to priorities and demands of the gram sabha.

It is now widely known that after the introduction of mandatory wage payment through bank and post offices to ensure transparency, the poor sections of the society have been brought into the organized sector and in many cases they have been provided with better access to rural credit. Despite this advantage, there are some constraints in implementation of the practice of institutional payment of wages.[9] Poor network coverage of banks and post offices, non-streamlined system of record keeping at the banks and post offices, ignorance and illiteracy of the workers, lack of necessary paper work in banks and post offices, and finally low cash limit coupled with inadequate staff in the branch post offices are creating problems for the poor and marginalized categories taking part in the scheme.

Another major problem is the question of leakage and misappropriation in the scheme for which it has received serious criticism. The CAG audit report[10] and other studies have identified that copies of muster rolls were not available for public scrutiny in many gram panchayats. Moreover, muster rolls are not updated regularly and in many worksites muster rolls are not available, rather *kachcha* entries (handwritten *chits*) are maintained for keeping records of attendance of workers. CAG report further suggests that in many cases wage payments are made to workers who either have no job cards or to those who do not actually undertake work at worksite. Double payments have also been noticed. Social audit and grievance redressal mechanism is a double-edge sword of the programme to protect corruption and ensure transparency and accountability. It is found that absence of frequent and effective social audit by gram sabha is a major constraint in proper implementation of the scheme.[11] It is also necessary to strengthen the grievance redressal mechanism to address issues of corruption as well as problems sometimes arising in the process of implementation. While the Act provides that each state is to formulate grievance redressal rules, only a few state government have prepared the same.[12] A summary of the major issues faced in the implementation process is reproduced below in the following table:

Table 4 *Major Issues in Implementation Identified in Field Studies*

Indicator	*Issues*
Demand of Work	Lack of awareness about the provision of demand work
	Dated receipt not given to applicants for work
	Demand for work not recorded by states
	Work not provided within 15 days
	Job-seekers denied employment
	Unemployment allowance not paid
Planning of Works	GSs not convened or not enough participation
	GSs' involvement in plan preparation is minimal, its role is often confined to a formality of approving what has already been done by the block
	Choice of works not oriented towards the priorities envisaged under MGNREGA
	Inadequate shelf of works for execution through the year or poor planning
	Lack of capacity in GP and shortage of technical staff with GPs for planning
	Technical sanction and administrative sanctions not obtained
Worksite Management	Worksite facilities not available
	MRs not available in worksites or not properly maintained
	JCs not with beneficiaries or not updated
	Measurement not being done on time
	Improper supervision or allocation of work
	Presence of machinery or contractor
	Fake entries tampered MRs
Quality of Works	Poor planning results in poor results (plantations made but no arrangement for watering meant plants died, etc.)
	Several works left incomplete
	Shortage of staff a serious issue in ensuring technical quality and durability

Cont'd...

...Cont'd

	Some works, like roads, required machinery and tractors to ensure durability
Wage and Wage Payments	Delays in payment; in some panchayats, delays cross 2–3 months
	So Rs Not accurately determined
	Long gaps between work and measurement also cause delays in wage payments
	Shortage of funds at block level also reportedly a cause of delayed wage payments
	Increases in task rates made at the state level do not translate into similar increases at GP level because it does not have the capacity to rework the estimates and engineers who can do so are too few in number
	Banks/Post Offices do not have branches/staff, etc. to cater to MGNREGA
	Fudging of MRs/ghost workers (workers that do not exist yet are shown as beneficiaries)
Other Admin -istrative Constraints	Poor maintenance of records like employment register
	Poor ICT infrastructure for monitoring (including computers, Internet connectivity)
Transpa-rency and Social Audit	Social audit not conducted
	Reports and documents show that there are:
	No active vigilance committees
	No vigilance committees
	In case social audits done, no records made available of the event
	Ineffective or non-existent grievance redressal mechanisms.

Source: Ministry of Rural Government, Government of India

And Miles to Go ...

During the financial year that ended in March 2013, 4.93 crore households were provided employment out of 5.1 crore demanding the same in which 225.07 crore person-days were generated. Country's average number of days against which employment was provided stood at 45.6 and a total number of 49.87 lakh households enjoyed the benefits of 100 days' work throughout the year.[13] Undoubtedly, this is a remarkable achievement in terms of resources but the achievement simultaneously demands a horizontal watchdog mechanism, besides the approach of top-down delivery. Under a such a situation, the Government of India along with the state governments are regularly monitoring the programme for better delivery of provisions and stoppage of the leakage. A new set of guidelines, keeping in view the existing bottlenecks, prepared by Dr Mihir Shah, a member of Planning Commission and his associates, has been released. This is expected to rectify the defects in the delivery mechanism. Apart from this, initiatives, reforms and several other measures have been undertaken by the central government in recent past.

On the other hand, success of this delivery mechanism depends a lot on the functioning of the constitutionally designed panchayats. Several studies across the country reveal that the real monitoring of this programme is gradually going beyond the control of the PRIs. Unfortunately, in many cases, the right to work has been converted into the right of attendance only.

To overcome these problems, there is the need for an enlightened citizens' forum at the grassroots level which will act as a watchdog of the programme. The intervention is required at the village level initially during the phase of planning, followed by proper resource mapping and identification of felt needs of the villagers in a long-term perspectives. Unplanned execution of the scheme may lead to a situation when there will be no pond or *hapa (*pond-less villages) or any other traditional water body in the village to excavate or re-excavate. Hence, there is the urgency in identifying a clear definition of sustainable community asset, which may vary from village to village, state to state. For this purpose, actual growth or decline of assets in a particular village and its people will have to be documented at the first instance. Second important requirement is the development of knowledge-base of the village workers about the basis of the scheme. In this sphere, the NGOs and CBOs like SHGs may take a leading role. Besides conventional IEC activities, new models of awareness generation will have to be identified at the field levels. Third and most important intervention is the creation of motivation among the villagers towards regular social audit and dissemination of proper and sufficient information from the programme implementing agencies.

All these will not happen overnight. No community planning in any country has ever succeeded without socio-political intervention. It is a prolonged and time-consuming process. Therefore, the most important intervention is to build up social mobilization which only can drive the engine to the desired goal and destination as intended in the objective statement and basic principles of the Act.

Notes

1. Government of India, *Draft Operational Guidelines*, New Delhi: Ministry of Rural Development, Mihir Shah Committee on MGNREGA, February 2012.
2. P. Dutta, R. Murgai, M. Ravallion and D. van de Walle, 'Does India's Employment Guarantee Scheme Guarantee Employment?', *Policy Research Paper*, Washington, DC: World Bank, 2012.
3. R. Jha, R. Gaiha and M.K. Pandey, 'Net Transfer Benefits under India's Rural Employment Guarantee Scheme', *Journal of Policy Modeling*, Vol. 34, No. 2, 2011.
4. S. Mangatter, 'Does MGNREGA Strengthen Rural Self Employment in Bolpur Sub-Division (West Bengal, India) ', Master's thesis, submitted at the Philipp University, Germany, 2011.
5. N. Pani and C. Iyar, *Evaluation of Impact of Process in MGNREGS in Karnataka*, Bangalore: National Institute of Advanced Studies, 2011.
6. C. Dheeraja and H. Rao, *Changing Gender Relation: A Study of MGNREGA Across Different States*, Hyderabad: NIRD, 2010.
7. Government of India, National Sample Survey Organization (NSSO), Survey of MGNREGA, 2010–11.
8. Government of India (CAG), *Performance Audit Report*, No. 11, 2008.
9. K. Bhatia and A. Adhikari, 'NREGA Wage Payments: Can We Bank on the Banks?', *Economic and Political Weekly*, 2 January 2011.
10. Government of India (CAG), *Performance Audit Report*, 2008.
11. T. Shah, S. Verma, R. Irdu and P. Hemant, 'Asset Creation through Employment Guarantee?: Synthesis of Case Studies in Nine States of India', Anand, India: International Water Management Institute, 2010.
12. Jean Dreze, 'The Accountability Gap', in Reetika Khera (ed.), *The Battle for Employment Guarantee*, New Delhi: Oxford University Press, 2011, pp. 266–269.
13. Government of India, website of the Ministry of Rural Development.

Index